THE COMMERCIAL PIL

ELECTRONICS
LOGIC and AUTO-FLIGHT
INSTRUMENTS

THE COMMERCIAL PILOT'S STUDY MANUAL SERIES

Vol. 3

ELECTRONICS LOGIC and AUTO-FLIGHT INSTRUMENTS

MIKE BURTON

Airlife
England

Copyright © 1997 Mike Burton

First published in the UK in 1997
by Airlife Publishing Ltd

British Library Cataloguing-in Publication Data
  A catalogue record for this book
  is available from the British Library

ISBN 1 85310 781 6

All rights reserved. No part of this book may be reproduced or transmitted in
any form or by any means, electronic or mechanical including photocopying,
recording or by any information storage and retrieval system, without permis-
sion from the Publisher in writing.

Typeset by Phoenix Typesetting, Ilkley, West Yorkshire.
Printed in England by Livesey Ltd, Shrewsbury.

Airlife Publishing Ltd
101 Longden Road, Shrewsbury SY3 9EB, England.

Contents

CONTENTS

CONTENTS

1

The Electron

1.1 Introduction

Anyone concerned with aviation is aware of the increasing use of electricity in modern aircraft systems and recognizes the importance of a thorough understanding of electrical principles.

In the study of physics, the electron theory of the structure of matter explains the fundamental nature of matter. A more detailed examination of this theory is necessary to explain the behaviour of the electron as it applies to the study of basic electricity.

1.2 Matter

Matter can be defined as anything that has mass (weight) and occupies space. Thus, matter is everything that exists. It may exist in the form of solids, liquids, or gases. The smallest particle of matter in any state or form, that still possesses its identity, is called a molecule.

Substances composed of only one type of atom are called elements. But most substances occur in nature as compounds, that is, combinations of two or more types of atoms. Water, for example, is a compound of two atoms of hydrogen and one atom of oxygen. A molecule of water is illustrated in Fig 1-1. It would no longer retain the characteristics of water if it were compounded of one atom of hydrogen and two atoms of oxygen.

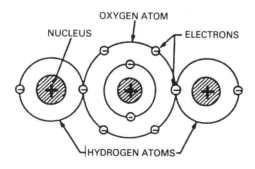

Figure 1–1 A water molecule.

1.3 The Atom

The atom is considered the basic building block of all matter. It is the smallest possible particle that an element can be divided into and still retain its chemical properties. In its simplest form, it consists of one or more electrons orbiting at high speed around a centre, or nucleus, made up of one or more protons, and, in most atoms, one or more neutrons as well. Since an atom is so small that some 200,000 could be placed side by side in a line 1 inch long, it cannot be seen; nevertheless, a great deal is known about its behaviour from various tests and experiments.

The simplest atom is that of hydrogen, which is one electron orbiting around one proton, as shown in Fig 1-2. A more complex atom is that of oxygen (see Fig 1-3), which consists of eight electrons rotating in two different orbits around a nucleus made up of eight protons and eight neutrons.

An electron is the basic negative charge of electricity and cannot be divided further. Some electrons are more tightly bound to the nucleus of their atom than others and rotate in an imaginary shell or sphere close to the nucleus, while others are more loosely bound and orbit at a greater distance from the nucleus. These latter electrons are called 'free' electrons because they can be freed easily from the positive attraction of the protons in the nucleus to make up the flow of electrons in a practical electrical circuit.

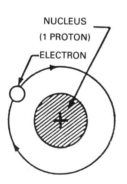

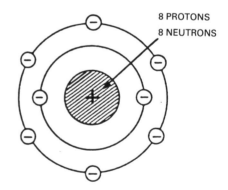

Figure 1-2 Hydrogen atom.   Figure 1-3 Oxygen atom.

The neutrons in a nucleus have no electrical charge. They are neither positive nor negative but are equal in size and weight to the proton. Since a proton weighs approximately 1,845 times as much as an electron, the overall weight of an atom is determined by the number of protons and neutrons in its nucleus. The weight of an electron is not considered in determining the weight of an atom. Indeed, the nature of electricity cannot be defined clearly because it is not certain whether the electron is a negative charge with no mass (weight) or a particle of matter with a negative charge.

Electricity is best understood in terms of its behaviour, which is based in part on the charge an atom carries. When the total positive charge of the protons in the nucleus equals the total negative charge of the electrons in orbit around the nucleus, the atom is said to have a neutral charge. If an atom has a shortage of electrons, or negative charges, it is positively charged and is called a positive ion. If it possesses an excess of electrons, it is said to be negatively charged and is called a negative ion.

1.4 Electron Movement

In a state of neutral charge, an atom has one electron for each proton in the nucleus. Thus, the number of electrons held by the atoms making up the various elements will vary from one, in the case of hydrogen, to 92 for uranium.

The electrons revolving around a nucleus travel in orbits, sometimes called shells or layers. Each shell can contain a certain maximum number of electrons, and if this number is exceeded, the extra electrons will be forced into the next higher, or outer, shell.

The shell nearest the nucleus can contain no more than two electrons. In an atom containing more than two electrons, the excess electrons will be located in the outer shells. The second shell can have a maximum of eight electrons. The third shell can hold up to 18 electrons, the fourth 32, etc. It should be noted, however, that in some large complex atoms electrons may be arranged in outer shells before some inner shells are filled.

1.5 Static Electricity

Electricity is often described as being either static or dynamic. Since all electrons are alike, these words do not actually describe two different types of electricity; rather, they distinguish between electrons at rest and those in motion. The word static means 'stationary' or 'at rest', and refers to the deficiency or to the excess of electrons. Originally it was thought that static electricity was electricity at rest because electrical energy produced by friction did not move. A simple experiment, such as running a dry comb through hair, will produce cracking or popping sounds, indicating static discharges are taking place. The charges thus built up consist of electrons transferred to the comb as the result of friction. The discharge is caused by the rapid movement of electrons in the opposite direction from the comb to the hair as the charges neutralise each other. In the dark it is possible to see these discharges as tiny sparks.

Static electricity has little practical value, and often causes problems.

It is difficult to control and discharges quickly. Conversely, dynamic, or current electricity, is generated and controlled easily and provides energy for useful work. A summary of that part of the electron theory dealing with charges will help explain static electricity. All electrons are alike and repel each other. Similarly all protons are alike and repel each other. Electrons and protons are not alike, but attract each other. Hence, the fundamental law of electricity is that like charges repel and unlike charges attract.

1.6 Generation of Static Electricity

Static electricity can be produced by contact, friction or induction. As an example of the friction method, a glass rod rubbed with fur becomes negatively charged, but if rubbed with silk, becomes positively charged. Some materials that build up static electricity easily are flannel, silk, rayon, amber, hard rubber, and glass.

When two materials are rubbed together, some electron orbits of atoms in one material may cross the orbits or shells of the other, and one material may give up electrons to the other. The transferred electrons are those in the outer shells or orbits and are called free electrons.

The effects of static electricity must be considered in the operation and maintenance of aircraft. Static interference in the aircraft communication systems and the static charge created by the aircraft's movement through the air are examples of problems created by static electricity. Parts of the aircraft must be 'bonded' or joined together to provide a low-resistance (or easy) path for static discharge, and radio parts must be shielded. Static charges must be considered in the refuelling of the aircraft to prevent possible igniting of the fuel, and provision must be made to ground the aircraft structure, either by static-conducting tyres or by a grounding wire.

1.7 Electrostatic Field

A field of force exists around a charged body. This field is an electrostatic field (sometimes called a dielectric field) and is represented by lines extending in all directions from the charged body and terminating where there is an equal and opposite charge.

To explain the action of an electrostatic field, lines are used to represent the direction and intensity of the electric field of force. As illustrated in Fig 1-4, the intensity of the field is indicated by the number of lines per unit area, and the direction is shown by arrowheads on the lines pointing in the direction in which a small test charge would move, or tend to move, if acted upon by the field of force.

Either a positive or negative test charge can be used, but it has been arbitrarily agreed that a small positive charge will always be used in determining the direction of the field. Thus, the direction of the field around a positive charge is always away from the charge, as shown in Fig 1-4, because a positive test charge would be repelled. On the other hand, the direction of the lines about a negative charge is towards the charge, since a positive test charge is attracted towards it.

Figure 1-5 illustrates the field around bodies having like charges. Positive charges are shown, but regardless of the type of charge, the lines of force would repel each other if the charges were alike. The lines terminate on material objects and always extend from a positive charge to a negative charge. These lines are imaginary in fact and are used diagramatically to show the direction a real force takes.

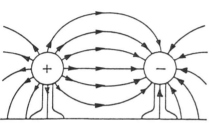
Figure 1–4 Direction of electric field around positive and negative charges.

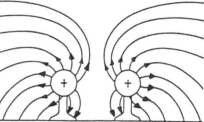
Figure1–5 Field around two positively charged bodies.

1.8 Electromotive Force

The flow of electrons from a negative point to a positive point is called an electric current; this current flows because of a difference in electric pressure between the two points.

If an excess of electrons with a negative charge exists at one end of a conductor and a deficiency of electrons with a positive charge at the other, an electrostatic field exists between the two charges. Electrons are repelled from the negatively charged point and are attracted by the positively charged point.

The flow of electrons of electric current can be compared to the flow of water between two interconnected water tanks when a difference of pressure exists between two tanks. Figure 1-6 shows the level of water in tank A to be higher than the water level in tank B. If the valve in the interconnecting line between the tanks is opened, water will flow from tank A into tank B until the level of water is the same in both tanks. It is important to note that it was not the pressure in tank A that caused the water to flow; rather, it was the difference in pressure between tank A and tank B that caused the flow. When the water in the two tanks is at the same level, the flow of water ceases because there is no longer a difference of pressure.

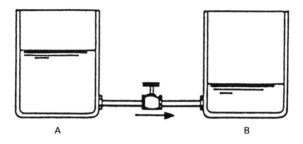

Figure 1–6 Difference of pressure.

This comparison illustrates the principle that causes the electrons to move, when a proper path is available, from a point of excess electrons to a point deficient in electrons. The force that causes this movement is the potential difference in electrical energy between the two points. This force is called the electrical pressure or the potential difference or the electromotive force (electron-moving force) which can all be considered the same thing. Electromotive force, abbreviated emf, causes current (electrons) to move in an electric path or circuit. The practical unit of measurements of emf, or potential difference, is the volt. The symbol for emf is the capital 'E'.

If the water pressure in tank A of Fig 1-6 is 10 psi and the pressure in tank B is 2 psi there is a difference in pressure of 8 psi. Similarly, it can be said that an electromotive force of 8 volts exists between two electrical points. Since potential difference is measured in volts, the word 'voltage' can also be used to describe amounts of potential difference. Thus, it is correct to say that the voltage of a certain aircraft battery is 24 volts, another means of indicating that a potential difference of 24 volts exists between two points connected by a conductor.

1.9 Current Flow

Electrons in motion make up an electric current. This electric current is usually referred to as 'current' or 'current flow', no matter how many electrons are moving. When the current flow is in one direction only, it is called direct current. Later in the study of electrical fundamentals, current that reverses itself periodically, called alternating current, will be discussed. In the present study all references are to direct current.

Since an electric current may consist of varying numbers of electrons, it is important to know the number of electrons flowing in a circuit in a given time. Electrons can be counted by measuring the basic electrical charge on each electron. Since this charge is very small the unit of measurement of it, for practical purposes, has to be correspondingly large. Called the Coulomb, this unit defines the accumulated charge on 6.28 billion electrons. When this quantity of electrons flows past a given point in an electrical circuit, one ampere of current is said to be flowing in the circuit. Current flow is measured in amperes or parts of amperes by an electrical instrument called an ammeter. The symbol used to indicate current in formulas or on schematics is the capital letter 'I', which stands for the intensity of current flow.

Figure 1–7   Electron movement.

The drift of free electrons must not be confused with the concept of current flow that approaches the speed of light. When a voltage is applied to a circuit, the free electrons travel but a short distance before colliding with atoms. These collisions usually knock other electrons free from their atoms, and these electrons travel on towards the positive terminal of the wire, colliding with other atoms as they drift at a comparatively slow rate. To understand the almost instantaneous speed of the effect of electric current, it is helpful to visualize a long tube filled with steel balls as shown in Fig 1-7.

It can be seen that a ball introduced in one end of the tube, which represents a conductor, will immediately cause a ball to be emitted at the opposite end of the tube. Even if the tube were long enough to reach clear across the country, this effect could still be visualized as being instantaneous. Thus, electric current flow can be viewed as occurring instantaneously, even though it is the result of a comparatively slow drift of electrons.

2

Basic Electrical Principles

2.1 Introduction

The modern conception of electricity, is based on the electron theory, a brief description of which is given in Chapter One. In accordance with this theory an electric current is defined as an orderly movement of electrons from one part of a circuit to another.

To obtain this movement of electrons in a simple circuit it is necessary first to have a source of electrical pressure such as a battery, sometimes called an accumulator, or a generator, and secondly, a complete external electrical circuit, comprising a system of conductors (wires) connected to that source of electrical pressure.

In such a circuit the flow of current is conventionally visualized as being from the positive terminal (+) of the source of electrical pressure, through the system of conductors, to the negative (–) terminal. *The actual movement of electrons, is however, in the opposite direction.* Each electron, being a minute electrical charge of electricity, is always attracted to a positive charge, therefore, the electron flow is from the negative terminal to the positive terminal.

2.2 Conductors and Insulators

A conductor is a material in which electrons are only loosely attached to their groups, so that application of electrical pressure causes these free electrons to move through the material in the direction of the electromotive force, that is the source of pressure such as the battery or the generator.

In general all metals can be classed as conductors, while some non-metallic materials such as carbon and acids also conduct electricity. Some materials permit the movement of electrons more freely than others, and the measure of ease with which they do so is known as their conductance. Metals such as copper and aluminium, for example, have high conductivity and are generally used for electrical conductors (wires).

Conductance is therefore the standard of comparison between different conducting materials; the reciprocal of conductance, ie resistance, is, however, used in calculations.

Insulators, which are also known as dielectrics, are materials in which electrons are so firmly attached to their groups that little or no electron flow takes place when electrical pressure is applied. At normal pressure such materials are considered as non-conductors. If however, the applied pressure is progressively increased a point is reached at which the material breaks down and passes current. The ability of a known thickness of insulating material to resist, or prevent, such breakdown is called its dielectric strength.

Although there is no perfect non-conductor, materials such as rubber, cotton, porcelain and bakelite are termed non-conductors or insulators; pure distilled water is also a non-conductor.

2.3 Electrical Pressure, Current, and Resistance

Three primary conditions exist in the simple electrical circuit. Firstly the electrical pressure; secondly, the flow of electrical current; and thirdly, the degree with which materials conduct electricity.

(a) Electrical Pressure

The electrical pressure which causes an electric current to flow in a circuit is known as the electromotive force (emf). It may be produced in three ways:

(1) By chemical action, as in a primary cell battery.

(2) By heat, as in a thermocouple.

(3) Mechanically, as in a generator.

The difference in electrical pressure which exists between any two points in the circuit is known as the potential difference (PD), as distinct from the total emf required to drive the current through the complete circuit.

(b) Current

The current in a circuit is the rate of flow of electricity. The practical unit of quantity of electricity is the Coulomb, which is approximately equal to 6.3×10^{18} electrons. The current in a circuit is therefore the number of coulombs per second flowing past a definite point in that circuit.

(c) Resistance

The opposition to the flow of electrons in a conductor in an electrical circuit is known as the resistance, and it is measured in ohms. Resistance depends on three factors:

(1) The cross sectional area of the conductor.

(2) The length of the conductor.

(3) The material from which the conductor is manufactured.

Therefore, where it is required to keep the opposition to the flow of the electricity to a minimum, the conductor with the largest practical cross sectional area, the shortest length, and made from a low resistant material, such as copper, is used.

Conductors made of high resistance materials, such as eureka, which offer considerable resistance to the flow of electricity, are deliberately used as resistances where it is required to resist, or restrict, the flow of current.

It must be noted that the resistance of a conductor is only constant at constant temperature. The resistance of all pure metals increases with increased temperature, whereas that of carbon decreases. The fraction by which the resistance of a conductor increases for each degree centigrade rise of temperature above a definite temperature (usually 20°C) is called the thermal coefficient of resistance of the material.

2.4 Units of Measurement

(a) Standard Units

The value of the three conditions noted above is expressed by the following standard units:

(1) The Volt is the unit of difference of electrical pressure. A Potential Difference (PD) of one volt exists between two points in an electrical circuit, when one Joule of work is done in moving one Coulomb of electricity from one point to the other.

(2) The Ampere is the unit of rate of flow of electric current. A current of one ampere is the rate of flow of electricity of one coulomb per second past a definite point in the circuit.

(3) The Ohm is the unit of resistance. It is that resistance which permits a current of one ampere to flow when a PD of one volt is applied across it.

(4) Multiple and Submultiple Units. In addition to the standard units, it is convenient to have larger and smaller units of measurement. The relationship between such multiples and submultiples and the standard unit is indicated by the use of the following prefixes:

2.5 Ohm's Law

In a DC (Direct Current) electrical circuit the ratio between the applied electrical pressure and the current flowing is constant at constant temperature. That is:

$\dfrac{E}{I}$ is a constant, and this constant is the resistance of the conductor.

This relationship between emf current and resistance is expressed by 'Ohms Law' which states that the current in a circuit is directly proportional to the pressure and inversely proportional to the pressure and inversely proportional to the resistance of the circuit. Thus, other factors remaining constant, if the pressure is doubled the current is doubled; if the resistance is doubled the current is halved. Ohms Law can be expressed as equation:

$$\text{Current in Amperes} = \frac{\text{emf in Volts}}{\text{Resistance in Ohms}}$$

In symbols $\quad I \quad = \dfrac{E}{R}$

If any two of these quantities are known therefore the third can be found by transposing the symbols, ie:

$$R = \frac{E}{I} \text{ or } E = IR \text{ or } I \times R.$$

2.6 Resistance in Simple Circuits

(a) Series Connection

Conductors connected end to end to form a single circuit are said to be in series. In a series circuit the value of the current is the same at all points and depends on the total resistance of the circuit and the applied emf. The PD across each resistance is proportional to the value of that resistance.

The total resistance of several resistances in series is equal to the sum of the individual resistances, ie:

$$R_t = r_1 + r_2 + r_3 + \ldots$$

(b) Parallel Connections

Conductors joined so that they provide alternative paths for the current are said to be in parallel. In a parallel circuit the voltage is common to each path, and the current in each path is proportional to the resistance of that path. The total current equals the sum of the individual currents. If several resistances are connected in parallel, the reciprocal of their total resistance $\frac{I}{R}$ is equal to the reciprocals of the individual resistances, ie:

$$\frac{I}{R_t} = \frac{I}{r_1} \quad \frac{I}{r_2} \quad \frac{I}{r_3} \quad \frac{I}{r_4}$$

The total resistance which is calculated from the above expression, is always less than the lowest value of the individual resistances.

Note: Any one path is a shunt to the remainder.

See Fig 2-1 for examples.

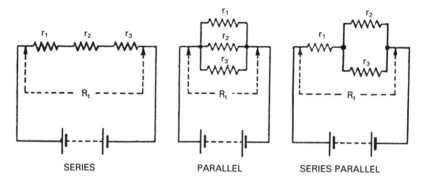

SERIES   PARALLEL   SERIES PARALLEL

Figure 2–1 Resistance arrangements.

(c) Series Parallel Combinations

To find the total resistance of a circuit containing both parallel and series connections, first find the equivalent value resistance of the parallel banks, as described previously in 2.6 (b), and then add this to the total value of other resistances connected in series.

2.7 Voltage Drop

When current flows, energy is absorbed in overcoming the resistance of the conductor and this energy is converted into heat. The loss of electrical energy results in a drop in electrical pressure along the conductor known as voltage drop. This difference in pressure between two points in a circuit is measured in volts (E).

Voltage drop in a circuit is calculated by Ohms law, ie E IR. It is important in circuits carrying heavy loads, that is, heavy currents, since a large current (I) causes a correspondingly large voltage drop.

Since voltage drop occurs in cables, the effective voltage at the terminals of equipment connected to the ends of those cables, is less than the applied voltage at the supply ends and is calculated as follows:

Effective voltage = Applied Voltage – Voltage Drop.

Therefore when wiring circuits the current carrying capacity of the cables must be sufficiently large in comparison with the current flowing to avoid excessive voltage drop and overheating of the cables.

2.8 Power and Energy

(a) Power
Power is the term used for the rate of doing work. The electrical unit of power is the Watt, and the power available from a source of supply is the product of emf in Volts and the current in Amperes, ie Watts = Volts × Amps, or Power E × I watts.

Where the value of the voltage is not known, power can be calculated from the expression:

Power = $I^2 R$ watts (since E = IR).

or if the current is not known,

Power = $\dfrac{E^2}{R}$ (since I $\dfrac{E}{R}$)

The equation Power = I^2R also represents the power lost in overcoming the resistance of the conductor and in producing heat.

The watt is too small for practical use where the power involved is large, and the unit adopted therefore is the kilowatt (1000 watts).

The mechanical unit of power, the Horsepower, is equivalent to 746 watts.

Therefore a kilowatt = $\dfrac{1000 \text{ watts}}{746}$ = 1.34 horsepower.

(b) Energy
Energy is the capacity for doing work; it is therefore measured in the same units as are used for work, ie Joules, and is represented by the symbol W (Work).

The Joule is defined as the work done when a current of one ampere flows between any two points in one second due to a pressure of one volt. The power expended will thus be one watt, and hence 1 Joule = 1 watt-second, and

W = I^2Rt joules (or watt seconds).

13

A more convenient unit than the watt-second is the Watt Hour which is defined as one watt supplied continuously for one hour.

For aircraft use the most common term used is the kilowatt hour, and is equivalent to 1000 watt-hours.

2.9 Magnetism

(a) Properties

If a steel bar is magnetised it acquires the following properties:

(1) The ends attract pieces of iron and steel. These ends (where the force of attraction is greatest) are known as the poles of the magnet.

(2) The bar if freely suspended from its centre, will always come to rest parallel with the lines of force of the earth's magnetic field. The end which seeks the north pole of the earth is known as the north pole of the magnet, and the other the south pole.

(3) If a second magnet is brought near the suspended magnet the latter is either attracted or repelled according to the pole presented to it. Like poles repel and unlike poles attract each other.

(b) Magnetic Field

A field of magnetic influence exists in the space surrounding a magnet. As the distance from the magnet increases, the strength of the magnetic field decreases. The magnetic field is represented in a diagram by lines of force, of flux, which are assumed to have the following properties:

(1) They tend to contract in length.

(2) They never cross.

(3) They are deflected by, and tend to pass through, magnetic materials placed in the magnetic field. In doing so they induce magnetic properties in that material.

(4) They form a complete magnetic circuit running from a north pole to a south pole outside the magnet and completing the loop from the south pole to the north pole through the magnet.

(c) Magnetic Materials

Soft iron and steel are the main magnetic materials used to construct magnets.

(1) Soft iron is easily magnetised, but loses the greater part of its magnetism when the magnetising force is removed. It is used in electro-magnets.

(2) Steel retains the greater part of its magnetism and is used for permanent magnets. Steel is usually alloyed with the practically non-magnetic materials tungsten, chromium and cobalt, which give it still better magnetic properties.

(d) Definitions
The following terms and symbols will be encountered in dealing with magnetic circuits and materials:

(1) Flux Density
The strength of the magnetic field, ie the number of lines of force per square centimetre.

(2) Permeability
The property of the magnetic material of increasing flux density; it may be compared with conductivity in the electric circuit. The permeability of air is unity, while that of soft iron and steel varies between 200 and 1000.

(3) Reluctance
This may be compared with resistance in an electric circuit. The reluctance of a magnetic circuit is greatly increased by the existence of air gaps, which is why air gaps in electric machines are normally kept as small as possible.

(4) Saturation
A magnetic material has reached its saturation point when it is completely magnetised, ie when flux density cannot be further increased.

(5) Retentivity
The property possessed by a material of retaining magnetism after the magnetising force has been removed.

(6) Hysteresis
This is the lagging behind of magnetisation in a material as the magnetising force is removed, or reduced. The amount of magnetism retained by a material after the magnetising force has been removed is known as residual magnetism.

2.10 Effects of an Electric Current

The effects of the flow of electric current may be grouped under three headings:

(a) Magnetic Field

Current flowing through a conductor sets up a magnetic field. The direction of the current flow, and the direction of the lines of force around the conductor bear the same relationship to each other as do the thrust and the turn of a corkscrew.

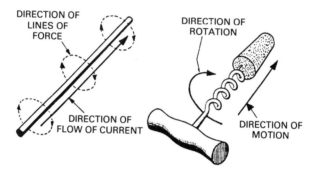

Figure 2–2 Corkscrew rule.

If a conductor carrying current, instead of being straight as above, is wound in the form of a coil or solenoid, a magnetic field is produced in and around the coil. The form of the field is similar to that of a bar magnet.

The polarity can be determined by imagining the solenoid to be grasped with the right hand, the fingers pointing in the direction of the current. The thumb then indicates the North pole. The polarity of the field reverses if the direction of current is reversed, and entirely disappears when the current is switched off.

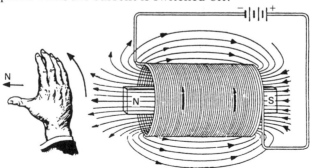

Figure 2–3 Polarity of a solenoid.

The strength of the magnetic field depends on the following factors:

(1)   The current in amperes.

(2)   The number of turns comprising the coil.

(3)   The length of the coil.

(4)   The permeability of the core.

Thus in an air-cored coil the flux density (B) is proportional to the magnetising force (H) expressed in ampere-turns per centimetre, ie the product of the current in amperes and number of turns in each centimetre length of the coil. Most electro-magnets consist of a solenoid wound on a core of soft iron or similar magnetic material, which offers an easier path to the lines of force; the flux density due to the ampere-turns/centimetre is thus increased by an amount depending on the permeability of the core.

Electro-magnets are used in relay switches and motor and generator field systems, the chief advantages of this type of magnet being a stronger magnetic field, which can also be controlled by variation of the current.

(b) Heating Effect

When current flows in a conductor the electrical power absorbed in overcoming resistance is converted into heat, causing a rise in temperature of the conductor. A steady temperature is reached when the heat lost per second by radiation, conduction and convection is equal to the heat gained per second from the current. The expression I^2RT joules (see paragraph 2.8, sub paragraph [b]) shows that the energy converted into heat is proportional to the product of the square of the current, the resistance in Ohms, and the time in seconds (Joule's law). Since 1 joule = 0.24 calories of heat, therefore:

Heat developed = $I^2Rt \times 0.24$ calories.

The actual rise in temperature depends on the nature of the conductor, ie its dimensions and the material of which it is made. For example, the rise in temperature is greater:

(1)   In a thin wire than in a thick wire carrying the same current.

(2)   In an iron wire than in a copper wire of the same gauge and carrying the same current.

Hence in general wiring the current carrying capacity of a conductor must always be sufficiently large in relationship to the current flow to prevent damage to the insulation of the conductor due to rise in temperature. Also electrical machines must be adequately ventilated, or otherwise cooled, to prevent overheating.

This heating effect is deliberately used in lamp filaments, heater elements and hot-wire ammeters.

(c) Chemical Effect

Certain substances, such as salts and acids, when dissolved in water conduct electricity and are known as electrolytes; dilute sulphuric acid is a typical electrolyte. The conductors by which the current enters and leaves the solution are known as electrodes and are termed the anode and cathode respectively. The passage of the current decomposes the solution into its constituent ions, the process being known as electrolysis. These ions are of two kinds, some being negatively charged and the others positively charged. The former are attracted towards the positive anode, whilst the latter travel with the current towards the cathode. Gases are also evolved at the electrodes.

This principle is applied in electro-plating, the essentials being an anode of the plating metal and an electrolyte suitable for the type of plating; the article to be plated forms the cathode. The passage of current dissolves plating metal from the anode into the electrolyte whence it is deposited on the surface of the cathode. The amount of metal deposited is proportional to the current and the time for which it flows. The amount of any particular metal deposited by one coulomb of electricity is known as the electro-chemical equivalent of the ion of that metal.

Other practical applications of the chemical effect of electric current are secondary cells and electrolytic meters. In the latter case the current flow is calculated by the amount of metal deposited, ie:

$$I = \frac{\text{Weight of metal deposited}}{\text{Electro-chemical equivalent} \times \text{time in seconds}}$$

Hence the definition of the ampere as that current which will deposit 0.001118 gramme of silver per second from a solution of silver nitrate.

2.11 Electro-magnetic Induction

The principle of electro-magnetic induction is used in electrical machines whenever an electric current is produced by means of a magnetic field. When a permanent magnet is lowered into a coil (Fig 2-4), lines of force cut the turns of wire. If the two ends of the coil are connected to a galvanometer the instrument pointer will deflect to indicate that an emf is being induced in the coil and that current is flowing. The pointer returns to the central position as soon as the relative motion between the magnet and coil ceases. This relative motion must always be such that the lines of force move across the conductors at an angle; if they move parallel to the conductors no emf is induced.

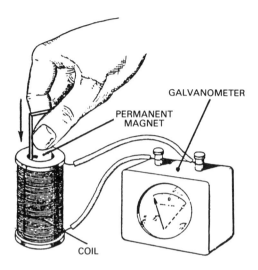

Figure 2–4 Electro-magnetic induction.

When the magnet is withdrawn the pointer is again deflected, but in the opposite direction. In both cases the direction of the induced current is such that the electro-magnetic field opposes the movement of the magnet.

The principles of electro-magnetic induction are summarised by two laws:

(a) Faraday's Law
Which states that the value of the induced emf is proportional to the rate of change of flux linkage: eg an emf of 1 volt is induced when the rate of change is:

100,000,000 (ie 10^8) lines of force per second.

(b) Lenz's Law
Which states that in electro-magnetic induction the induced currents have a direction such that their reaction tends to stop the motion which produces them.

2.12 Inductance

Inductance (symbol L) is that property possessed by any circuit, such as a coil, where a change of current is accompanied by a change in the strength of a magnetic field.

(a) Self-Inductance

When the current through a coil varies, the resultant movement of the surrounding lines of magnetic force induces an emf in the turns of the coil. This induced emf is in a direction such that it opposes the changing condition in the circuit (Lenz's law). Thus on closing the switch in an inductive DC circuit the self-induced (or back-) emf opposes the applied emf and causes a gradual rise in current to its maximum steady value, while the magnetic field surrounding the coil is being established. On opening the switch the collapse of the magnetic field tends to maintain the flow of current, and if a resistance is connected in parallel with the inductance a decaying current flows through it while the energy stored in the magnetic field is being returned to the circuit (Fig 2-5). If there is no resistance in parallel, the tendency to maintain the flow of current creates an arc at the switch contacts at the instant of opening.

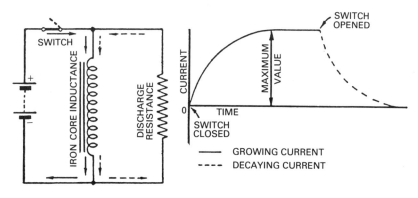

Figure 2-5 Current in inductive circuit (Growth and Decay).

The unit of inductance is the Henry (H) and a circuit has an inductance of 1 Henry if an emf of 1 volt is induced in the circuit when the current changes at the rate of 1 ampere per second.

Iron-cored inductances, or chokes, are generally used in rectifier circuits for smoothing out variations in direct current obtained from an AC supply.

(b) Mutual Inductance

If two coils are placed so that when current is passed through one of them the resultant magnetic flux links with the other coil, any variation of the current in the first coil causes an emf to be induced in the second coil. The coils are known as the primary and secondary coils respectively, and are said to have mutual inductance. The unit of measurement is the Henry, and the mutual inductance of two coils is 1 Henry when an emf of 1 volt is induced in the secondary due to the primary current changing at the rate of 1 ampere per second.

The principle is used in transformers, ignition coils, magnetos and similar apparatus.

2.13 The Condenser

Any two conductors separated by an insulator form a condenser (or capacitator) and, when a PD is applied across them, have the property of storing an electric charge; this property is known as capacitance.

The simple condenser consists of two sheets of metal foil separated by a thin strip of waxed paper or mica, termed the plates and the dielectric respectively. When a momentary current flows into the condenser a PD is established across its plates. Since the dielectric contains no free electrons this current cannot flow through it, but the PD sets up a state of stress in the atoms comprising it. For example, in the circuit shown in Fig 2-6, on placing the switch in position 1 a rush of electrons – known as the charging current – occurs from plate A through the accumulator to plate B, and ceases when the PD between the plates is equal to the PD of the accumulator. When the switch is opened the plates remain positively and negatively charged respectively, since the atoms of plate A have lost electrons while those at B have a surplus; thus electrical energy is stored in the condenser in the form of an electric field existing between the plates due to the force of attraction between the opposite charges on them. When the switch is moved to position 2 the plates are short-circuited and the surplus electrons at the negatively charged plate rush back to the positively charged plate until the atoms of both plates are electrically neutral and no PD exists between them. This discharging current is in the reverse direction to the charging current as indicated by the centre-zero ammeter.

Both the charging and discharging currents are at a maximum at the commencement of charge and discharge respectively, and gradually fall to zero. Increase in the value of the resistance (R) decreases the initial maximum value of the current, but increases the duration of the charge and discharge; this principle is used in time bases. Note that the current flows only when applied PD is changing.

Excessive PD across the plates causes a spark to occur between them and punctures the insulation, ie the condenser 'breaks down'. The maximum permissible working voltage (DC) is therefore marked on condensers, and depends on the thickness and dielectric strength of the insulating material used.

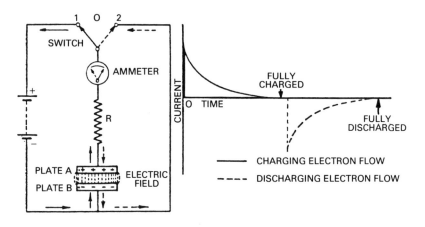

Figure 2–6 Condenser principle.

2.14 Capacitance

The capacitance (C) of a condenser is the ratio between the charge in coulombs (Q) retained by the condenser and the PD in volts between the plates, ie:

$$\text{Capacitance in Farads} = \frac{\text{Charge in coulombs}}{\text{P D in volts}} \text{ or } C = \frac{Q}{V}$$

The Farad (F) is the unit of capacitance and is the capacitance of a condenser in which a charge of 1 coulomb raises the PD between the plates by one volt. The Farad is too large for practical values and the microfarad (mid or μF $= 10^{-6}$F) is generally used.

(a) Capacitance of Condenser

The capacitance of a condenser is directly proportional to:

(1) The area of the plates: eg the greater the number of plates connected in parallel the larger the capacitance.

(2) The dielectric constant of the insulator between the plates: eg that of air is unity, and that of mica 5 (approximately);

and is inversely proportional to:

(3) The thickness of the dielectric: the thinner the dielectric the greater the capacitance for the same area of plate.

(b) Condensers in Parallel

If the effective area of the plates is increased, the total capacity is increased, and is the sum of the individual capacities, ie:

$C_t = C_1 + C_2 + C_3 +$ etc.

(c) Condensers in Series

If the thickness of the dielectric is increased the total capacity is decreased, being less than the capacity of any one of the individual condensers. It is calculated by the expression:

$\dfrac{1}{C_t} = \dfrac{1}{C_1} + \dfrac{1}{C_2} + \dfrac{1}{C_3} +$ etc.

Key Points to Remember

Theory

(1) The unit used to measure the Potential Difference (PD), or Electromotive Force (emf), is called the VOLT.

(2) The unit used to measure the rate of current flow of Electricity is called the AMPERE.

(3) The unit used for measuring resistance is called the OHM.

(4) The unit used for measuring electrical power is called the WATT.

(5) If the voltage in a current is doubled, then the current will double.

(6) OHM's LAW states that the current flowing in a circuit depends on the applied voltage and the resistance.

$$I = \frac{V}{R} \qquad V = IR \qquad R = \frac{V}{I}$$

(7) Power used in any circuit can be calculated by using one of the following:

$$P = VI \qquad P = I^2 R \qquad P = \frac{V^2}{R}$$

(8) The TOTAL power consumed by a circuit is found by the SUM of the power consumed by each individual component.

(9)   To find the power consumption of individual components only the values V, I and R for *that part* of the circuit must be used.

(10)   If a number of resistances are connected in SERIES, the TOTAL resistance would equal the sum of the individual resistances.

(11)   If a number of resistances are connected in PARALLEL, the RECIPROCAL of the TOTAL resistance is the SUM of the RECI-PROCALS of the individual resistances.

(12)   The total AMPERAGE flow of a number of circuits in PARALLEL can be calculated by the SUM of all the amperage of ALL the components in the circuits.

(13)   To find the value of Electrical HP:

$$Watts = Volts \times Amperes$$

(14)   A Voltmeter measures emf.

(15)   An Ammeter measures current flow and is connected in series so that if it fails it will not affect the generator output.

Fuses and Circuit Breakers

(1)   The reason for fitting fuses and circuit breakers in aircraft electrical circuits is to provide a safety measure when the circuit is overloaded.

(2)   A tripfree circuit breaker that has tripped due to overload can be reset but MUST not be held in.

(3)   Assuming a fuse has failed in flight, and investigation shows that the circuit is 'opened circuit', the pilot should switch circuit OFF and replace the failed fuse with one of the correct rating ONCE only.

(4)   A thermal circuit breaker works on the differential expansion of metals.

(5)   If the load current of a circuit is 120 Watts 40 Volts, the fuse size would be 5 Amps.

ie $\dfrac{W}{V} = Amp + 100\%$ $\dfrac{120}{40} = 3 + 100\% = 6\ Amp\ (nearest$
$rating\ -5A)$

(6)   A fuse is said to be 'blown' when excessive heat from an overload melts the fuse wire.

(7)   In a single pole electrical circuit, a 'short' between a conductor and the aircraft structure will result in the appropriate fuse blowing.

(8)   A short circuit on a double pole electrical circuit could be caused by bridging of the conductors.

(9)   Loss of electrical insulation could cause a short circuit between the conductor and earth.

General

(1)   An inertia switch on an aircraft operates during an emergency or crash landing.

(2)   With the left side of the master switch (labelled ALT) in the OFF position and the engine running above altimeter cut-in speed, the engine alternator will not be supplying power to the bus-bar.

(3)   If, in flight, the electrical services are ON and the overvolt red warning light comes ON, the ammeter will indicate minus values.

(4)   In a simple electrical circuit, when the power trimming devices are in parallel, then the total current consumer is equal to the sum of the current taken by the devices.

Section 2   Test Yourself Questions

1. Resistance in a conductor:
    (a)   increases with increase of temperature.
    (b)   reduces with increase of temperature.
    (c)   remains constant at all temperatures.
    (d)   varies in an irregular manner with temperature change.

                                                        Ref 2.3.

2. Electrical pressure:
    (a)   is measured in amps.
    (b)   is the emf
    (c)   is the rate of current flow.
    (d)   is measured in ohms.

                                                        Ref 2.3.

3. The rate of doing work of an electrical component is measured in:
    (a)   volts.
    (b)   ohms.
    (c)   amps.
    (d)   watts.

                                                        Ref 2.8.

4. Energy:
    (a)   is the voltage available.
    (b)   is the current rate.
    (c)   is the capacity for doing work.
    (d)   is the capacity to store power.

                                                        Ref 2.8.

5. Resistance is:
    (a) $E \times I$
    (b) $R - I$
    (c) $E - I$
    (d) $\dfrac{E}{I}$

                                                        Ref 2.5.

3

Elementary Principles of DC Generators and Motors

3.1 Electro-magnetic Induction

A generator is a machine which converts mechanical power into electric power. It consists of a magnetic field in which conductors are rotated in such a manner that they cut the magnetic lines of force.

If a conductor is moved in a magnetic field, in a manner such that it cuts lines of force, an emf is induced in that conductor. Alternatively, if the conductor is held stationary and the magnetic field is moved or varied in intensity, an emf is similarly induced in the conductor. A voltmeter connected across the two ends of the conductor will read the value of the emf induced, and if a closed circuit is connected across the two ends of the conductor a current will flow.

Fleming's Right-Hand Rule is a simple means of determining the direction of an induced emf. If the first finger of the right hand is pointed in the direction of the magnetic field, and the thumb in the direction of motion of the conductor relative to the magnetic field, then the middle finger, held at right angles to both the thumb and first finger, indicates the direction of the emf and current.

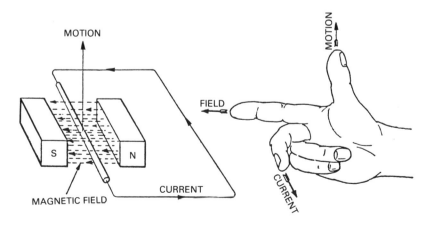

Figure 3–1 Fleming's Right-Hand Rule.

3.2 emf Induced in a Rotating Loop

The simplest form of generator consists of a loop of wire, known as an armature, rotating in a permanent magnetic field. Connection to the external circuit is made by brushes pressing on two slip rings connected to the ends of the coil (see Fig 3-2).

During rotation the two sides of the loop cut the magnetic field in opposite directions. The emfs induced are therefore in opposite directions, but, since the conductor forms a complete loop, they assist each other, so that the total emf – across the slip rings – is the sum of the two. The value of the emf varies during rotation, according to the number of lines of force cut by the conductors during a given time; this depends both on the angle at which the conductors are moving across the magnetic field, and on the speed of rotation.

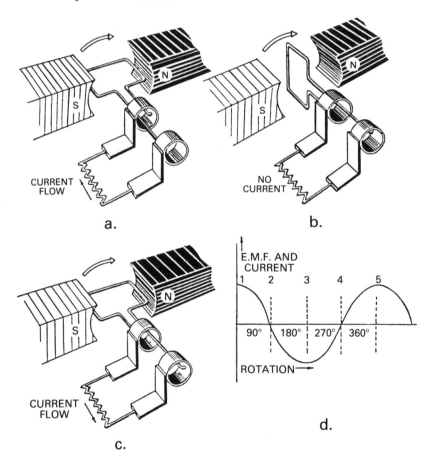

Figure 3–2 Production of alternating current.

In Fig 3-2a the sides of the loop are moving at right angles to the field, cutting the maximum number of lines of force, and the induced emf is at a maximum in one direction: this corresponds to position 1 in Fig 3-2d which shows the rise and fall of the induced emf. As the loop rotates the induced emf falls, until the sides of the loop are moving parallel to the field as at Fig 3-2b when, for an instant, no lines of force are cut and the emf is zero; this corresponds to position 2 in Fig 3-2d. Continued rotation causes the sides of the loop to move into the field and the emf rises until it again reaches a maximum, in the position shown in Fig 3-2c. Since the relative motion between each side of the loop and the magnetic field was reversed at the position shown in Fig 3-2d, this second maximum emf is in the opposite direction to the first maximum and is shown at position 3 in Fig 3-2d. With continued rotation the sides of the loop once again move parallel to the magnetic field, and as no lines of force are being cut, the induced emf again falls to zero as at position 4. After one complete revolution the loop reaches its original position in the field and the emf is once again maximum as at position 5.

The direction of the emf and polarity of the slip rings therefore reverse as the sides of the loop move alternately under the influence of a north and south pole. The direction of the current flow in the external circuit therefore also changes direction and is known as an alternating current.

3.3 Production of Direct Current

To change the alternating current in the rotating loop into a uni-directional or direct current in the external circuit, the ends of the loop are connected to both halves of a split ring. This forms a simple commutator, the halves being insulated from each other and known as segments. The loop is connected to the external circuit by two brushes placed on opposite sides of the commutator.

In Fig 3-3a no emf is induced in the loop and no current flows in the external circuit. In Fig 3-3b maximum emf is induced in the loop and current flows in the external circuit in the direction indicated. In Fig 3-3c the emf has fallen to zero and the segments are moving on to the opposite brushes. In Fig 3-3d the emf in the loop has risen to a maximum in the opposite direction, but since the commutator segments are under opposite brushes the current flows in the same direction in the external circuit. Fig 3-3e completes one revolution and the emf is again zero.

The current always flows in the same direction in the external circuit, one brush always being positive and the other always negative.

The emf and current produced by a single loop falls to zero twice per revolution. A smoother flow of current can be obtained by increasing the number of loops and commutator segments. The loops are placed symmetrically around the axis of rotation. The emf induced in each loop

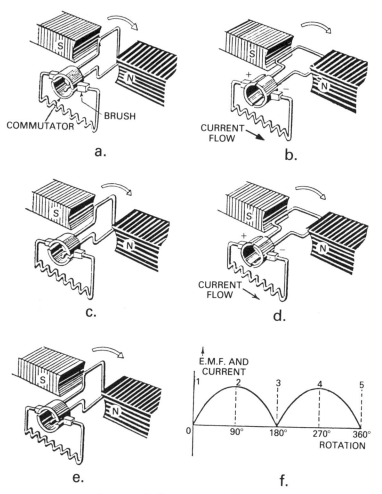

Figure 3–3 Production of direct current.

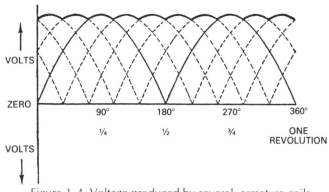

Figure 3–4 Voltage produced by several armature coils.

therefore reaches its maximum value slightly later than the preceding loop. The resultant emf at the brushes is fairly steady, and at no time falls to zero. The fluctuation in voltage becomes a ripple as indicated by the heavy line in the illustration (Fig 3-4).

3.4 Magnitude of the emf

The emf induced in a single loop of wire moving in a permanent magnetic field is too small to be of practical use. A higher emf can be obtained by using a coil of wire, consisting of several turns, each end being connected to a separate commutator segment; this is known as an armature coil. The emfs induced in the separate turns are all in the same direction, and combine to form a total emf at the brushes, equal to the sum of the emfs induced in each turn of the coil.

If an electro-magnet is used in place of the permanent magnet, variation of the current flowing through the magnet coils changes the strength of the magnetic field. For any given speed of rotation of the armature, the induced emf increases or decreases as the field strength is increased or decreased. If the speed of rotation is increased or decreased so a greater or smaller number of lines of force are cut in a given time and the induced emf increases or decreases.

Therefore the magnitude of an induced emf depends on three factors:
(a)   Number of conductors.
(b)   Speed of rotation.
(c)   Strength of the magnetic field.

In practice the number of conductors is fixed by the designer, and machines are usually driven at a constant speed by a governor-controlled prime-mover. The voltage is therefore usually controlled by varying the field strength by means of a variable resistance in the field circuit.

CONSTRUCTION OF DC MACHINES

3.5 The Magnetic Field System

To obtain an intense magnetic field, DC machines are constructed of magnetic materials. With the exception of a small air gap, separating the rotating armature from the stationary field system, a complete magnetic circuit is formed. The component parts of the magnetic field are as follows:

(a)   The Yoke is the circular frame of the machine and is made of cast iron, cast steel or rolled steel.

31

(b) The Pole Pieces are built up of steel laminations, and bolted on the inside of the yoke. Solid mild steel pole pieces with laminated pole shoes are sometimes used.

(c) The Field Windings are wound round the pole pieces, in a manner such that the polarity of adjacent poles is alternately North and South.

(d) The Armature Core is made up of thin iron laminations, mounted on a cast iron spider keyed to the shaft. It is slotted to take the armature windings and rotates inside the pole shoes, being separated from them by a small air gap.

3.6 The Armature

The armature is the practical application of the rotating loop of wire. It consists of a number of coils wound on the armature core; these are rotated in the magnetic field by a prime mover such as a petrol engine or electric motor; it includes the following parts:

(a) Armature Windings
In small machines each armature coil consists of several turns of copper wire, which are wound on a former to the correct shape. The coil is then insulated with varnished cambric and is fitted in the armature slots, which are lined with thin fibre. In larger machines copper strip conductors are used. Each end of each armature coil is connected to a separate segment of the commutator.

As the armature rotates, centrifugal force tends to throw the armature coils outwards. This is prevented by wire lapping, which holds the conductors in position in the armature slots.

(b) The Commutator
This is mounted at one end of the armature shaft and is built up of copper segments, insulated from each other by thin mica sheets. The whole assembly is insulated from but rotates with the armature shaft. The number of segments is equal to the number of armature coils. The armature coils are connected to the commutator by thin strips of copper known as 'risers' and soldered into slots in the segments.

(c) Exhaust Fan
For cooling purposes a fan is mounted on the opposite end of the armature shaft to the commutator.

(d) The Bearings
In large machines the armature shaft rotates in plain journal bearings

in the end plates. Small machines are usually fitted with ball or roller-bearings at each end.

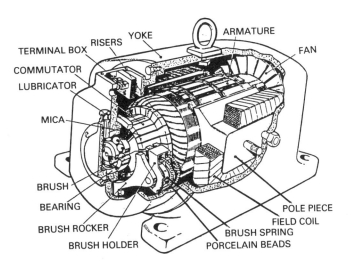

Figure 3-5 Construction of a DC machine.

3.7 Brushgear

Since the armature is rotating a rubbing contact is necessary to carry current away from the moving commutator and conductors, to the stationary external circuit. This is provided by the brushgear, which consists of the following parts:

(a) Brushes

These are usually made of carbon or graphite, and sometimes a mixture of copper and carbon to increase conductivity. When they are set radially to the commutator, the armature can be rotated in either direction. When the brushes are set at an angle to the commutator, the armature must be rotated in one direction only. The brushes are connected to the terminals by flexible copper leads, sometimes insulated with porcelain beads.

(b) Brush Holders

These are small brackets or boxes in which the brushes are mounted. A spring is fitted, which presses the brush on to the surface of the commutator, ensuring good electrical contact.

(c) Brush Rocker

The brush holders are sometimes mounted on an adjustable ring or rocker. The whole assembly may be turned relative to the commutator, until the brushes are in the best position for good commutation, with the minimum of sparking. This is known as rocking the brushes. The normal position is usually indicated by marks on the brush rocker and end frame.

Note:
Where four brushes are fitted, they are alternately positive and negative, those of the same polarity being connected to each other.

TYPES OF DC GENERATOR

3.8 Method of Field Excitation

Some small generators such as magnetos use a permanent magnetic field, but most generators have an electro-magnetic field. The following diagram shows a four-pole machine. The four brushes are resting on the commutator. The two positive brushes are connected together and to the positive terminal A. The negative brushes are also connected together and to the negative terminal AA (or A_1).

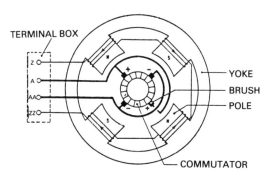

Figure 3–6 Armature and field connections.

The four field coils are usually connected in series and referred to as the field circuit, the ends being connected to the terminals Z and ZZ (or Z_1). The coils are so wound and connected that the poles are alternately North and South.

There are several methods of supplying the field current, and the characteristic of the generator largely depends on the method of field excitation. The characteristic of a generator is the relationship between the voltage at the generator terminals and the load current. In general the voltage of a generator tends to fall as the load current increases. Generators are named according to the manner in which the field and armature windings are connected; the various types are described in the following paragraphs.

Note: **Field Flashing**
A generator may lose its residual magnetism, that is the permanent magnetism within its magnetic poles, or become incorrectly polarised (reversal of polarity), due to heat, shock loads or reverse current flow. This can be corrected by passing direct current through the field windings by connecting a battery to the field circuit. This is known as Field Flashing.

3.9 Separately Excited Generator

The field winding is connected to an external source of supply such as a small DC generator known as the exciter. The field current remains constant irrespective of the load connected to the generator. When a load is switched on current flows through the armature, therefore the terminal voltage falls slightly as the load is increased due to voltage drop in the armature windings.

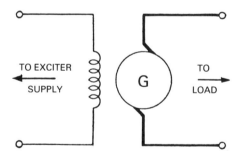

Figure 3–7 Separately excited generator.

(a) **Voltage Regulation**
The current flowing through the field circuit, and therefore the strength of the magnetic field, can be controlled by varying the voltage of the exciter. If the armature speed is kept constant, increase in the field current causes an increase in the generated emf; decreased field current causes a decrease in the generated emf.

(b) Use

This type of machine is used where complete control of the field current and voltage is required over a large range.

3.10 Shunt-wound Generator

The field winding is connected in parallel with the armature and with the external load circuit. It is therefore energised by part of the armature current. The field coils contain a large number of turns of wire and are of relatively high resistance, thus taking a small current.

When the armature is rotated the conductors cut the weak magnetic field due to the residual magnetism in the poles. A small emf is generated and, since the field is connected across the armature, a current flows through the field coils, thus increasing the magnetic flux. This causes a further rise in emf and a further rise in field current and so on. Therefore when no external load is connected, the field is fully excited, and the terminal voltage is at a maximum. A shunt generator must be allowed to 'build up' before connecting the load.

Variation of the load on a shunt generator causes a small variation in the terminal voltage; as the load increases the voltage falls. If a constant load is applied the terminal voltage takes up a steady value. If the generator is overloaded the voltage falls considerably.

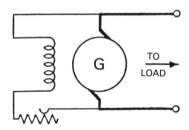

Figure 3–8 Shunt-wound generator.

(a) Voltage Regulation

This is obtained by inserting a variable resistance known as a field regulating resistance (Voltage Regulator) in series with the field winding as shown in the diagram. Variation of the resistance increases or decreases the field current, causing a corresponding variation of the magnetic field and therefore of the generated emf.

(b) Use

Shunt generators are used to supply loads such as accumulator charging. They are used as engine-driven generators on aircraft.

3.11 Series-wound Generator

The field winding is connected in series with the armature and load, therefore the current flowing in the series field is the load current. To reduce voltage drop in the field, the resistance of the winding is low and the number of turns small. Since the field is in series with the armature, no current flows through it until an external circuit is connected. On open circuit the small emf generated is due to residual magnetism in the field system.

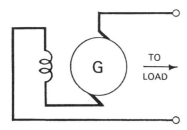

Figure 3–9 Series-wound generator.

As the load is increased more current flows through the field coils and increases the strength of the magnetic field. In a series machine the terminal voltage therefore increases almost proportionately with increase in load current until the maximum output is reached.

The generator is unsuitable for normal use and has no service application. In mains supply systems it is sometimes necessary to compensate for resistance drop in long cables, and a series generator can be connected in series with the main circuit to step-up the voltage; these generators are known as boosters.

3.12 Compound-wound Generator

In this type of generator a combination of shunt and series field excitation is used. The machine has a shunt winding connected in parallel with the armature, with a low resistance series winding – connected in series with the load – producing the same polarity and wound on the same pole pieces. As the load is increased the current in the series winding increases, resulting in an increased field strength, which compensates for the fall in voltage, which occurs in a plain shunt generator (see paragraph 10). If the series winding is so designed that the terminal voltage is maintained almost constant, the machine is said to be 'level-compounded'. If the number of turns is greater, the voltage rises as the load is increased and the machine is said to be 'over-compounded'.

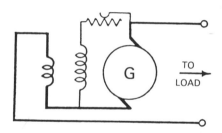

Figure 3–10 Compound-wound generator.

(a) Voltage Regulation

A rheostat is connected in series with the shunt field circuit. It is used for small voltage adjustments by increasing or decreasing the field current. Its range is usually smaller than in a shunt machine, as the main voltage regulation is automatically carried out by the series field winding.

(b) Use

This is the most common form of industrial generator and is used for fluctuating loads such as lighting and traction. A level-compounded generator is used wherever a constant terminal voltage is required with varying loads. When power is transmitted over long distances, an over-compound generator is used to compensate for voltage drop in the cables, and to maintain a constant voltage at the end of the feeders.

3.13 Rating

The rating of a generator is the output in watts or kilowatts that a machine will supply; this is limited by the rise in temperature which occurs in the machine due to electrical losses. The rating is calculated by the maker and is given, either directly in watts or indirectly in amps and volts (watts = amps × volts), on the rating plate attached to the machine; it gives all or part of the following information:

(a) Number of the generator and its type of winding.

(b) Voltage and type of supply (DC or AC).

(c) Pressure between terminals in volts.

(d) Current in amperes.

(e) Speed in revolutions per minute.

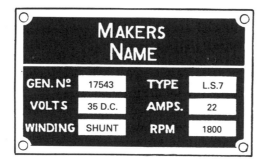

GEN. N°	17543	TYPE	L.S.7
VOLTS	35 D.C.	AMPS.	22
WINDING	SHUNT	RPM	1800

Figure 3–11 Rating plate.

The rating plate shows that the machine is a direct current, shunt-wound generator, with a normal working voltage of 35 volts and a maximum load of 22 amps, when it is driven at a speed of 1800 rpm. Its rating is 35 volts × 22 amps = 770 watts.

3.14 Parallel Operation of Shunt Generators

In multi-engined aircraft shunt generators are sometimes connected in parallel so that the load is shared equally between them. The principle is illustrated in the diagram Fig 3-12, the generators are connected to common positive and negative mains through double-pole switches. The

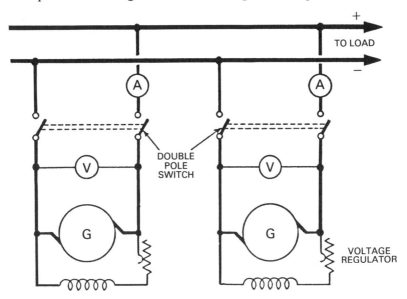

Figure 3–12 Shunt generators in parallel.

terminal voltage of each generator is controlled by a Voltage Regulator. An ammeter and voltmeter are connected in each generator circuit.

One generator is run up to speed – the required voltage being obtained by adjusting the field regulating resistance – and is connected to the load by closing the double-pole switch. To bring the second generator into operation it must first be run up to speed, and its voltage adjusted to the same value as the first generator before closing its double-pole switch.

Adjust the field regulating resistance until the load is equally shared between the generators as indicated on the ammeters. If the voltage of one generator falls, the other generator drives current through it in a reverse direction, causing it to act as a motor. The whole load is thus thrown on to the first generator, which may consequently be overloaded.

On disconnecting one generator, adjust the field regulating resistance until the ammeter reads zero before opening the double-pole switch.

ELEMENTARY MOTOR PRINCIPLES

3.15 Action of a Motor

The electric motor is a machine for converting electrical energy into mechanical energy, its function being the reverse of a generator. There is no difference in construction between a DC generator and a DC motor and if an external supply is connected to the terminals of a DC machine current flows through the armature and field windings and the armature revolves.

Figure 3-13 shows one conductor, on the armature of a DC machine, under a North pole. Current is flowing in the conductor in the direction 'into the paper'. A magnetic field is set up round the conductor in a clockwise direction (Corkscrew rule). It is seen that on the left of the conductor this field and the main magnetic field oppose one another; on the right-

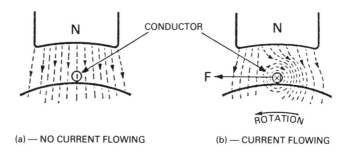

(a) — NO CURRENT FLOWING   (b) — CURRENT FLOWING

Figure 3–13 Motor principle.

hand side they assist one another. The result is that lines of force of the main magnetic field, Fig 3-13a, become distorted, Fig 3-13b. Bearing in mind the elastic properties of magnetic lines of force, and regarding them as stretched elastic threads, a mechanical force is exerted on the conductor in the direction F, and the armature rotates in an anti-clockwise direction.

Paragraph 3.1 illustrates Fleming's Right-Hand Rule for a generator; Fleming's Left-Hand Rule applies in the same manner to a motor: the left hand first finger points in the direction of the magnetic field; the middle finger points in the direction of current flow in the conductor, the thumb shows the direction in which the conductor moves.

The action of the commutator reverses the direction of the flow of current in each armature conductor as it passes under the influence of the next pole, which is of opposite polarity. Thus the mechanical force on each conductor is always in the same direction and the armature continues to rotate so long as the supply is connected.

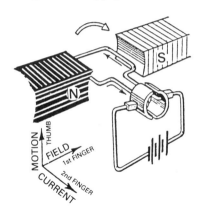

Figure 3–14 Fleming's Left-Hand Rule.

3.16 Back emf

The resistance of the armature windings of most motors is very low, usually being less than 1 ohm. If this were the only opposition offered to the current, in say a 220 volt supply, the current would be extremely high. This, however, is not the case. Immediately the armature of a motor starts rotating, the armature conductors cut the main magnetic field and an emf is induced in them as in a generator. This emf always opposes the emf applied to the terminals of the motor and is thus known as the 'Back emf'. The current which actually flows through the armature therefore depends on the effective emf, which is the difference between the applied emf and the back emf.

3.17 Speed of a DC Motor

The speed and current consumption of a motor automatically adjust themselves to the mechanical load. When the load is increased the speed falls, causing the back emf to fall also. The effective emf is therefore increased and a greater current is taken from the supply. This variation of speed with load is known as the 'speed characteristic' of the motor, and, as in a generator, this characteristic depends on the method by which the field is excited and motors are named accordingly.

The speed of a motor can be controlled over a wide range by variation of the current flowing through the field coils; this is done by connecting a variable resistance in the field circuit. In any DC motor, weakening of the field results in an increase in armature speed, whilst strengthening the field decreases the rpm.

TYPES OF DC MOTORS

3.18 Shunt-wound Motor

The field winding is connected in parallel with the armature. The field is therefore directly across the supply and it is of a fairly high resistance. If the supply voltage is maintained constant the field strength remains constant. The armature is also connected across the supply and since it is of low resistance, a shunt motor must not be started by connecting it directly to the mains because a heavy current will flow through the armature windings. To limit the starting current a resistance is connected in series with the armature until the speed of the motor generates sufficient back emf to limit the working current to a safe value. The driving power (torque) of a shunt motor is small on starting and on low speeds.

The speed of a shunt motor is controlled by a variable resistance connected in series with the shunt field windings. If the resistance in the circuit is increased the speed is increased and vice versa (see paragraph 3.19).

When a load is applied the reduction in speed from 'no load' to 'full load' is very small, and the shunt motor can be considered a constant speed machine. This type of motor is generally used where the load does not vary greatly and where an approximate constant speed is required, eg workshop lathes.

3.19 Series-wound Motor

In this type of motor the armature and field windings are in series with each other so that – unlike the shunt motor – the armature and field currents are the same. The combined resistance of the armature and field is very small and a large current flows on starting. This can be controlled by a resistance – in series with the circuit – which is gradually cut out as the speed rises. For some purposes, eg engine starting, no starting resistance is used and the circuit is designed to carry heavy currents.

The speed of a series motor varies considerably with the mechanical load applied, running slowly on heavy loads and fast on light loads. It is important that a series motor be permanently connected to the load, because if the load is removed the motor races at dangerously high speeds.

Since this type of motor has a high starting torque it is used for engine starting, cranes and traction work.

3.20 Compound-wound Motor

The motor has two field windings, one shunt connected and the other connected in series with the armature, both being wound on the same pole pieces. In the more common type of compound motor the series field is wound so that is produces the same polarity as the shunt field and, as the load increases, so the influence of the series field increases. Compound motors have a speed/load characteristic between that of shunt and series motors depending on the relative strengths of the two windings.

If the influence of the series field is small the motor has a shunt characteristic at first, but as the load is increased the speed falls more rapidly than that of a shunt motor. If the series field is predominant the motor has a high starting torque – that is, a series characteristic – but the small shunt winding limits the no load speed to a safe value.

The speed of a compound motor is controlled by connecting a variable resistance in series with the shunt field; as the resistance in circuit is increased the speed increases.

Compound motors are used to drive cranes and machinery, where the load fluctuates.

OPERATION OF DC SHUNT MOTORS

3.21 Motor Starter

To limit the current, when starting a DC machine, a variable resistance is placed in series with the armature. On starting the maximum resistance is in the circuit, and as the armature gathers speed the resistance is gradually decreased until it is finally cut out altogether.

Starter resistances are usually of the faceplate type, with the components mounted on an insulated panel. The resistance is tapped at several points, which are connected to contact studs on the faceplate; a moving arm makes contact with these studs. The moving arm is normally held in the off position by a spring and is held in the full-on position by an electro-magnet known as the no-volt coil. An overload release consisting of an electro-magnetic or thermal switch is incorporated and releases the handle – which flies back to the off position – if an excessive current flows. Connections to the starter are made by three terminals marked Z (field), L (line) and A (armature).

3.22 Shunt Motor Installation

A DC shunt motor circuit consists of a main switch and fuses, starter, and in some cases a reversing switch. Before the supply is connected the motor, starter, and switch casings must be connected to a good earth. One line from the supply is connected through the main switch to the terminal L on the starter; the other line is connected to the terminals AA and ZZ on the motor. The A terminal on the starter is connected to the other side of the motor armature at A terminal, and the Z terminal is connected to the corresponding Z terminal (shunt field) on the motor.

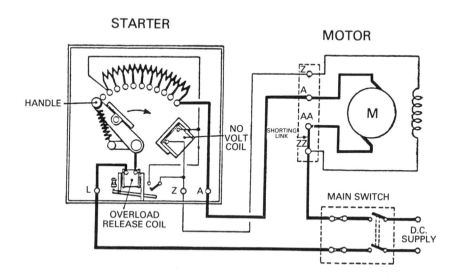

Figure 3–15 DC Shunt motor and starter.

3.23 Starting

Before starting, the speed regulator – if fitted – must be set in the position of minimum resistance. To start the motor, close the main switch, and move the starter handle slowly from the OFF to the ON position, by which time the motor should be running at full speed.

3.24 The Basic DC Circuit

The following is a brief explanation of the principles and operation of a basic DC system. This should be read in conjunction with Fig 3-16.

This system uses a shunt-wound DC generator.

(a) Generator

In order that voltage can be induced into the armature loop, two basic functions are required:

(1)   The armature loop or conductor must be in motion, ie rotated.

(2)   A magnetic field must exist between the magnetic poles.

The armature is rotated by the engine, normally via a drive shaft or a drive belt similar to a car generator drive system, causing the armature loop to cut the lines or magnetic force between the magnetic poles.

On engine starting the initial excitation, that is, the initial magnetic field, is provided by residual magnetism retained by permanent magnets within the core of the magnetic poles.

Normal or operational excitation is provided by electro-magnetic coils or windings wound onto the magnetic poles and known as the field windings.

Current will not flow in the field windings, in the example shown, until the generator produces current flow, hence the need for initial excitation.

The generator produces Alternating Current which, through the method of collection of the current through a commutator, becomes DC. More recent types of DC system may use a Rectifier to perform this function.

The flow of current from the generator, the generator output, will in the main be determined by the demands of the various circuits. These circuits, serving specific service loads, are connected to a bus-bar, the distribution point. The generator supplies its current to the bus-bar.

The output of the generator is indicated on an Ammeter, this measures the current flow in Amperes (Amps). The majority of the output flows to the bus-bar, some however flows to the field windings via the Voltage Regulator to create the required magnetic field.

Note:
The ammeter used to indicate generator output is normally termed the Load Ammeter or Generator Load Ammeter.

(b) The Voltage Regulator

The stronger the field current, that is current flowing to the field windings, the greater the output of the generator. The flow of current to the field windings is controlled by the voltage regulator which is a form of variable resistor.

The Voltage Regulator is designed to operate at a set value giving the generator a constant voltage or pressure output. Normally, for each 12 volts required in the system, the generator will produce 14 volts; ie for a 24 volt system the generator will produce 28 volts, etc. The additional output is required to make up for losses in the system and to provide enough additional voltage to recharge the battery in flight.

If the generator voltage is insufficient, it is said to be undervolting, if it is producing too great an output, it is said to be overvolting.

In operation, therefore, if the generator is overvolting the magnetic field between the poles is too strong, the voltage regulator will then sense this from the generator output, increase its resistance, reducing the field current to the magnetic poles, and therefore reduce the output of the generator.

(c) Cut-Out

Before the engine is started, electrical supply will be provided by the battery. This is achieved by switching on the Master Switch, and or, the Battery Master Switch. This action connects the battery to the bus-bar. As current will flow through the lines of least resistance, there is a danger the battery will discharge through the generator, possibly damaging its windings, rather than supply the bus-bar. To prevent the battery discharging to the generator, the Cut-Out or Battery Cut-Out is fitted.

As shown in simple form, the cut out has a switch which will remain open until the generator produces, usually ½ volt more than battery output, and then the switch will close connecting the generator to the bus-bar. The generator can now be said to be 'on line', that is, when it is connected to the bus-bar.

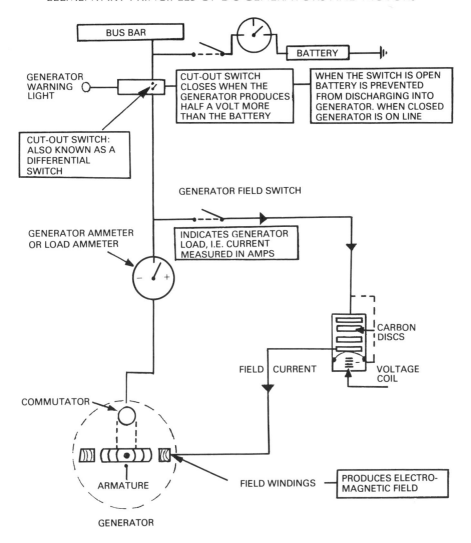

Figure 3–16 Basic DC supply switch.

(d) Generator Warning Light

The generator warning light is usually a red warning light displayed in the cockpit. It indicates when the generator fails or is not 'on line'. It operates in conjunction with the cut out and unless the cut out switch is closed the warning light will illuminate.

(e) Battery Ammeter

The Battery Ammeter indicates the rate of charge or discharge of the battery.

(f) Batteries

With the exception of light aircraft, there is normally more than one battery fitted and they are virtually always fitted in parallel to provide a greater ampere/hour capacity.

Additional Notes on the DC Supply.

(1) Normally there is only one load ammeter fitted in the cockpit regardless of the number of generators. Each generator has a sensor which transmits the current flow rate to the indicator in the cockpit. The ammeter in the cockpit has a mode switch which allows the pilot to select the load indication required, ie select generator No 1 load or No 2 etc.

(2) The Battery Ammeter is coupled in the same way as the load ammeter.

(3) The Voltage Regulator is sometimes fitted with a Trimmer Resistor which allows fine adjustment to increase or decrease the generator output from the cockpit.

(4) A Thermistor may also be fitted to the voltage regulator to compensate for variations of resistance due to temperature changes.

(g) Load Sharing Generators

Load sharing or paralleling of generators, that is when two generators are supplying the same bus-bar (as may occur on some twin-engined aircraft) requires in a DC supply system the voltage in each generator to be exactly, or within fine limits, the same. To achieve this the two generators are connected to each other via the voltage regulators by what is termed an equalizing circuit. Each end of the equalizing circuit is coupled to an equalizing coil in the voltage regulator which ensures the main voltage coils, which essentially control the field current, produce the same voltage in each regulator.

It should be noted that, when two generators are paralleled, it is normally for safety purposes, so that in the event of one generator failing the serviceable generator can provide all the requirements of the circuits. In such circumstances, should one generator fail, the voltage the other serviceable generator receives is unchanged; the load on the serviceable generator, however, will double.

The current at the bus-bar will remain the same as the loads and services switched on remain the same.

(h) Load shedding

It is possible, in flight, that a generator may not produce its maximum voltage due perhaps to a minor fault, such as an accumulation of dirt on the slip rings or brushes. This may be indicated by flickering of the generator warning light, or the generator trips out in that the cut out switch opens as the battery is now providing a greater voltage than the generator, therefore the generator warning light will remain on. Bringing the generator back on line can be achieved by reducing the load, ie switching off non essential services. The switching off of loads is termed load shedding.

(i) Circuit Protection

Each individual circuit will be protected against damage in the event of a fault, usually by one of two methods:

(1)   A Fuse.

(2)   A Circuit Breaker.

On some circuits both of these devices may be fitted in series with the load, normally between the switch and the load. Under normal circumstances spare fuses must be carried on the aircraft as a mandatory requirement. The pilot may replace a fuse that had blown once, should it blow a second time the engineer should be consulted. The circuit breaker must be treated in the same way as a fuse in that if it trips out it may be reset by the pilot once, then the engineer should be consulted. When a fuse is replaced, only a fuse of the same type and value should be used. Remember, fuses are rated in Amps.

(j) Re-setting Circuit Breakers

(1)   Non-trip free type

As with all types of fuse and circuit breaker, they cause the circuit to be broken, or become open circuited, in the event excessive heat is generated in the conductor. The excessive heat will cause the metal wire to melt in a fuse and/or the bi-metal strip in a circuit breaker to disrupt the continuity of the conductor.

When re-setting the non-trip free circuit breaker the reset button must be pushed in and then finger pressure immediately released. It must never be held in to prevent it tripping out or the circuit may overheat and fire may result.

(2)   Trip Free Circuit Breaker

This type is designed so that it cannot be inadvertently held in.

Section 3   Test Yourself Questions

Generators and Motors

1. Fleming's Right Hand Rule is normally applied to:
   (a) generators.
   (b) motors.
   (c) magnetic fields around conductors.
   (d) transformers.

Ref 3.1.

2. Maximum emf is induced in the loop of an armature when the loop:
   (a) cuts the lines of magnetic flux at 90°.
   (b) cuts the lines of magnetic flux at 45°.
   (c) is moving parallel to the lines of magnetic flux.
   (d) cuts the lines of magnetic flux at 270°.

Ref 3.2.

3. The magnitude of the emf in a generator is dependent upon:
   (a) the size of the magnetic poles.
   (b) the number of armatures.
   (c) the strength of the magnetic field.
   (d) the cross sectional area of the conductors in the field.

Ref 3.4.

4. Voltage is controlled in a shunt wound DC generator by:
   (a) a variable resistor.
   (b) varying the rpm of the generator.
   (c) a parallel variable resistor.
   (d) control of the loads or services.

Ref 3.10.

5. DC generators are rated in:
   (a) KVA.
   (b) VA.
   (c) KVAR.
   (d) KW.

Ref 3.13.

6. In any DC motor:
   (a) the field is kept constant.
   (b) weakening of the field causes armature speed to increase.
   (c) weakening of the field causes armature speed to reduce.
   (d) weakening of the field will have no effect on armature speed.

Ref 3.18.

7. In a shunt-wound motor:
   (a) the field windings are in series with the armature.
   (b) the field windings are in parallel with the motor.
   (c) the field windings are connected to an external power source.
   (d) the field windings are connected to the bus-bar.

Ref 3.19.

8. A shunt-wound motor:
   (a) can be considered to be a constant speed machine.
   (b) has a high starting torque.
   (c) is started by connection to mains or high voltage.
   (d) is started by connection to high voltage batteries.

Ref 3.19.

9. To limit the current, when starting a DC motor:
   (a) a variable resistor is fitted in parallel with the armature.
   (b) a variable resistor is fitted in parallel with the field.
   (c) a variable resistor is fitted in series with the armature.
   (d) a variable resistor is fitted in series with the field.

Ref 3.22.

10. If a speed regulator is fitted to a motor, the speed switch must, before starting, be set to:
   (a) max rpm.
   (b) off.
   (c) min rpm.
   (d) disconnect.

Ref 3.24.

4

Aircraft Batteries

4.1 Introduction

As has been established in previous chapters there are two primary sources of electrical energy used on modern aircraft.

(a) The generator, which converts mechanical energy into electrical energy.

(b) The battery, which converts chemical energy into electrical energy.

During normal engine operation, electrical energy is taken from the generator, which itself is driven by the engine. Most engines, however, are initially started with the use of electrical power and such power must be stored until required for use. The most common method of storage is the electrical battery. Such batteries may also be used to provide emergency power in the event of generator failure.

Batteries may be divided into two basic types:

(a) The primary, or elementary, cell battery which is non-rechargeable and disposed of when all chemical energy has been used.

(b) The secondary cell or rechargeable type battery.

The majority of aircraft batteries are of the rechargeable type and are of Lead-Acid, or the more common Nickel-Cadmium, construction.

4.2 The Lead-Acid Type Battery

This type of battery is very similar to those used in cars. The cells are connected in series. Each cell contains positive plates of lead peroxide, negative plates of spongy lead, and electrolyte consisting of sulphuric acid and distilled water. In discharging, the chemical energy stored in the battery is changed into electrical energy; in charging, the electrical energy supplied to the battery is changed to chemical energy and stored. It is possible to charge a storage battery many times before it deteriorates permanently.

When new the battery is initially charged from an electrical supply before the battery is fitted to the aircraft. Under normal operational conditions energy is used from the battery to provide electrical power for pre-start checks and to physically start the engine. After the engine has started, the generator, besides providing power to the various systems, will also provide power to recharge the battery to ensure it is fully charged ready for the next time its electrical supply is required.

4.3 Lead-Acid Battery Construction

Figure 4-1 shows an example of the basic construction of a lead-acid battery. Each plate consists of a framework which is called a grid, and is made from lead and antimony, to which the active material (spongy lead, or lead peroxide) is attached. The positive and negative plates, item (1) on Fig 4-1, are so assembled that each positive plate is between two nega-tive plates. Therefore the end plate in each cell is a negative plate. Between the plates are porous separators (7) which keep the positive and negative plates from touching each other and shorting out the cell. The separators have vertical ribs on the sides facing the positive plates. This construction permits the electrolyte to circulate freely around the plates. In addition, it provides a path for sediment to settle to the bottom of the cell.

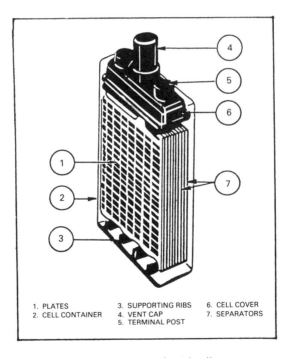

1. PLATES	3. SUPPORTING RIBS	6. CELL COVER
2. CELL CONTAINER	4. VENT CAP	7. SEPARATORS
	5. TERMINAL POST	

Figure 4–1 Lead-acid cell.

Each cell is sealed in a hard rubber casing through the top of which are terminal posts and a hole into which is fitted a nonspill type vent valve, or cap, see item (4). The hole provides access for testing the strength of the electrolyte and adding, or topping up with distilled water. The vent plug permits gases to escape from the cell with a minimum leakage of electrolyte, regardless of the position of the aircraft in flight or on the ground. Figure 4-2 shows the construction of the vent plug. In level flight, the lead weight permits venting of gases through a small hole. In inverted flight, this hole is covered by the lead weight. Vent ducts are normally provided to remove such gases that may vent from the battery directing them to atmosphere.

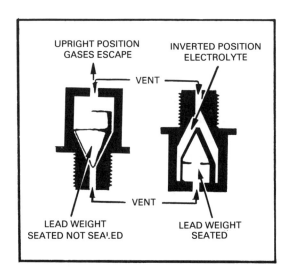

Figure 4–2 Nonspill battery vent plug.

The individual cells of the battery are connected in series by means of cell straps. The complete assembly is enclosed in an acid resistant metal container, termed the battery box, or compartment, which serves as electrical shielding and provides mechanical protection. The battery box has a removable top and also has a vent tube connection at each end. When the battery box is installed in the aircraft, a vent tube is attached to each vent tube connection. One tube is the intake tube and is exposed to the slipstream, the other is the exhaust vent tube and is attached to the battery drain sump, which is a glass jar containing a felt pad moistened with a concentration of sodium bicarbonate in solution. With this arrangement, the airstream is directed through the battery compartment, or box, where the gases are picked up, neutralized in the sump, and then expelled overboard without damage to the aircraft.

4.4 Lead-Acid Type Battery Ratings

The voltage of a battery is determined by the number of cells connected in series to form the battery. Although the voltage of a single cell, when just removed from a battery charger is approximately 2.2 volts, a lead-acid cell is normally rated at only 2 volts, because it soon drops to that level after removal from the charge supply. A battery rated at 12 volts consists of six cells connected in series, and a battery rated at 24 volts is composed of twelve cells.

The capacity of an aircraft storage battery is rated in ampere hours (amperes furnished by the battery times the amount of time current can be drawn). This rating indicates how long the battery may be used at a given rate before it becomes completely discharged.

Theoretically, a 100 ampere-hour battery will furnish 100 amperes for one hour, 50 amperes for two hours, or 20 amperes for five hours. Actually, the ampere output of a particular battery depends on the rate of discharge. Heavy discharge current heats the battery and decreases its efficiency and total ampere hour output. For aircraft batteries, a period of ten hours has been established as the discharge time rating battery capacity. This time of ten hours is however only a basis for rating and does not necessarily mean the length of time during which the battery is expected to furnish current. Under actual service conditions it is possible that a battery may completely discharge in a matter of minutes, or it may never discharge if the generator provides sufficient charge.

The ampere-hour capacity of a battery is dependent upon its total effective plate area. Connecting batteries in parallel will increase their ampere-hour capacity and connecting batteries in series increases the total voltage but not the ampere-hour capacity. In multi engined aircraft where more than one battery is used, the batteries are usually connected in parallel. The voltage is equal to that of one battery, but the ampere-hour capacity is increased. The total capacity is the sum of the ampere-hour ratings for the individual batteries.

4.5 Factors Affecting Lead-Acid Battery Life

Various factors cause deterioration of a battery and shorten its service life. These include over-discharging, which causes excessive sulphation and too rapid charging or discharging, resulting in overheating of the plates and shedding of active material. The accumulation of shedded material, in turn, causes shorting of the plates and results in internal discharge. A battery that remains in a low or discharged condition for a long period of time may be permanently damaged. In addition to causing deterioration of the battery, these factors also decrease battery capacity.

4.6 Operation of Lead-Acid Cells

A lead-acid cell contains positive plates coated with lead peroxide (PbO_2); negative plates made of lead (Pb); and liquid electrolyte, consisting of sulphuric acid (SO_4) and water (H_2O). During discharge, lead sulphate ($PbSO_4$) is formed on both the positive and negative plates, the acid content of the electrolyte is decreased, and its water content increased. As discharge continues, the amount of lead sulphate on the plates increases until the sulphate coatings become so thick that the weakened electrolyte cannot effectively reach the active materials (lead and lead peroxide). When this happens, chemical reaction is retarded and the output of the cell reduced. In practice, the cell is not permitted to be discharged to this extent because thick coatings of lead peroxide are difficult to remove in charging. Additionally, a cell approaching a state of total discharge is of little use because the high internal resistance caused by the coatings of sulphate on its plates reduces the current to a value too low for practical use.

When a cell is being charged, lead sulphate is removed both from the positive and the negative plates, and sulphuric acid is again formed. In the process, the water content of the electrolyte is decreased and the density of the electrolyte increased. The open circuit voltage of a lead-acid cell, that is, its voltage when there is no load drawing current, is approximately 2.2 volts.

This voltage is the same for every lead-acid cell regardless of its plate size and remains at this value until the cell is practically dead, regardless of its state of discharge. When the cell approaches total discharge, its voltage begins to drop rapidly.

The closed circuit voltage of a cell, that is, its voltage under load, decreases gradually as the cell is discharged. This gradual decrease in terminal voltage is due to a gradual increase in the internal resistance of the cell caused by sulphation of the plates. At the end of normal discharge, the internal resistance of a lead-acid cell is more than twice as high as it is when fully charged. The difference between the open circuit and closed circuit terminal voltages is due to the voltage drop inside the cell. This is equal to the current the load draws multiplied by the internal resistance in the cell. The discharging voltage that a lead-acid cell can supply under closed circuit conditions is therefore equal to the open circuit voltage of the cell minus the internal resistance drop in the cell.

To give a high discharge current and a high terminal voltage under load, a battery must have low internal resistance. This characteristic can be achieved through extensive plate area. Each cell therefore contains several sets of plates. All the positive plates of a cell are connected by one connecting bar, and all the negative plates by another. Thus, the plates are connected in parallel, further decreasing the internal resistance of the cell. The open circuit cell voltage is not affected: it remains the same as that of a single pair of plates.

4.7 Lead-Acid Battery Testing Methods

The state of charge of a storage battery depends upon the condition of its active materials, primarily the plates. However, the state of charge of a battery is indicated by the density of the electrolyte and is checked by a hydrometer, an instrument which measures the specific gravity (weight as compared with water) of liquids.

The hydrometer most commonly used consists of a small sealed glass tube weighted at its lower end so it will float upright. Within the narrow stem of the tube is a printed scale with a range of 1.100 to 1.300. The depth to which the hydrometer sinks in the electrolyte is determined by the density of the electrolyte, and the scale value indicated at the level of the electrolyte is its specific gravity. The more dense the electrolyte, the higher the hydrometer will float; therefore, the highest number on the scale (1.300) is at the lower end of the hydrometer scale. In a new, fully charged aircraft storage battery, the electrolyte is approximately 30 percent sulphuric acid and 70 percent distilled water (by volume) and is 1.300 times as heavy as pure water.

During discharge, the solution (electrolyte) becomes less dense and its specific gravity drops below 1.300. Specific gravity readings between 1.300 and 1.275 indicates a high state of charge, a medium state of charge would be between 1.275 and 1.240, and a low state of charge between 1.240 and 1.200.

Aircraft batteries are generally of small capacity but are subject to heavy loads. The values specified for state of charge are therefore rather high. Hydrometer tests are made periodically on all storage batteries installed in aircraft. An aircraft battery in a low state of charge may have perhaps 50 percent charge remaining, but is nevertheless low in the face of heavy demands which would soon exhaust it. A battery in such a state of charge is considered in need of immediate recharging. Aircraft batteries are given a serviceability check every three months and must achieve a minimum rate of efficiency of 80 percent. The state of charge of an aircraft battery must be checked every three months and in general before each flight.

When a battery is tested for serviceability using a hydrometer, the temperature of the electrolyte must be taken into consideration. The specific gravity readings on the hydrometer will vary from the actual specific gravity as the temperature changes. No correction is necessary when the temperature is between 70°F and 90°F since the variation is not great enough to be considered. When temperatures are greater than 90°F or less than 70°F. It is necessary to apply a correction factor. Most hydrometers are supplied with a correction chart, or scale.

The specific gravity of a cell is reliable only if nothing has been added to the electrolyte except occasional small amounts of distilled water to replace that lost as a result of normal evaporation. Hydrometer readings should always be taken before adding distilled water, never after. This is necessary to allow more time for the water to mix thoroughly with the electrolyte and to avoid drawing up into the syringe a sample which does not represent the true strength of the solution.

Extreme care should be exercised when making the hydrometer test of a lead-acid battery cell. The electrolyte should be handled very carefully, for sulphuric acid will burn clothes and skin. If the acid does come into contact with the skin the area should be treated by a thorough washing with clean water and the area treated with bicarbonate of soda.

Care should also be taken to avoid spillage of electrolyte and, or, acid onto aircraft structure as severe corrosion to the affected area may result if the area is not treated immediately after the spillage.

4.8 Lead-Acid Battery Charging Methods

A storage battery may be charged by passing direct current through the battery in a direction opposite to that of the discharge current. Because of the internal resistance in the battery, the voltage of the external charging source must be greater than the open circuit voltage. For example, the open circuit voltage of a fully charged 12-cell lead-acid type battery, is approximately 26.4 volts (12×2.2 volts), but approximately 28 volts are required to charge it. This larger voltage is required for charging because of the voltage drop in the battery caused by the internal resistance. Hence, the charging voltage of a lead-acid battery must equal the open circuit voltage plus the internal resistance drop within the battery.

Batteries are charged by either the constant voltage or constant current method. In the constant voltage method, a motor generator set with a constant regulated voltage forces the current through the battery. In this method, the current at the start of the process is high but automatically tapers off, reaching the value of approximately one ampere when the battery is fully charged. The constant voltage method requires less time and supervision than does the constant current method.

In the constant current method, the current remains almost constant during the entire charging process.

This method requires a longer time to charge a battery fully and, towards the end of the charging process, presents the danger of overcharging if care is not exercised.

In the aircraft, the storage battery is charged by direct current from the aircraft generator system. This method of charging is the constant voltage method, since the generator voltage is held constant by use of a voltage regulator.

When a storage battery is being charged, it generates a certain amount of hydrogen and oxygen. Since this is an explosive mixture, it is important that measures be taken to prevent ignition of the gas mixture. During the charging process the vent caps should be loosened and left in place. No open flames, sparks, or other sources of ignition should be permitted in the vicinity. Before connecting or disconnecting a battery to be charged, always turn off the power at the main supply source.

Note:
The action of loosening vent caps during charging applies only to batteries being charged in a servicing bay situation and not when the battery is being charged by normal process in the aircraft.

4.9 Nickel-Cadmium Batteries

The primary advantages of the Nickel-Cadmium battery, usually referred to as the ni-cad battery, are its low maintenance cost, excellent reliability, good starting capability, and a short recharge time coupled with a long life.

4.10 Nickel-Cadmium Cell Construction

As in the lead-acid battery, the cell is the basic unit of the ni-cad battery. It consists of positive and negative plates, separators, electrolyte, cell vent and cell container. The plates are constructed as porous plaques on which nickel hydroxide has been deposited. In both cases the porous plaque is obtained by sintering nickel powder to a fine wire mesh screen. Sintering is a process which fuses together extremely small granules of powder at a high temperature. After the active positive and negative materials are deposited on the plaque, it is formed and cut into the proper plate size. A nickel tab is then welded to a corner of each plate and the plates are assembled with the tabs welded to the proper terminals. The plates are separated from each other by a continuous strip of porous plastic. The electrolyte used in the ni-cad battery is a 30 percent solution (by weight) of potassium hydroxide (KOH) in distilled water. The specific gravity of the electrolyte remains between 1.240 and 1.300 at room temperature. No appreciable changes occur in the electrolyte during charge or discharge; as a result, the battery state of charge cannot be determined by a specific gravity check of the electrolyte using a normal hydrometer. The electrolyte level should be maintained just above the level of the plates.

4.11 Operation of Nickel-Cadmium Cells

When a charging current is applied to a ni-cad battery, the negative plates lose oxygen and begin forming metallic cadmium. The active material of the positive plates, nickel hydroxide, becomes more highly oxidized. This process continues while the charging current is applied, or until all the oxygen is removed from the negative plates and only cadmium remains. Towards the end of the charging cycle the cells emit gas. This will also occur if the cells are over-charged. This gas is caused by decomposition of water in the electrolyte into hydrogen at the negative plates and oxygen at the positive plates. The voltage used during charging, as well as the temperature, determines when gassing will occur. In completely charging a nickel-cadmium battery, some gassing, however slight, must take place; thus some water will be used.

The chemical action is reversed when discharging takes place. The positive plates slowly give up oxygen, which is regained by the negative plates. This process results in the conversion of the chemical energy into electrical energy. During discharge the plates absorb a quantity of the electrolyte. On recharge the level of the electrolyte rises and, at full charge the electrolyte will be at its highest level. Therefore distilled water should only be added when the battery is fully charged.

4.12 Precautions to Note with Ni-cad Batteries

For servicing purposes, a separate storage and maintenance area should be provided for nickel-cadmium batteries. The electrolyte is chemically opposite to the sulphuric acid used in a lead acid battery. Fumes from a lead acid battery can contaminate the electrolyte of a ni-cad battery.

This precaution of keeping the two types completely separate should be extended to equipment, tools and syringes. Acid must not be allowed near a ni-cad battery.

The potassium hydroxide electrolyte used in ni-cad batteries is extremely corrosive. When handling the electrolyte protective goggles, gloves and rubber aprons should be used. Suitable washing facilities should be provided in case the electrolyte is spilt on clothing or skin. Such exposures should be rinsed immediately with clean water or a boric acid solution. In an emergency vinegar or lemon juice may be used.

4.13 State of Charge and Charging

Since the electrolyte does not react chemically with the cell plates, the specific gravity of the electrolyte does not change appreciably. Therefore, it is not possible to determine the state of charge of the battery with a hydrometer; nor can the charge be determined by a voltage test because the voltage of a ni-cad battery remains constant during 90 percent of the discharge cycle.

Charging can be accomplished by either the constant voltage or constant current method. For constant potential charging, maintain the charging voltage constant until the charging current decays to 3 amperes or less and ensure that the battery cell temperature does not exceed 100°F. For constant current charging, start the charge and continue until the voltage reaches the desired potential; reduce the current level to 4 amps; continue charging until the desired voltage is reached or until the battery exceeds 100°F and the voltage begins to decline.

4.14 Thermal Runaway

Normally batteries are able to perform to their rated capacities when temperature and the charging rates are within their specified values. Should these values be exceeded, however, a condition known as thermal runaway can occur.

When this happens, there will be violent gassing, the electrolyte will boil, and damage will occur to the battery case and plates through melting. All of this may also result in damage to the aircraft structure and the electrical system.

Batteries generally have a low thermal capacity and this results in rapid heat dissipation which in turn causes internal resistance to decrease. When being charged, therefore, a lower resistance will allow a greater charge rate, higher temperature still, and the runaway condition is achieved. Some aircraft, in particular those which use nickel-cadmium batteries, have temperature sensing devices to warn the pilot of a pending runaway condition. In some systems the battery is automatically isolated, in others the battery must be isolated manually.

Section 4   Test Yourself Questions

Batteries

1. As a lead-acid battery is taken off charge, the maximum state of charge in an individual cell will be:
   (a) 2.0V.
   (b) 12.0V.
   (c) 12.2V.
   (d) 2.2V.

Ref 4.4.

2. A one hundred ampere/hour battery will furnish 50 Amps for:
   (a) 1 Hour.
   (b) 30 Minutes.
   (c) 2 Hours.
   (d) 50 Hours.

Ref 4.4.

3. The electrolyte of a lead-acid battery is:
   (a) Sulphuric acid and water.
   (b) Hydrochloric acid and distilled water.
   (c) Sulphuric acid and distilled water.
   (d) Potassium hydroxide and distilled water.

Ref 4.4.

4. The acid content of the electrolyte in a lead-acid battery is:
   (a) 70% by weight.
   (b) 30% by volume.
   (c) 30% by weight.
   (d) 70% by volume.

Ref 4.4.

5. If the electrolyte of a ni-cad battery is spilt on the skin:
   (a) it can be considered harmless.
   (b) the area should be treated with boric acid.
   (c) the area should be treated with sodium bicarbonate.
   (d) the area should be treated with potassium hydroxide.

Ref 4.12.

5

Basic Electrical Components

5.1 Introduction

The basis of an electrical circuit is the item of equipment, usually termed the 'load', and the cable connecting it to the electrical supply, but in practice such simplicity is rarely encountered as it may be necessary to provide a means of stopping and starting the flow of current (switch), controlling the amount of current flowing (rheostat), safeguarding the circuit from damage by excessive current (fuse), while it is also advantageous to provide points at which a number of cables can be connected together (terminal or plug). Simple components that fulfil the requirements mentioned, are as follows:

5.2 Cable

The electric current necessary to operate electrical equipment is conveyed from a source of supply, eg generator or battery, by means of a conductor. To confine the current to its proper path, it is necessary to sheath conductors with an insulating material. Such a sheathed conductor is termed an electric cable. A conductor which is sheathed only with enamel or fibre (silk, cotton, or rayon) is not classed as cable, but as 'insulated wire'.

A cable consists of one or more sheathed conductors, known as cores, and an outer protective covering. The conductor of each core is usually made of a number of strands of tinned copper wire, although other metals, such as aluminium and steel are occasionally used for special purposes. To facilitate circuit tracing and fault location, the insulation of each core of multi-core cable is appropriately coloured.

The number of strands and the gauge of the wire of a cable depend on its current-carrying capacity and the degree of flexibility required. Therefore, when renewing a cable, the replacement cable must be of similar specification to that removed, otherwise serious damage to the cable may occur.

The outer covering of the cable which binds the cores together, is primarily protective, and the materials used for it are chosen with a view to the conditions under which the cable will be used. Among the materials employed are cellulose, cotton braiding treated with varnish, tough

63

rubber, plastic (polyvinyl chloride – pvc), copper wire braiding, and lead sheathing.

(a) Fitting

The following are general points that are observed when fitting cables:

(1)   When stripping back the outer covering to expose the cores, the insulation of the cores must not be cut or damaged.

(2)   When stripping back the core insulation to prepare the wire for connection, cutting of the wire strands must be avoided; the strands must not be cut to facilitate fitting a connector. Every strand must be in circuit when the cable is connected.

(3)   Where a cable connector is not used, the core strands must be twisted together and looped under the washer of the terminal screw in a clockwise direction. This will ensure that tightening the screw does not tend to unhook the wire.

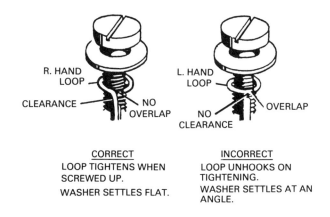

Figure 5–1 Direct screw connection.

(4)   If a connector is to be soldered to a cable, resin must be used as a flux. All other fluxes are corrosive and are not permitted for electrical work; a special wire type solder with a resin core is usually used.

(5)   When installed, cables should be supported throughout their length without undue slackness. Supporting clips and cleats must be lined with insulating material to protect the cables from chafing.

(b) Faults

Electrical failures in simple circuits are attributable to one or more of four main causes: short-circuits, insulation failure, loss of continuity, and incorrect connection of cables.

(1)   Short-circuits

Can be regarded as an abnormal decrease of resistance causing excessive current to flow; this results in overheating, blowing of fuses, and possibly damage to insulation. They can be caused by breakdown of insulation, loose strands of wire between adjacent cable ends and terminals, metal swarf or metallic dirt collecting between 'live' portions of equipment, or by mechanical damage to cables or components.

(2)   Insulation Failure

Can be caused by hydraulic fluid, oil, grease, gasoline, kerosene, dampness, etc, chemical action, chafing or abrasion of cables, and overheating of conductors due to excessive current.

(3)   Loss of Continuity

Can be regarded as an abnormal increase of resistance in the circuit, restricting or stopping the flow of current. Can be caused by partial breakage of the conductor, eg when several strands of a flexible conductor are broken at the cable end, by badly soldered joints, by loose terminals, or by dirty or uneven contact surfaces.

Note:
Badly soldered joints are usually referred to as 'dry' joints.

(4)   Incorrect Connection of Cables

This class of fault has its origin in bad workmanship; it should never occur in a circuit which is installed or serviced by a competent mechanic. This fault is certain to cause either non-operation or inefficient operation of the circuit; it may easily cause serious damage to cables or equipment by short-circuit faults.

Note:
Faults in electrical equipment observed by an airframe mechanic must be reported immediately to the electrical tradesman.

5.3 Switches

Switches are used to complete or interrupt a circuit, thereby starting or stopping the flow of current to the load. The simplest form of switch consists of two contacts which are insulated from each other, one connected to the supply, the other to the load, the gap between the two contacts being bridged when required by a movable metallic unit.

The movable unit, or 'movement', is generally spring loaded to ensure good contact and a quick opening action, both of which are necessary if sparking at the contacts is to be avoided. Most switches are operated by moving a knob or 'dolly', but rotary switches in which the handle is twisted are often used when it is necessary to guard against accidental operation.

Note:
Before operating any switch, ensure that the service affected is known.

Switches have an important function to perform; the following are general points to be observed for their efficient operation:

(a)   Examined frequently for signs of mechanical wear or damage by burning.

(b)   Contact surfaces are kept clean and free from all traces of pitting, burning or corrosion.

(c)   A switch which becomes erratic in its action (a fault caused by wear in the movement, or its pivots) is renewed immediately.

5.4 Fuses

Fuses are safety devices which are placed in circuits to protect them from excessive currents. If a circuit carries current in excess of that for which it was designed, the components of the circuit will become overheated. Such overheating may cause damage and fire.

A fuse usually consists of a short strand of wire which is positioned in a circuit so that all the current passes through it. If the current becomes excessive, the heat generated in the fuse will melt it and prevent the passage of further current. The current at which the fuse melts depends on the diameter of the wire and the material of which it is made.

Figure 5–2 Types of aircraft fuse.

A blowing fuse produces a spark, and to avoid the risk of fire or explosion, which might occur if gasoline fumes are present, aircraft fuses are totally enclosed in glass tubes fitted with brass end caps. Stamped on the end cap is the value of permissible current allowed to flow. The fuse fits into two contact clips in a fuse box; terminal screws at the base of the clips serve to connect the fuse with the circuit.

The following points are noted when checking or renewing fuses:

(a)   A blown fuse indicates a fault in the circuit; the fuse may be replaced by the pilot ONCE, if it blows again, the engineer must be consulted.

(b)   Care must be taken to ensure that replacement fuses are of the same value as those removed. Because it is dangerous, it is strictly forbidden to replace a blown fuse by one of higher rating.

(c)   Fuses are inspected periodically and renewed if the wire shows signs of sagging or discolouration.

Current Limiters
Current limiters are designed primarily for use in circuits of a heavy duty nature such as a starter motor circuit. Such circuits carry high voltage values and the current limiter will limit the current to some pre-determined amperage value. The current limiter will take a considerable overload and generally have a high melting point.

Figure 5–2a   Current Limiter.

Limiting Resistors
This type of protection device is more commonly found in DC circuits where the initial current surge is very high. They are often fitted to starter motor and inverter circuits, or circuits containing high capacitive loads.

5.5 Rheostats

The rate of flow of current in a circuit is dependent on the voltage applied to the circuit and upon its resistance. Normally, the voltage applied is constant, and any variation of current must be obtained by varying the resistance of the circuit. Rheostats, which are simply variable resistances, are used for this purpose.

Most rheostats consist of a length of high-resistance wire wound on a former, with a sliding contact which varies the effective length of resistance wire in the circuit. The rheostat has two terminals, one connected to one end of the resistance wire, and the other to the sliding contact or, in some instances, to the contact and to the end of the wire.

Dimmer Switch
Many rheostats used in lighting circuits to control the brilliancy of the lamps, are so designed that the sliding contact can be moved beyond the end of the resistance wire, thus breaking the circuit. This arrangement, which is in effect a combination of switch and rheostat, is utilised in dimmer switches which are often used on aircraft instrument panels.

5.6 Relay Switches

The switches mentioned in the previous paragraphs are all of the direct-operating type, but for many purposes it is advantageous to use switches that can be remotely controlled. These switches, known as relay switches, are operated by an electro-magnet, comprising a solenoid and soft iron armature connected to a separate electrical control circuit.

Relay switches can be regarded as belonging to one or other of two groups, eg, heavy duty or control relays. The former are often used in heavy-current starter motor circuits, while control relays form an essential part of many automatic control systems.

(a) Heavy Duty Relay
The main problem when operating large motors on low-voltage systems is one of voltage drop in the supply cables, due to the large current involved. The use of a remotely controlled switch permits the cables to be run directly from the supply to the motor; by reducing the length of cable, the voltage drop is correspondingly reduced.

Figure 5-3 shows a starter motor circuit using a heavy duty relay. When the control push-button is pressed, a current flows through the solenoid to energise the electro-magnet. The plunger (armature) is drawn into the hollow core of the solenoid, causing the heavy copper contact-plate to bridge the two fixed contacts and thus complete the circuit to the motor.

When the control push-button is released, the electro-magnet is de-energised. The spring is then able to return the armature and contact plate to their original positions, thus interrupting the circuit to the motor.

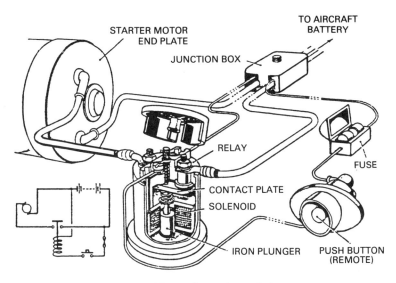

Figure 5–3 Heavy duty relay switch.

(b) Control Relay

These relays operate on the same principle as the heavy-duty type, ie by electro-magnet, but their contact assembly is of light construction, since the current to be handled by the contacts is relatively small. The solenoid winding is generally of high resistance enabling the relay to be energised continuously, if required, without overheating.

Many variations of contact assembly are in use, ranging from single-pole switch-action to four-pole action. For example, in the fire extinguishing circuit the relay may control four circuits, the contacts being either opened or closed on energising the magnet. Relays having a selector-switch action, ie opening one circuit and closing another when energised, are often used for control of electro-hydraulic valves, etc.

Note:
Although a solenoid and armature are used both in relays and in valves, the armature in the relay operates contacts, and the armature in the valve operates the valve element.

5.7 Filament Lamps

A piece of metal which is heated to a bright red will not only radiate heat, but it will also emit a certain amount of light. This property of light-emission due to temperature is termed incandescence. As stated, an electric current passing through a conductor has a heating effect; if this effect is great enough, the conductor will become incandescent and give off light. This is the principle of the filament lamp.

(a) Construction

The lamp consists of a thin thread (filament) of wire, usually made of tungsten, enclosed in a glass envelope from which all air has been evacuated. The glass envelope is necessary, otherwise oxygen contained in the atmosphere would combine with the heated filament, which would disintegrate almost immediately. Lamps constructed in this manner are known as vacuum lamps.

Tungsten melts at 3400°C, but in a vacuum evaporation of the metal, which causes blackening of the glass envelope with a reduction in light-emission, sets in at 2000°C. To enable the filament to be worked at high temperatures, thus increasing the efficiency of the lamp, the glass envelope may be filled with an inert gas, eg argon or nitrogen – which will not combine with other elements. These types of lamp are termed gas-filled, and have a light-output per watt approximately double that of a corresponding vacuum lamp.

(b) Classification

Filament lamps are classified according to the voltage of the supply for which they are designed, and their rate of consumption in watts. To describe a lamp in terms of voltage alone is inadequate; 24-volt lamps range from small indicator lamps of 3 watts consumption to large searchlight lamps taking 900 watts. Wattage alone is likewise insufficient: the description must include both terms, eg 24 volts, 6 watts; 230 volts, 100 watts.

A further classification point is the type of end cap fitted to the lamp, through which electrical connection is made to the filament. The diameter of the end cap is measured in millimetres. The most common types of cap are as follows:

(1) Edison Screw Cap

These are centre-contact caps of the form shown in the illustration, the metal screw portion forming one contact. The large contact area makes this cap suitable for heavy-current lamps, while the certainty of alignment of contacts is an added advantage.

(2) Bayonet Cap

This is the most common type of cap met with in British lamps. It may be either a centre contact, double contact or treble contact; its chief advantage is the ease with which it can be inserted and withdrawn from the lamp-holder.

(3) Pre-focus Cap
This cap is used in light fittings where focus is important and must be pre-set by the manufacturer, rather than by local adjustment. Typical uses are in searchlights, landing lamps, signalling lamps, etc.

PRE-FOCUS   EDISON SCREW   BAYONET

Figure 5–4 Types of lamp cap.

5.8 Bonding

During flight a static electrical charge is induced into metallic parts of an aircraft, and any intermittent contact between parts of different potential may cause sparking with consequent risk of fire; sparking also interferes with radio reception.

To prevent these hazards, and to provide a large constant-capacity earth to increase radio efficiency, every metal component of an aircraft is bonded (electrically-interconnected) so that the potential throughout the aircraft structure is uniform. Wooden and composite aircraft have earthing strips of tinned copper extending along the main components and connected to a common earth terminal; each metal component is bonded to the copper strip by means of a bonding lead of braided flexible copper wire. All-metal aircraft are bonded satisfactorily without the use of an earthing strip as the airframe structure serves for this purpose.

To obtain continuity throughout the aircraft, bonding leads, strips of brass or copper, or copper gauze are connected to or interposed between metal components, though with clean metal-to-metal joints additional contact is not necessary. Component parts that are removable from the aircraft are provided with bonding terminals to which the bonding lead is connected.

71

Note:
Before removing an airframe component, ensure that the bonding has been disconnected, and after fitting a component, ensure that the bonding is reconnected.

Electrical Conducting Tyres
When the aircraft lands, induced static electricity would tend to pass from the aircraft to the earth and cause a spark. To prevent this happening, aircraft nose and tail wheel tyres are specially constructed of rubber composition of low resistance, thus providing a path to earth for the static electricity.

ELECTRICAL SUPPLY IN AIRCRAFT

5.9 Introduction

Certain items in aircraft, such as radio and radar equipment, lighting equipment, and many types of aircraft instrument depend entirely for their operation on a suitable electrical supply.

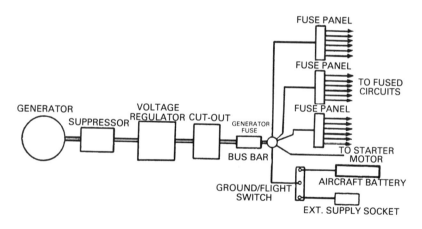

Figure 5–5 Single generator installation.

Remote control and operation of other items can be accomplished much more simply by electrical means than by manual, hydraulic or pneumatic methods. Furthermore, most safety devices, and almost all automatically-controlled equipment are dependent wholly, or in part, on electricity for their operation.

Electric cables are more flexible, less bulky, less vulnerable, and much easier to repair or renew than are hydraulic or pneumatic pipelines, or flexible mechanical drives. Other advantages in the use of electrical equipment include the following:

(a) Cleanliness.

(b) Lightness and compactness of electrical components, so saving weight and space.

(c) Electrical components obviate complicated linkages.

(d) Quicker response of components.

(e) Pressurization efficiency increased.

5.10 Suppressor

As stated, the main electrical supply in aircraft is provided by one or more DC generators driven, through gearing, by the aero-engines; an emergency supply, available in the event of generator failure is provided by a battery.

Sparking at the brushes of a generator results in the radiation of electro-magnetic waves, which interfere with radio reception. Such radiation may take place not only from the generator, but also from any circuit connected to it. The interference may also be conducted along the wiring to the power unit of the radio equipment, if this is supplied from the general distribution point (bus-bar).

Prevention of radio interference is achieved in two stages. The generator is totally enclosed in a metallic casing, and the supply cables from the generator are either sheathed with metal braid or are enclosed in a metal conduit (sleeve); this prevents direct radiation. To prevent interference being conducted along the wiring, suppressors are fitted to the ends of the 'screened' cables as close to the generator as possible.

5.11 Voltage Regulator

The voltage supplied by the generator must remain constant if the electrical equipment is to operate with maximum efficiency. Since the generator speed is directly proportional to the speed of the aero-engine, some form of automatic voltage control is necessary; this is achieved by the use of a voltage regulator.

With the use of a voltage regulator, the output voltage of a shunt-wound DC generator can be regulated by automatic control of the field current. If, for example, the voltage rises because of increased speed or decreased load, the field current is reduced accordingly.

Voltage control is usually obtained through a voltage regulator in which a pile of carbon washers, held together by spring pressure, is connected in series with the generator field winding. Any fluctuation of voltage varies the spring pressure, thereby varying the resistance of the field and adjusting the field current to cancel out voltage variation.

5.12 Cut-out

The aircraft battery is intended to supply current in the event of generator failure, and must therefore be connected to the distribution bus-bar at all times, unless the whole installation is out of service or an external supply is being applied to the bus-bar. Under normal operating conditions, with the generator output voltage at its correct level, the battery takes a small charging current, and the entire load is supplied by the generator.

In the event of the generator voltage falling below the battery voltage, the entire load will fall on the battery, and the generator will take a reverse current which, because of the low resistance of the generator armature, would be quite heavy and cause damage to the armature windings and discharge of the battery.

It is, therefore, essential that the generator is not connected to the bus-bar until the generator voltage exceeds the battery voltage, and that the generator should be disconnected from the bus-bar whenever a sizable reverse current begins to flow through its windings. These functions are done, automatically, by the cut-out. In this case the cut-out switch will open when generator output falls ½ volt below battery output.

5.13 Distribution

All aircraft loads, with the exception of starter motors, are supplied through protective devices. Simple fuses of suitable rating are used for the smaller load circuits; the fuses are generally grouped in covered fuseboxes or on covered panels supplied from the distribution bus-bar. Large circuits are often fed through thermal circuit breakers; these replace the normal type of fuse and consist of a special switch which opens automatically if unduly heavy current is carried; they can be re-set by hand or electrically, after the circuit fault has been rectified.

Most modern aircraft are wired on the 'single-pole' system. In this system, one terminal (usually the negative) of the battery, generator and each item of electrical equipment is connected to the metal of the airframe at selected 'earthing' points. A saving of cable results from this method, as the return path of the current is through the metal of the airframe, also fault location is simplified.

The distribution of electric current to all electric components of an aircraft is arranged, via cables, as follows:

(a) Bus-bars

These are the main points receiving electric current from generator and battery.

(b) Distribution Panels

These incorporate or are connected to a bus-bar, and provide electric current to separate circuits. They usually contain fuses. Distribution panels must be fitted with covers; any covers missing must be reported to the electrical tradesman.

(c) Conduits

These contain the cables, thus providing protection and facilitating cable grouping. Damaged conduits must be reported to the electrical tradesman.

(d) Plugs and Sockets

These are used at all points where frequent disconnection is necessary, eg wing roots, portable electric components, etc. They also assist in efficient pressurisation of the aircraft, eg at bulkheads, etc. Before removing any airframe component, ensure that plugs and sockets are not fitted. If fitted, the plug and socket must be disconnected by the electrical tradesman.

(e) Terminal Block

These provide a simple means of connecting cables, but wherever possible are replaced by plugs and sockets.

5.14 External Supplies

When servicing and testing the electrical equipment of aircraft prior to flight, and when starting aircraft fitted with electric starters, the current demand is extremely heavy. The capacity of the aircraft battery is insufficient to meet these demands, and an independent external supply is connected to the aircraft installation.

The external supply is obtained from batteries, or an engine-driven generator, mounted on a wheeled truck, termed an electric servicing trolley or ground power unit. This supply unit is connected to the aircraft external supply socket by a heavy cable and plug. To isolate the aircraft battery from the bus-bars when the external supply is connected, a switch, termed a ground/flight switch may be fitted in the circuit. When this switch is set to 'Ground', the aircraft battery is isolated; when it is set to 'Flight' the aircraft battery is in circuit.

In modern aircraft, the ground/flight switch is replaced by a special plug on the end of the external supply cable and a special socket on the aircraft which, when engaged, automatically isolates the aircraft battery. With this type of circuit, a manually-operated battery isolating switch is usually provided in the cockpit which enables the pilot to switch off the electric current from the battery in an emergency, eg crash-landing, thus minimising fire risk.

Some aircraft are fitted with relays in circuit with the inertia switch, which isolates the battery automatically should the aircraft crash land.

Notes:

(1)   Irrespective of the setting of the battery isolating switch or ground/flight switch, essential services such as fire extinguishing, dinghy release, etc, are not isolated as they are connected, via switches, direct to the aircraft battery.

(2)   Ground power must be switched off when connecting to or disconnecting from the aircraft.

ELECTRICAL INDICATORS

5.15 Introduction

As a means of attracting attention and conveying information to the pilot, various types of electrical indicator are situated in the cockpit.

(a) Warning Lights
May be used to indicate fuel, oil, or cabin pressure failure, power failure, position of alighting gear, fire warning, etc.

(b) Electro-magnetic Indicators
To indicate fuel contents, oil temperature, engine speed, flap position, etc.

(c) Buzzer
This audible warning device, which warned the pilot that the alighting gear was in a retracted or unlocked position when he attempted to throttle back the engines, has been superseded on most aircraft by a warning light.

Where it is sufficient to know that a component is UP or DOWN, or a system is ON or OFF, warning lights are used. When more detailed information is required such as the amount of movement, variation in contents or pressure, electro-magnetic indicators are used, though on modern aircraft warning lights are being replaced, where possible, by electro-magnetic indicators.

5.16 Warning Lights

Warning lights consist of small filament lamps fitted behind coloured screens. Dependent on the type of circuit, the lamps may be illuminated by operation of a pressure switch, relay, microswitch, or flame detector switch.

Pressure Switch
With this type of switch, when installed to indicate pressure failure, the pressure exerted on a plunger opens the contacts and the warning light is OFF. Should the pressure fail, the plunger, assisted by a spring, closes the contacts and the warning light comes ON.

Relay
The relay consists of a solenoid which, when energised, moves an armature. Dependent on the purpose of the relay, contacts operated by the armature may be closed or opened, thus initiating the warning light. As a power failure warning device, the main relay opens when the generator fails and connects the warning light relay to the battery, thus energising its solenoid which attracts the armature. Contacts operated by the armature close, and the power failure warning light is illuminated by current from the battery.

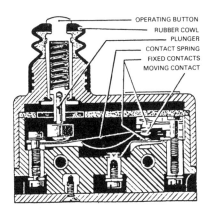

Figure 5–6 Microswitch.

Microswitch

The term 'micro' has no bearing on the size or current-carrying ability of the switch, but refers to the very short travel (0.025in approx) of the operating plunger. The switch consists of a spring-loaded plunger which, when depressed, causes internal switch contacts to operate with a snap action by a flat spring to which they are fitted. Any further depression of the plunger is termed 'over-travel', and is taken up by the plunger spring.

One of the many uses of microswitches is to operate the alighting gear warning lights. The microswitches are situated on the airframe structure so that when the alighting gear moves, the plungers are depressed or released, and contacts initiate the warning lamps. Microswitches are also often used as external limit switches, eg by opening the electrical circuit when movement of an actuator has reached its allotted travel.

Flame Detector Switch

One type of flame detector switch consists of an expansion tube of alloy steel housing contacts mounted on a special spring-bow assembly (Fig 5-7). At normal temperature, the spring-bow assembly is under compression so that the springs are bowed and the contacts are open. When heat is applied, the steel tube expands to a greater extent than the spring-bow assembly; the compression is eased, the contacts close and so complete the circuit to the warning lamp.

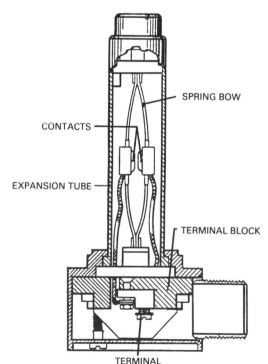

Figure 5–7 Resetting type flame detector.

A subsequent drop in temperature recompresses the spring-bow assembly, opens the contacts and causes the warning lamp to go out. This switch is termed a resetting type flame detector.

5.17 Electro-magnetic Indicators

To convey measurement of position, contents or pressure to remotely situated indicators, various electrical methods of transmission are used in aircraft. The Desynn system here described, which can be adapted to indicate all these measurements, consists of an indicator and transmitter electrically connected to each other and energised by the aircraft direct current supply, (Fig 5-8). When the transmitter mechanism is moved, the indicator pointer follows the movement.

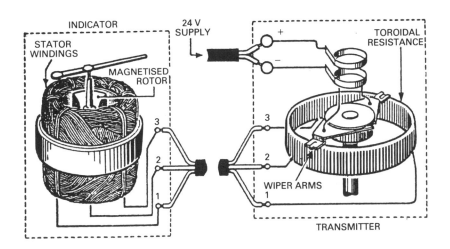

Figure 5–8 Desynn transmission system.

The transmitter consists of an endless coil of resistance wire wound on a ring-shaped former, the assembly being termed a 'toroidal resistance'. The resistance is tapped at three equidistant points, and conductors from these points lead to the indicator. A central spindle in the transmitter carries two wiper arms which bear on the toroidal resistance at diametrically opposite points. The arms are insulated from each other at the spindle, but are connected, via sliding contacts, to the electrical supply.

The indicator consists of a soft iron stator and a magnetised rotor. Disposed around the stator are three windings which, for functional purposes, may be considered as three coils placed 120 degrees apart. One end of each coil is connected to a transmitter tapping, and the remaining three ends are connected together. The rotor is a two-pole magnet mounted on a pivoted spindle at the centre of the stator; the indicating pointer is secured to the rotor spindle.

Since the wiper arms of the transmitter are connected to the power supply, current will enter the toroidal resistance at the positive arm and divide, half flowing to the negative arm in a clockwise direction and the other half flowing to it in an anti-clockwise direction. With a supply voltage of 24 volts, the progressive drop in voltage around the resistance will be as indicated in Fig 5-9. The tapping to which coil 'A' is connected is at 24 volts potential, whilst coils B and C are at 8 volts respectively. Current will flow from the higher to the lower potential, ie in through A and out via B and C. By applying the grasp rule, it can be seen that coil A will establish a north polarity at its inner end, and coils B and C south polarities. The resultant field at the centre of the stator will hold the rotor in the position shown.

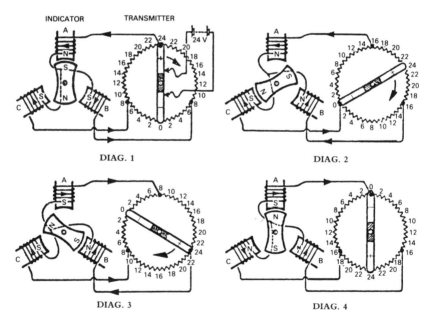

Figure 5–9 Desynn operating principle.

In diagram 2, the wiper arms have rotated 60 degrees clockwise. Potentials fed to the indicator coils are now, coil A – 16 volts, coil B – 16 volts, coil C – 0 volts. Current will flow in through A and B, and out through C creating north polarities at A and B and a south polarity at C.

The rotor aligns itself with the field as shown; the rotor has moved through the same angle as the wiper arms. Similarly, in diag 3 and 4 it may be seen that as the wiper arms continue to rotate, the indicator rotor will follow them.

Note:
To demonstrate the operation of the Desynn electrical indicator, 60 degree steps of the wiper arms have been used, but intermediate positions on the indicator are similarly obtained.

Position Indicators
These are used to indicate to the pilot and engineer the attitude or setting of remote movable components such as air brakes, flaps, trimming tabs, etc.

The transmitter is mounted near and coupled to the component, so that when the component is moved the transmitter spindle is rotated. The transmitter is electrically connected to an indicator in the cockpit and to the electrical supply. As the component moves, the transmitter operates the indicator which follows the movement and provides a continuous indication of the position of the component.

Note:
Should the power to the instrument fail, an 'off-scale' device consisting of a weak magnet situated near the rotor, attracts the rotor and moves it to a position where the pointer is held off the scale. The pilot will then be aware that the instrument is not working.

Electrically all transmitters are similar to that previously described, but mechanically they differ to suit the components to which they are coupled. Three types are in use, the toroidal resistance in each being housed above the drive.

(a) Direct Drive
The wiper arms of direct drive transmitters are driven directly from a central spindle in the transmitter. When the spindle is coupled with the component, an angular displacement of the component will cause a similar displacement of the wiper arms. The indicator dial is calibrated in degrees of rotation. (Fig 5-10).

(b) Radial Arm Drive
Where small angular movements are to be measured, a radial arm drive transmitter is used (Fig 5-11). It is connected to the moving component by a link which is attached to the end of a radial arm. A sector and pinion gear is built into the transmitter, so that a small displacement of the radial arm will cause a relatively larger displacement of the wiper arms. A tensioned spring is mounted on the central

spindle to take up play between the gears and in the connecting linkage, so that no lost motion will occur when the direction of movement is reversed.

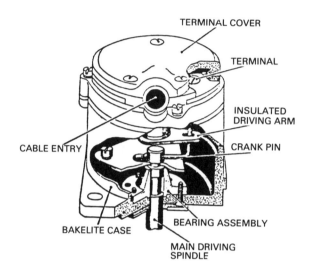

Figure 5–10 Direct drive.

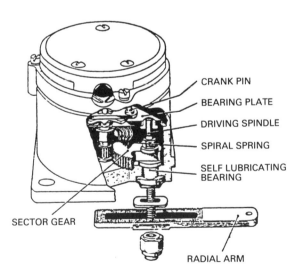

Figure 5–11 Radial arm drive.

(c) Pushrod Drive

The pushrod drive transmitter (see Fig 5-12) is designed for use in conjunction with linear actuating gear. It is coupled to the moving member by a connecting rod which screws into the end of the push rod and is locked by a locknut. The pushrod has a rack cut into its surface which engages with a pinion on the central spindle of the transmitter. When the pushrod is operated, the rack rotates the spindle which moves the wiper arms over the toroidal resistance. A tensioned spring is fitted to the spindle to prevent lost motion between the rack and pinion.

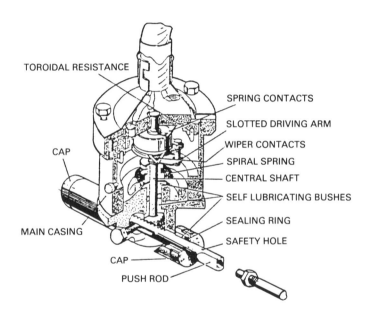

Figure 5–12 Pushrod drive.

Fuel Contents Gauge

The Desynn fuel contents gauge provides a continuous indication of the quantity of fuel in the tank of an aircraft. Where several fuel tanks are fitted, a separate gauge system is used for each tank. Each system comprises a tank unit and an indicator. A float on the tank unit operates a transmitter; the float responds to the level of fuel in the tank and positions the wiper arm of the transmitter accordingly. The transmitter is electrically connected to an indicator in the cockpit and to the electrical supply.

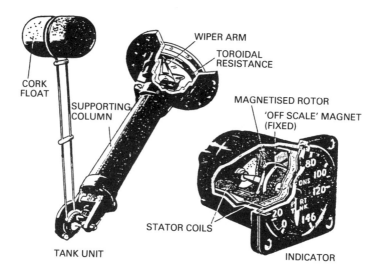

Figure 5–13 Fuel contents guage.

Since the fuel level is taken as a measure of the contents of the tank, the size and shape of the tank must be considered. Each tank unit and indicator is therefore designed and calibrated to suit a specific type of tank, and the appropriate tank part number is marked on both the tank unit and the indicator.

The cork float of the tank unit is attached to the end of a light steel arm, which is pivoted from a cylindrical supporting column. The arm is geared to a spindle which passes through the column to connect with a transmitter housed in a recess at the other end of the column. When the float arm rises and falls with the level of fuel in the tank, the spindle turns the wiper arms of the transmitter so that the arms always occupy a position corresponding to the fuel level. Limit stops prevent the float arm from touching the sides of the tank at the two extreme positions.

Where the mark number of a fuel gauge system is starred, eg Mk 4B*, it denotes that a low level warning device is fitted. This consists of a contact assembly housed in the transmitter head of the tank unit and a warning light in the cockpit. When the fuel level becomes low, contact is made by the movement of the wiper arms, and the warning lamp lights.

Pressure Gauge

The system comprises a transmitter unit and an indicator. The transmitter is installed near the engine and connected to the pressure system by a short flexible pipe. The indicator is mounted on the instrument panel in the cockpit. The transmitter is electrically connected to the indicator and to the electrical supply.

The indicator is similar to the Desynn indicators previously described, but the transmitter unit contains a pressure sensitive device coupled to a micro-transmitter. (Fig 5-14)

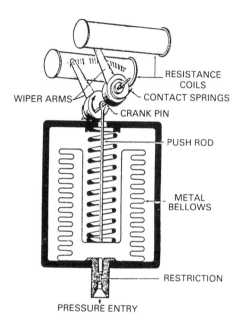

Figure 5–14 Oil pressure transmitter.

The pressure sensitive device is located in the lower part of the unit and consists of a corrugated metal bellows and a control spring. Pressure is fed into the bellows from a union at the bottom of the transmitter, and the bellows expand against the thrust of the spring. Movement of the bellows is conveyed to the micro-transmitter by a pushrod. To prevent pump pulsations affecting the bellows, the bore of the inlet union is restricted.

The micro-transmitter is a development of the toroidal type, and consists of two cylindrical resistance coils, mounted side by side, and two wiper arms which make sliding contact with them. Tappings from the coils are arranged and connected so that the device responds in a similar manner to the toroidal transmitter, but is more sensitive to small movements of the wiper arms. The arms are operated by a crank pin, to which the bellows movement is applied; current is conveyed to the arms by two spiral springs.

For each pressure, the bellows locate the wiper arms in a definite position relative to the resistance coils. The output from the transmitter, which depends upon the position of the wiper arms, is conveyed to the indicator which registers the pressure in lb/sq in.

To prevent mechanical vibration affecting the transmitter mechanism, the unit is supported in a special anti-vibration mounting. The mounting consists of a metal strap suspended on three springs in an outer cradle. The cradle is rigidly secured to the aircraft, and the transmitter is held by the floating strap which grips the transmitter body when a clamping screw, on the strap, is tightened. (Fig 5-15)

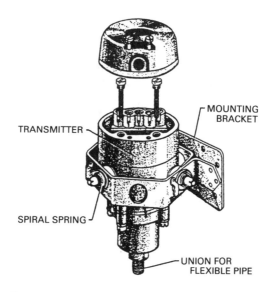

Figure 5–15 Transmitter in anti-vibration mounting.

ELECTRICALLY-OPERATED VALVES

5.18 Introduction

The operating force of these types of valve is obtained by the use of an electro-magnet which consists of a soft iron or steel armature, housed in a non-ferrous metal sleeve, around which a wire is wound to form a coil or solenoid.

Various methods of control of the valve are available. For example, the electric current may be introduced by manual switch if the valve is to be in continuous use, or a push-button for intermittent operation. Where automatic control is necessary, a thermostat or pressure switch can be used.

5.19 Pilot Valve

This valve may be included in a hydraulic system to facilitate the selection of a service by remote control. Pressure fluid is admitted at the radial inlet ports and thence to the holes in the valve seat. When the solenoid is energised, the armature is displaced vertically by magnetic attraction, and the valve element, which is pinned to the armature, is lifted off its seat. Pressure fluid then escapes past the valve element and out of the valve through the outlet port. (See Fig 5-16).

When the solenoid is de-energised, the armature and valve element are returned to their original positions by a spring. The valve element is thus held on its seat, closing the inlet port until the solenoid is again energised.

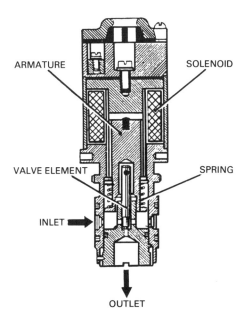

ARMATURE SOLENOID VALVE ELEMENT SPRING INLET OUTLET

Figure 5–16 Pilot valve.

5.20 Two-way Selector Valve

This valve is used to direct a flow of fluid to a specific service, or alternatively allow fluid from that service to pass to a return line. The electric current to a solenoid operates a pilot valve which directs fluid to control the movement of a slide valve; this in turn directs the main flow of fluid through the selector. (See Fig 5-17).

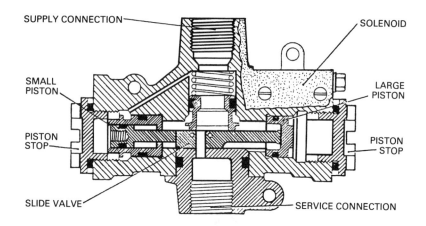

Figure 5–17 Two-way selector valve.

When the solenoid is de-energised, the spindle in the pilot valve is held away from the ball valve by its spring. Fluid from the supply connection then passes along drillings to the pilot valve, forces the ball valve against the return seat, flows past the ball valve and through a drilling to the bore for the large actuating piston. Simultaneously, supply fluid flows from the supply connection direct to the bore for the small actuating piston. The difference in surface area of the pistons causes a greater force to be applied at the large piston and move the slide valve to align its slot with that of the connection block; supply fluid then flows to the service connection.

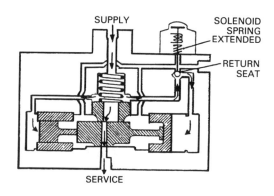

Solenoid De-Energised.

When the solenoid is energised, its plunger pushes the spindle of the pilot valve to thrust the ball valve against the pressure seat. The fluid from the supply connection is thus cut off from the bore for the large piston and the pressure on this piston is relieved through the open return seat. Supply fluid flows directly through a drilling to the bore for the small piston, with the result that the slot of the slide valve is moved out of alignment with the slot of the connection block.

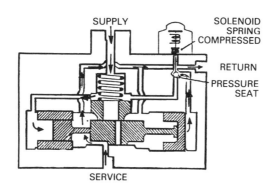

Solenoid Energised.

The flow of the supply fluid through the selector is thus cut off and the return fluid at the service connection passes round the end of the slide valve and through a drilling to the return connection.

5.21 Four-way Selector Valve

This valve is used to direct the flow of fluid to one of two services and simultaneously to open the return line for the other service. (Fig 5-18). The electric current to either of two solenoids operates a corresponding pilot valve controlling the movement of a slide valve. With both solenoids de-energised, the slide is in a neutral mid-position and there is no flow of fluid through the unit.

When both solenoids are de-energised, the spindle in each pilot valve is held away from the ball valve by its spring. Fluid from the supply connection then passes along drillings to both pilot valves, forces the ball valves against their return seats, flows past the ball valves and through drillings to the bores of the centralising and actuating pistons.

The fluid pressure, acting equally on both pistons, maintains the slide valve in the central position. Fluid cannot flow through the unit as the

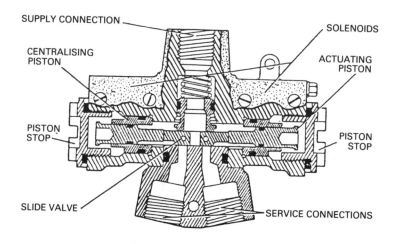

Figure 5–18 Four-way selector valve.

slot of the slide valve is midway between the two slots in the connection block.

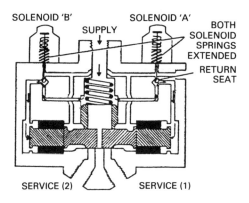

Both Solenoids De-energised.

With the energising of one solenoid, for example solenoid B, its plunger pushes the spindle of the pilot valve to thrust the ball valve against the pressure seat. The fluid from the supply connection is thus cut off from the bore of the relevant actuating piston, and the pressure on this piston is relieved through the open return seat. The pressure acting on the opposite actuating piston moves the slide valve along the main bore, and the idle actuating centralising pistons are moved to contact the piston stop; fluid at this end flows to the return connection.

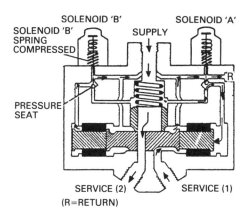

Solenoid 'B' Engergised.

The slot in the slide valve is now aligned with one of the slots in the connection block and fluid from the supply connection flows to the relevant service connection. With the offset movement of the slide valve, one of the oblique drillings is uncovered and return fluid from the other service connection flows through this drilling to the return connection.

When the solenoid is de-energised, the spring of the pilot valve assembly withdraws the spindle from the ball valve. Fluid in the pressure line forces the ball valve on to the return seat and equal pressure is again applied to the pistons. Whilst the slide valve is offset from the centre, the pressure is applied at one end to the combined areas of the actuating and centralising pistons, both of which are in contact with the slide valve.

Only the actuating piston is in contact with the slide valve on the opposite side and, therefore, the pressure is effective only on this piston area. The differential loading moves the slide valve towards the central position. When the moving centralising piston has reached the limit of its travel, the pressure becomes effective only on the actuating piston and thus becomes equal at each end.

The slide valve, which is then centralised, ceases to move, and in this position the slot in the slide valve is midway between the slots in the connection block. Fluid is therefore trapped in the pipe lines from the service connections until a new selection is made.

Note:
The operation of solenoid A is similar in principle to solenoid B, but the flow of fluid to and from the service connections is reversed.

ACTUATORS

5.22 Introduction

Electrical units that are capable of exerting reversible linear movement, or a reversible turning effort are known as electrical actuators and are used in many aircraft installations where remote control is required, eg, operation of flaps, trimming tabs, canopy hood, bomb doors, etc. Dependent on their function, actuators are termed either rotary or linear, both of which contain a small electric motor to supply the necessary power. They are self-contained units, and are close-connected to the equipment to be operated.

5.23 Motor

To obtain reversibility in operation, the majority of actuators are powered by a small split-field series motor, ie a motor having two field windings wound in opposite directions. Electrical connections are made from both fields to a switch mechanism, situated in the cockpit, which enables a changeover to be made from one field to the other, so causing a reversal of rotation of the motor.

The speed of rotation and the amount of rotary movement of the output shaft of the motor depend on its design. For example, the output shaft of a rotary actuator designed for operation of fuel cocks may be required to turn at 3 rpm, and be limited to an angular travel of 90 degrees. The output shaft of a canopy actuator may turn at 50 rpm, without limitation to angular travel, while a cowl gill actuator shaft may turn at 12 rpm and be restricted in travel to a pre-determined number of complete revolutions.

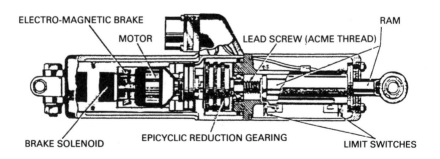

Figure 5–19 Linear actuator.

5.24 Gearing

The speed of the motor may be over 15,000 rpm, and to reduce the speed of the output shaft suitable reduction gearing is used. This gearing may be either or both of two types, epicyclic or multi-stage spur gearing. The gearing reduction ratio of a normal multi-stage spur type can be as low as 21,000:1, and a normal epicyclic type 625:1. Rotary actuators designed for low-speed small-angle operation are usually fitted with multi-stage spur type gears, while linear actuators are fitted with epicyclic gearing or a combination of both gears.

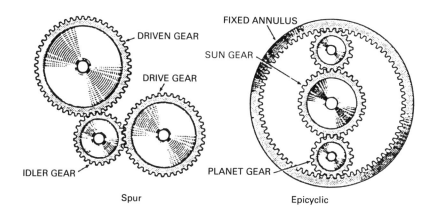

Figure 5–20 Types of reduction gearing.

Annulus Release

In some types of actuator, the first annulus gear may be 'floating' and have an annulus release incorporated. This device, which may be either mechanically or electrically-operated, enables an alternative form of drive to be applied to the load should the electrical supply to the actuator fail. When an alternative drive is not provided, the annulus release may be fitted to allow the component to move to the 'safe' position, eg if the electrical supply fails, the airstream would move cowling gills to the fully open position, thus preventing overheating of the engine, (see Fig 5-21).

With the electrically-operated type, the first annulus gear is held stationary by the metal head of an electro-magnetic plunger, thus permitting transmission of the drive to the ram. The metal head is three-sided and has two holes for guide pins, which prevent the plunger from being rotated when meshed with the teeth on the outside of the annulus. If the electrical supply to the actuator fails, the electro-magnet is de-energised

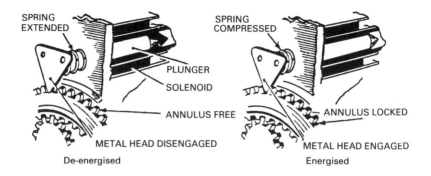

Figure 5–21 Annulus release.

and the metal head withdrawn by spring pressure, thus the first annulus gear is free and disconnects the drive between motor and ram.

5.25 Lead Screw Threads

In the linear actuator, the motor is coupled through reduction gearing to a lead screw, which extends or retracts a ram or plunger. The thread of the lead screw mates with a corresponding thread in the ram. The lead screw is located axially and can only turn. The ram is prevented from turning, but has freedom of movement in a linear direction, thus the rotary motion of the motor is converted into linear movement of the ram.

Screw-thread of the acme type is usually used in the smaller types of actuator, but a high-efficiency thread that may be termed a 'ball bearing thread' is used in large, powerful actuators. This latter thread consists of two grooves which contain steel balls and replaces the conventional male and female threads; a recirculating device ensures that the steel balls are fed continuously into the grooves as the ram extends or retracts. To prevent rotation of the ram, steel balls are sometimes located in depressions in the outer surface of the ram and travel in slots formed on the inside of the ram housing.

5.26 Limit Switches

To prevent excessive load on the motor at full extent of travel of the output shaft, or ram, and to control the movement, some form of limit switch is fitted. Limit switches also enable the pilot to make selection without having to worry if full travel will be exceeded. Rotary actuators whose output shafts are designed to rotate not more than one revolution, are usually fitted with internal limit switches; where the movement is greater, external switches (similar to micro switches) are operated by the airframe component. In both instances, the switches automatically cut off the electrical supply to the motor when the output shaft or ram has reached its allotted position.

5.27 Electro-magnetic Brake

After a limit switch operates and cuts off the electrical supply, the motor would tend to continue to rotate due to inertia, but this override or over-travel, is prevented by an electro-magnetic brake. The brake illustrated in Fig 5-22 consists of a brake drum integral with the first sun gear. Screwed to the intermediate housing is an eight-pole brake spider, the solenoid of which is connected in series with the armature of the motor. Across the top of each of the four pairs of pole shoes (only two pairs illustrated) is a cork-lined brake shoe. To maintain pressure between the pole shoes and the inside periphery of the brake drum, small helical springs are fitted.

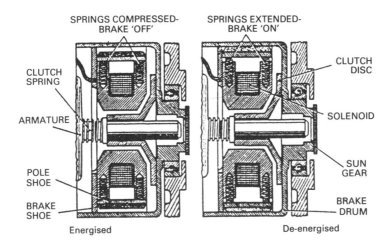

Figure 5–22 Electro-magnetic brake.

When the brake solenoid is energised, the pole shoes are attracted, the springs compressed and the brake shoes drawn clear of the brake drum, thereby allowing the motor to rotate the gearing. Immediately the electrical supply is switched off, either by operation of the control switch, or by the limit switches, the brake solenoid is de-energised and the brake shoes released. The springs then extend and force the brake shoes against the brake drum, thereby preventing override.

5.28 Clutch

To prevent damage to the motor, which can be caused by excessive load on the output shaft, the drive from the motor to the reduction gearing may pass through a spring-loaded clutch. This allows the motor to slip in the event of excessive overloading of the output shaft.

5.29 Indicator

Indication of the position of the actuated component may be shown on the actuator by wording, eg OPEN and SHUT, or there may be additional contact surfaces incorporated in the actuator limit switches which are connected by electrical wiring to a panel-mounted indicator in the cockpit.

Section 5   Test Yourself Questions

Components

1. A fuse may be replaced by the pilot:
   (a)   only after consulting an engineer.
   (b)   once, then the engineer must be consulted.
   (c)   never, it must always be replaced by an engineer.
   (d)   twice, and then the engineer must be consulted.

Ref 5.4.

2. A Rheostat is:
   (a)   a temperature control device.
   (b)   a remote automatic manual switch.
   (c)   a variable resistor.
   (d)   a temperature indicator.

Ref 5.5.

3. A Relay:
   (a)   is a form of mechanical switch.
   (b)   is a form of electro-magnetic switch.
   (c)   is a form of connector.
   (d)   is a form of temperature-sensing device.

Ref 5.6.

4. Bonding:
   (a)   ensures electro-static potential difference is maintained.
   (b)   ensures electro-static potential difference is minimised.
   (c)   is used to reduce radio interference.
   (d)   is used to earth negative connectors.

Ref 5.8.

5. In the event that generator voltage falls below battery voltage:
    (a)   reverse current to the generator is prevented by the cut-out.
    (b)   the generator will remain connected to the bus-bar.
    (c)   the battery will automatically be disconnected from the bus-bar.
    (d)   the cut-out will disconnect the battery from the system.

Ref 5.12.

6. A microswitch is an assembly:
    (a)   of very small dimensions.
    (b)   which has a very small movement to make or break a circuit.
    (c)   used for instrument contact only.
    (d)   used where one side of the structure is inaccessible.

Ref 5.16.

7. The limit switches of a linear actuator:
    (a)   limit the travel of the actuator.
    (b)   prevent excessive loads on the actuator.
    (c)   illuminate the actuator lights when the actuator is on.
    (d)   prevent overtravel of the actuator.

Ref 5.26.

8. Ground power:
    (a)   output must be the same as aircraft output before it is connected.
    (b)   output must be paralleled with aircraft output before it is connected.
    (c)   output must be on minimum before it is connected.
    (d)   must be 'off' before it is connected to the aircraft.

Ref 5.14.

9. Generator voltage:
    (a)   is controlled by the cut-out.
    (b)   is controlled by the voltage regulator.
    (c)   is controlled by the number of magnetic poles.
    (d)   is controlled by the rpm of the engine.

Ref 5.11.

10. When a ground/flight switch is set to:
    (a)   'ground', power is supplied for ground operations.
    (b)   'ground', power is off.
    (c)   'flight', power is off.
    (d)   'ground', the electrical circuits are earthed to ground.

Ref 5.14.

6

The Generation of Alternating Current

6.1 Introduction

Modern aircraft utilize electrical power to operate an ever-increasing number of aircraft systems and sub-systems, and the power requirements for a modern airliner are such that considerable advantage may be gained from the use of alternating generators, otherwise known as alternators. The saving of weight and space in modern aircraft is of the utmost importance, and in the electrical sense, with the use of alternating current (AC) devices, considerable savings can be made in both. In particular, the use of AC generators and motors are particularly advantageous as they are generally smaller and simpler than their DC equivalents. In the past brush wear, ie wear of the pick up points, has been a serious problem through arcing at altitude; this, however, in modern AC generators has been eliminated.

Another advantage is that most aircraft using 24 volt DC supply, have a requirement for a certain amount of 400 cycle AC. Supply voltages from AC sources can also be converted from higher to lower voltages or vice versa, with almost 100 per cent efficiency which is a major advantage.

6.2 Comparison of AC and DC

Some of the principles, characteristics and effects of AC are similar to those of DC. Equally, there arc a number of differences and these are explained later. Direct current flows in one direction only, and has constant polarity. The only change of magnitude occurs when the circuit is switched on or off, (See Fig 6-1).

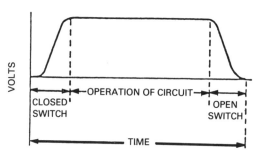

Figure 6–1 DC Waveform.

Alternating current on the other hand, changes direction and therefore polarity at regular intervals. It increases in value at a definite rate; decreases to zero having completed a half cycle, then repeats the process but in a negative sense in the other direction. This is referred to as a full 360 degrees cycle and is sinusoidal in form; there is therefore a current flow in one direction for half the cycle, and a flow in the opposite direction for the second half of the cycle. See Fig 6-2.

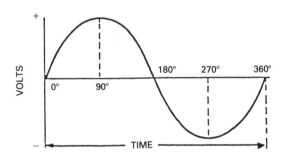

Figure 6–2 AC Waveform.

6.3 Sine Wave

In Fig 6-3 the origin of sine wave is shown in diagrammatic form. If OP rotates in the direction shown at a constant angular velocity w, the length of ON will vary according to OP sin wt where t equals time of rotation. OP is regarded as a vector of the same magnitude as Yo, the projection therefore of OP on Oy, will show instantaneous value of a quantity which is alternating sinusoidally, and the peak value will be Yo.

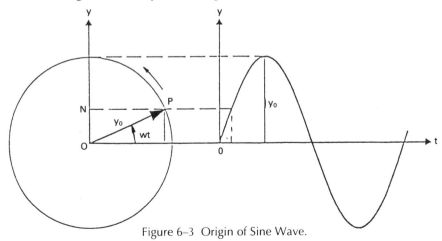

Figure 6–3 Origin of Sine Wave.

6.4 Principles of Generating Electricity

Following the discovery that an electric current flowing through a conductor creates a magnetic field around the conductor, the English scientist Faraday showed that the reverse was also true: that is, if a conductor were passed through a magnetic field then a voltage would be induced in the conductor and current would flow.

Figures 6-4a, b and c demonstrate these principles.

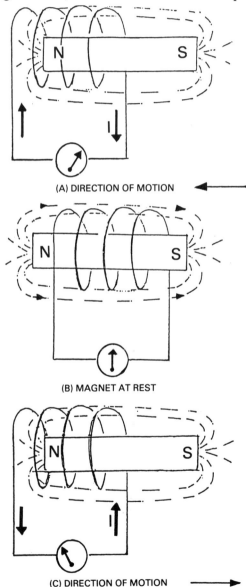

(A) DIRECTION OF MOTION

(B) MAGNET AT REST

(C) DIRECTION OF MOTION

Figure 6–4 Principle of Current Generation.

Figure 6-4a shows a bar magnet being moved through a coil of wire, ie a conductor, in the direction shown by the arrow. As the lines of force of the magnetic field move through the coil, an electromotive force or voltage is induced in it, and a current will flow in the circuit in the direction shown, and will be measured by the galvanometer.

When the magnet is withdrawn from the coil, a voltage will again be induced, and a current will flow but in the opposite direction. Therefore it can be seen there will only be a voltage induced when there is relative motion between the magnetic field and the conductor.

As illustrated in Fig 6-5a and 6-5b, the maximum emf will be induced when the conductor cuts the lines of magnetic force of the magnetic field at right angles, (Fig 6-5a). Figure 6-5b shows the conductor moving parallel to the lines of magnetic force and so no emf will be induced, therefore no current will flow.

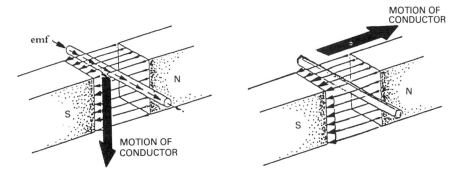

Figure 6–5a emf being induced.   Figure 6–5b No emf induced.

6.5 The Basic Principles of the AC Generator

In its simplest form an AC Generator, or Alternator consists of a coil rotating in a uniform magnetic field. See Fig 6-6.

The generator current which is induced in the rotating coil is fed from the coil in such a way that each side of the coil is always connected to the same terminal output, no matter what the orientation of the coil. This is achieved by the use of slip rings. Side W of the coil is attached to slip ring X. This rubs against brush Y which is connected to output terminal Z. Thus, W is always in electrical contact with Z. Similarly, side M of the coil is always in electrical contact with output terminal N, and therefore the alternating emf of the rotating coil appears at the output terminals.

As with the DC generator, the magnetic field of the AC generator is provided by an electromagnet. The coils of the electromagnet are called

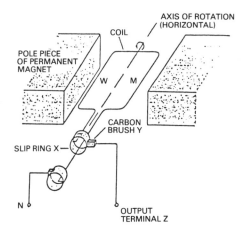

Figure 6–6 Principle of an AC Generator.

field coils, or field windings, and are wound onto soft iron poles. In the same way as the DC generator, the field windings are energised by direct current and normally controlled by a voltage regulator.

Figure 6-7 shows the basic operation.

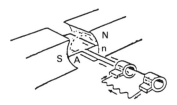

Figure 6–7a Inducing maximum voltage in an elementary generator.

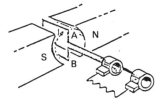

Figure 6–7b Inducing minimum voltage in an elementary generator.

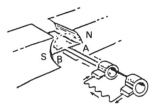

Figure 6–7c Inducing maximum voltage in the opposite direction.

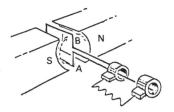

Figure 6–7d Inducing minimum voltage in the opposite direction.

Figure 6-7 shows a loop of wire, the conductor, rotating in a magnetic field in a clockwise direction.

In Figs 6-7a and 6-7b the position of the loop shows maximum and minimum induced voltages for the positive half cycle, whilst Figs 6-7c and 6-7d show the maximum and minimum voltage induction for the negative half.

This can now be related to Fig 6-8 which shows the complete waveform of alternating current which has been generated.

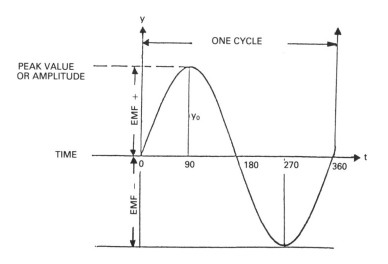

Figure 6–8 Output of an elementary generator.

6.6 Basic Construction and Operation

In the principles so far given in this chapter, the magnetic poles have been shown as stationary and the armature loop the rotating member. In reality modern AC generators normally have the armature fixed, or stationary, and the magnetic poles the rotating member. The primary reason for this is that the rotating slip rings need only be capable of handling the smaller of the two currents. In such an arrangement the armature becomes known as the stator and the magnetic poles the rotor. Fig 6-9 shows a comparison of the two arrangements, that is the rotating armature as used on most DC generators and the fixed armature, or stator, as used on most AC types.

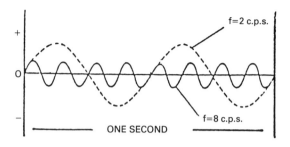

Figure 6–9 Cycle and frequency.

6.7 Generator or Alternator Frequency

Frequency can be defined as the number of cycles of an AC waveform generated per second, and the unit of frequency is the 'Hertz' (Hz). One Hertz is equal to one cycle per second.

The frequency of an alternator depends upon;

(a) the number of pairs of magnetic poles, and

(b) the speed of rotation of the rotor.

This may be found from: $\text{cps} = \dfrac{\text{rpm} \times \text{no of pairs of poles}}{60}$

For example, a six pole generator with a rotational speed of 8000 rpm would give:

$$\frac{8000 \times 3}{60} = 400 \text{ cps or } 400 \text{ Hz.}$$

For aircraft constant frequency systems, 400Hz has been adopted as the standard. There are essentially two types of AC generator used on aircraft with regard to frequency, the constant frequency, or constant speed type, as mentioned above, which is controlled to produce a frequency of 400Hz. The other type is uncontrolled, that is to say, Frequency Wild, and may produce a frequency between approximately 100Hz and 1200Hz. These types will be discussed in detail later.

6.8 Inductance

When alternating current flows through a coil of wire, the rise and fall of the current flow, first in one direction, and then in another, sets up an expanding and collapsing magnetic field about the coil. A voltage is induced in the coil which is opposite in direction to the applied voltage and which opposes any change in the alternating current. The induced voltage is called the counter electro-motive force (cemf), since it opposes the applied voltage.

This property of a coil to oppose any change in the current flowing through it is called inductance.

The inductance of a coil is measured in Henrys. In any coil, the inductance depends on several factors, principally the number of turns, the cross sectional area of the coil, and the material in the centre of the coil, or core. A core of magnetic material greatly increases the inductance of the coil.

It must be remembered, however, that even a straight wire has inductance, small though it may be when compared with that of a coil. AC motors, relays, and transformers contribute inductance to a circuit. Practically all AC circuits contain inductive elements.

The symbol for inductance in formulas is the capital letter 'L'. Inductance is measured in henrys (abbreviated h). An inductor (coil) has an inductance of 1 henry if an emf of 1 volt is induced in the inductor when the current through the inductor is changing at the rate of 1 ampere per second. However, the henry is a large unit of inductance and is used with relatively large inductors usually having iron cores. The unit normally used for small air core inductors is the millihenry (mh). For still smaller air core inductors the unit of inductance is the microhenry (μh).

If all other circuit values remain constant, the greater the inductance in a coil the greater the effect of self induction, or opposition to the change in the value of current. As the frequency increases, the inductive reactance increases, since the greater the rate of current change the more the opposition to change by the coil increases. Therefore, inductive reactance is proportional to inductance and frequency.

Inductors may be connected in a circuit in the same manner as resistors. When connected in series, the total inductance is the sum of the inductances in the inductors. When two or more inductors are connected in parallel, the total inductance is, like resistances in parallel, less than that of the smallest inductor.

Figure 6-10 shows an example of an inductor in a circuit.

6.9 Inductance Reactance

The opposition to the flow of current which inductances put in a circuit is called inductance reactance. The symbol for inductive resistance, or reactance, is X_L, and is measured in ohms, just as resistance is.

So $X_L = 2\pi fL$

where X_L = inductance reactance in ohms

f = frequency in cycles per second.

π = 3.1416.

In any circuit in which there is only resistance, the expression for the relationship of voltage and current is Ohm's Law.

$$\text{Current} = \frac{\text{Voltage}}{\text{Reactance}} \text{ or } \frac{IE}{{}^{x}L}$$

where ${}^{x}L$ = inductive reactance of the circuit in ohms.

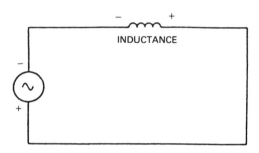

Figure 6–10 AC Circuit containing inductance.

6.10 Capacitance

Another important property in an AC circuit, besides resistance and inductance, is capacitance. While inductance is represented in a circuit by a coil, capacitance is represented by a capacitor.

Any two conductors separated by a nonconductor, called a dielectric, constitute a capacitor. In an electrical circuit a capacitor serves as a reservoir, or storehouse, for electricity.

Figure 6-11 shows a capacitor in a DC circuit and Fig 6-12 a capacitor in an AC circuit.

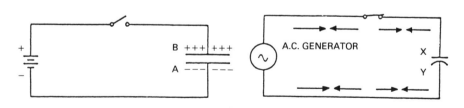

Figure 6–11 Capacitor in a DC circuit.

Figure 6–12 Capacitor in an AC circuit.

106

When a capacitor is connected across a source of direct current such as a storage battery, such as that shown in Fig 6-11 and the switch is then closed, the plate marked B becomes positively charged, and the plate marked A negatively charged. Current flows in the external circuit during the time the electrons are moving from plate B to A. The current flow in the circuit is at a maximum the instant the switch is closed, but continually decreases thereafter until it reaches zero. The current becomes zero as soon as the difference in voltage between A and B plates becomes the same as the voltage of the battery. If the switch is opened, the plates remain charged. However, the capacitor quickly discharges if it is short circuited.

The amount of electricity a capacitor can store depends on several factors, including the type of material of the dielectric. It is directly proportional to the plate area and inversely proportional to the distance between the plates.

If a source of alternating current is substituted for the battery, the capacitor acts quite differently from the way it does with direct current. When alternating current is impressed on the circuit as shown in Fig 6-12, the charge on the plates constantly changes. This means that electricity must flow first from Y clockwise around to X, then from X counterclockwise around to Y, then from Y clockwise around to X, and so on. Although no current flows through the insulator between the plates of the capacitor, it constantly flows in the remainder of the circuit between X and Y. In a circuit in which there is only capacitance, current leads the impressed voltage, by contrast with a circuit in which there is inductance, where the current lags behind the voltage.

The unit of measurement of capacitance is the Farad, for which the symbol is the letter 'f'. The Farad is too large for practical use and the units generally used are the microfarad (μf), one millionth of a Farad, and the micromicrofarad ($\mu\mu f$), one million millionth of a microfarad.

6.11 Capacitance Reactance

Capacitance, like inductance, offers opposition to the flow of current. This opposition is called capacitive reactance and is measured in ohms. The symbol for capacitive reactance is X.

The Equation:

$$Current = \frac{Voltage}{Capacitive\ Reactance} \quad or$$

$$I = \frac{E}{X_c}$$

is similar to Ohm's Law and the equation for current in an inductive circuit. The greater the frequency in a capacitive circuit, the less the reactance. Hence, the capacitive reactance:

$$X = \frac{I}{2\eta \times f \times C}$$

Where f = frequency in cps
C = capacity in Farads.
2η = 6.28.

6.12 The Phase Relationship of Current and Voltage in the Generation of Alternating Current

Figures 6-13a and 6-13b, show what is referred to as the phase relationship of voltage and current in a sinusoidal waveform.

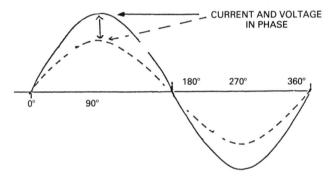

Figure 6–13a In phase current and voltage.

Figure 6-13a shows the voltage and current to be 'in phase', that is to say, the values of both are at their maximum and minimum at the same time. In a circuit with a purely resistive load, the voltage and current are in phase.

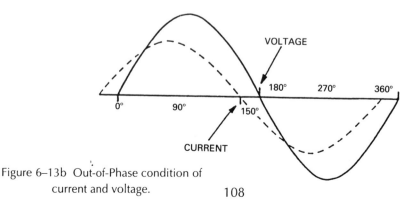

Figure 6–13b Out-of-Phase condition of current and voltage.

108

Figure 6-13b shows the current lagging the voltage by 30 degrees; they are said to be out of phase. In a circuit with an inductive load, the current lags behind the voltage by 90 degrees.

Phase Relationships in A.C. Circuits with Resistive, Inductive and Capacitive Loads

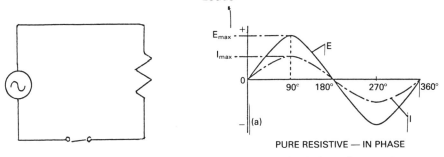

PURE RESISTIVE — IN PHASE

Figure 6–14a In a circuit with a purely resistive load, the voltage and current are in phase.

In a circuit with a capacitive load the current leads the voltage by 90 degrees.

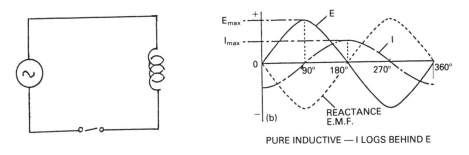

PURE INDUCTIVE — I LOGS BEHIND E

Figure 6–14b In circuit with an inductive load, the current lags behind the voltage by 90 degrees.

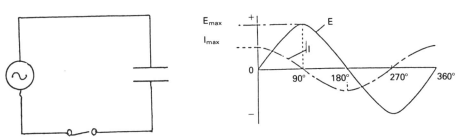

Figure 6–14c In a circuit with a capacitive load, the current leads the voltage by 90 degrees.

6.13 Root Mean Square Values

If an alternating current flowing in a circuit produces the same heating effect as a direct current of (say) 3A flowing in the same circuit, then the effective value of the alternating current is also 3A. In general, the effective value of the alternating current is equal to that direct current which results in the same expenditure of energy under the same conditions.

The energy, W, supplied in time, t, by an alternating current, I, flowing through a resistance, R, is given by the product of t and the average value of I^2R, ie

$$W = (I^2R)_{avge}\, t$$

since R is constant, this becomes

$$W = (I^2)_{avge}\, Rt$$

If (anticipating the result) the effective value of I is denoted by I_{RMS}, then W is equal to the energy supplied by a steady current of magnitude I_{RMS} flowing through a resistance R for time t, ie:

$$W = (I_{RMS})^2\, Rt$$

Therefore, from the above equations:

$$(I_{RMS})^2\, Rt = (I^2)_{avge}\, Rt$$

$$\text{ie } I_{RMS} = \sqrt{(I^2)_{avge}}$$

$$\text{ie } I_{RMS} = \sqrt{\text{average value of } I^2}$$

Thus, the effective value (denoted by I_{RMS}) is the root mean square (RMS) value and the reason for the notation is now clear. This equation holds for any alternating current, but the relationship between I_{RMS} and the peak value, I_0, depends on the nature of the AC.

Sinusoidal AC

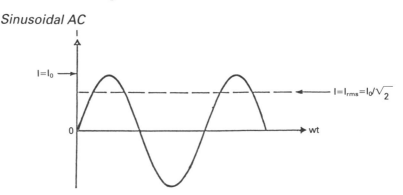

Figure 6–15 To illustrate the relationship between a sinusoidal alternating current and its RMS value.

From the above it can be shown that the root mean square values of AC current and voltage are:

$I_{rms} = I_o / \sqrt{2} = 0.7071_o$ and

$E_{rms} = E_o / \sqrt{2} = 0.707E_o$

6.14 Power Ratings of AC Generators

The power ratings of alternating current generators are usually given in kilovolt-amps (kVA) rather than kilowatts (kW) as in the case of DC generators.

The main reason for this is that in calculating the power, account must be taken of the difference between the true or effective power and the apparent power.

This difference arises from the type of circuit which the generator is to supply, and the phase relationships of voltage and current. This is expressed as a ratio termed the power factor (PF) and may be written as:

$$PF = \frac{\text{Effective power (kW)}}{\text{Apparent power (kVA)}} = \cos \text{ phase angle}$$

If the voltage and current are in phase as in a resistive circuit, the power factor is 100% of 'unity', the reason being that the effective power and apparent power are equal. Therefore a generator rated at 100 kVA in a circuit with a power factor of unity will have an output which is 100% efficient and exactly equal to 100 kW.

When a circuit contains inductance or capacitance, however, current and voltage will not be in phase; this will then make the PF less than unity.

Figure 6-16 shows a vector diagram for a current I lagging behind a voltage E, by an angle ϕ.

The current is resolved into two components at right angles to each other, one is in phase with E, and is given by $I \cos \phi$, and the other out of phase by 90 degrees or 'in quadrature', given by $I \sin \phi$. The in phase component is called the active 'wattful' or working component (kW), and the other is referred to as the idle, wattless or reactive component (kVAR).

The importance of these two components will become more apparent when, later, methods of load sharing between generators are discussed.

Most AC generators are designed to take a proportion of the reactive component of current through their windings. Some indication of this may be obtained from the information given on the generator data plate. As an example, the output rating may be specified as 40 kVA at 0.8 PF. This would mean that the maximum output in kW is 0.8 × 40 or 32 kW,

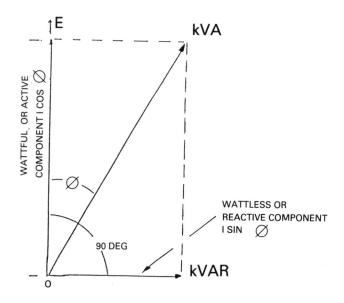

Figure 6–16 Current/Voltage.

but that the product of volts and amperes under all conditions of PF must not exceed 40 kVA.

6.15 Further Illustrations of Power in AC Circuits

In a DC circuit, power is obtained by the equation, $P = EI$, (watts equal volts times amperes). Thus if 1 ampere of current flows in a circuit at a pressure of 200 volts, the power is 200 watts. The product of the volts and the amperes is the true power in the circuit.

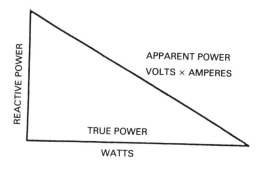

Figure 6–17 Power relations in AC circuit.

In an AC circuit, a voltmeter indicates the effective voltage and an ammeter indicates the effective current. The product of these two readings is called the apparent power. Only when the AC circuit is made up of pure resistance is the apparent power equal to the true power (Fig 6-17). When there is a capacitance or inductance in the circuit, the current and voltage are not exactly in phase, and the true power is less than the apparent power. The true power is obtained by a wattmeter reading. The ratio of true power to apparent power is called the power factor and is usually expressed in percent. In equation form, the relationship is:

$$\text{Power Factor (PF)} = \frac{100 \times \text{Watts (True Power)}}{\text{Volts} \times \text{Amperes (Apparent Power)}}$$

Problem:
A 220 volt AC motor takes 50 amperes from the line, but a wattmeter in the line shows that only 9,350 watts are taken by the motor. What is the apparent power and the power factor?

Solution:
Apparent power = Volts × Amperes
Apparent power = 220 × 50 = 11,000 watts or volt-amperes.

$$PF = \frac{\text{Watts (True Power)} \times 100}{\text{VA (Apparent Power)}}$$

$$PF = \frac{9350 \times 100}{11,000} = 85 \text{ or } 85\%$$

6.16 Rectification of AC

Rectification is the process of changing alternating current to direct current. When a semi-conductor rectifier, such as a junction diode, is connected to an AC voltage source, it is alternately biased forward and reverse, in step with the AC voltage, as shown in Fig 6-18.

In Fig 6-19, a diode is placed in series with a source of AC power and a load resistor. This is called a half-wave rectifier circuit.

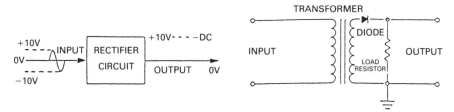

Figure 6–18 Rectification process.   Figure 6–19 Half-wave rectifier circuit.

The transformer provides the AC input to the circuit, the diode provides the rectification of the AC, and the load resistor serves two purposes: (1) it limits the amount of current flow in the circuit to a safe level, and (2) it develops an output signal due to the current flow through it.

Assume, as in Fig 6-20, that the top of the transformer secondary is positive and the bottom negative. With this polarity, the diode is forward-biased, resistance of the diode is very low, and current flows through the circuit in the direction of the arrows. The output (voltage drop) across the load resistor follows the waveshape of the positive half of the AC input. When the AC input goes in a negative direction, the top of the transformer secondary becomes negative and the diode becomes reverse-biased.

With reverse bias applied to the diode, the resistance of the diode becomes very great, and current flow through the diode and load resistor becomes zero. (Remember that a very small current will flow through the diode.) The output, taken across the load resistor, will be zero. If the position of the diode were reversed, the output would be negative pulses.

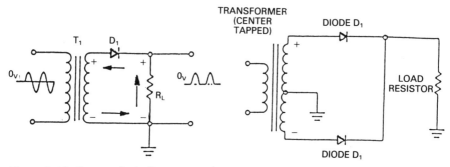

Figure 6–20 Output of a half-wave rectifier.   Figure 6–21 Full-wave rectifier.

In a half-wave rectifier, a half cycle of power is produced across the load resistor for each full cycle of input power. To increase the output power, a full-wave rectifier can be used. Figure 6-21 shows a full-wave rectifier which is, in effect, two half-wave rectifiers combined into one circuit. In this circuit a load resistor is used to limit current flow and develop an output voltage, two diodes to provide rectification, and a transformer to provide an AC input to the circuit. The transformer used in full-wave rectifier circuits must be centre tapped to complete the path for current flow through the load resistor.

Assuming the polarities shown on the transformer, diode D_1 will be forward-biased and current will flow from ground through the load resistor, through diode D_1 to the top of the transformer.

When the AC input changes direction, the transformer secondary will assume an opposite polarity.

6.17 Diode Bridge Rectifier Circuit

An advantageous modification to the full-wave diode rectifier is the bridge rectifier, see Figs 6-22a, b, c. The bridge rectifier differs from the full-wave rectifier in that it does not require a centre-tapped transformer, but does require two additional diodes.

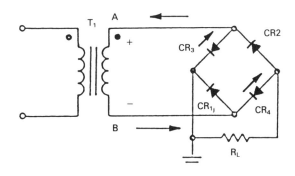

Figure 6–22a Diode bridge rectifier.

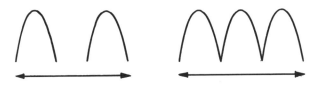

Figure 6–22b   Figure 6–22c

Half-wave and full-wave rectifier outputs
Elements used in rectifiers include: the *Semi-conductor* type, the *Silicon rectifier*, and the *Selenium* rectifier.

Section 6   Test Yourself Questions

1.   In an AC Generator:
    (a)   the moving member is termed the armature.
    (b)   the moving member is termed the inductance coil.
    (c)   the moving member is termed the rotational coil.
    (d)   the moving member is termed the rotor.

                                                          Ref 6.6.

2.   In a circuit with purely resistive loads:
    (a)   voltage leads current.
    (b)   current lags behind voltage.
    (c)   voltage and current are in phase.
    (d)   voltage lags behind current.

                                                          Ref 6.12.

3.   In an inductive circuit:
    (a)   voltage leads current.
    (b)   voltage and current are in phase.
    (c)   voltage lags behind current.
    (d)   current leads voltage.

                                                          Ref 6.12.

4.   In a capacitive circuit:
    (a)   voltage and current are in phase.
    (b)   voltage leads current.
    (c)   voltage lags behind current.
    (d)   voltage and capacitance are in phase.

                                                          Ref 6.12.

5.   In an AC Supply system, AC is converted to DC by:
    (a)   a commutator.
    (b)   an inverter.
    (c)   a rectifier.
    (d)   a transformer.

                                                          Ref 6.16.

7

AC Generators

7.1 Introduction

The following is a general description of the basic types of generator, or alternator, currently used on aircraft.

Alternating current generators are generally of two main types: those designed for operation over a wide variable speed and variable frequency range (frequency-wild generators), and those designed for constant speed and constant frequency operation (constant-speed generators).

7.2 Frequency-wild Generators

There are basically two categories: those used on small aircraft to provide a direct current voltage output, after rectification, and those used to provide an alternating current voltage output to supply systems that do not require a fixed frequency supply.

Figure 7-1 shows a generator, the output of which is rectified to provide direct current. Generators of this type are utilised in a variety of small aircraft requiring direct current as the primary power source. The main components of the generator are the rotor, the stator, and a rectifier assembly. The rotor consists of two extruded steel pole pieces pressed onto a shaft against each end of a field coil. Each pole piece has six 'fingers', so shaped that when the pole pieces are in position, the fingers mesh with, but do not touch, each other. Two slip rings are pressed onto one end of the rotor shaft and are electrically connected to the rotor field coil. The rotor is rotated by a driving belt and pulley driven by the engine, or by coupling the generator directly to the engine gearbox drive shaft. The stator comprises three star-connected coils wound around a laminated core; each end of each coil is connected to the rectifier assembly whilst the other ends are joined together to form the 'star' or neutral point. The rectifier assembly is located opposite the drive-end of the generator, and consists of six silicon diodes connected to form a full-wave bridge rectifier circuit.

Three of the diodes (negative) are mounted on the end frame, while the other three (positive) are mounted on a 'heat sink' plate on the inside of the end frame. Spring-loaded brushes are located inside the end frame and make contact with the rotor slip rings to complete the field or excitation coil circuit.

These small generators do not usually incorporate permanent magnets and are not self excited. They therefore require a supply of direct current from an independent source for the initial excitation of the rotor field windings. In the type illustrated in Fig 7-1, this is provided from the busbar of the electrical system of the aircraft when the battery, or an external power supply, is connected to that busbar. The current passing through the field coil circuit causes the fingers of the rotor pole pieces to become alternately north and south electro-magnetic poles. As it rotates, the magnetic field set up in the rotor poles induces a three-phase alternating voltage in the stator windings at a frequency dependent on rotor speed. The output is supplied to the rectifier assembly, and the direct current thus obtained is then supplied to the electrical system busbar, thereby maintaining excitation of the field coil. The rectified output is also fed to a voltage regulator which is pre-set to regulate the generator voltage, within the limits specified for the generator and the aircraft electrical system.

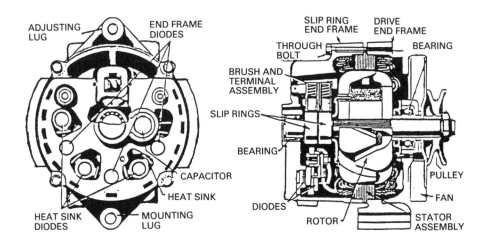

Figure 7–1 Example Small brushless DC generator.

Figure 7-2 shows a typical three-phase, frequency-wild generator, which is used in some aircraft for the supply of alternating current to electrical systems that do not require a fixed frequency supply, such as resistive load circuits for de-icing and anti-icing systems. This generator has a power output of 15 kVA at 208 volts, and its frequency and driven speed ranges are 335 to 535 Hz and 6700 to 10,700 rpm, respectively. The

AC GENERATORS

generator consists of two major assemblies: a rotor assembly and a fixed stator assembly. The rotor assembly has six poles, each of which is wound with a field coil; the coils terminate at two slip rings secured at one end of the rotor shaft. Three spring-loaded brushes are equi-spaced on each slip ring, and are contained within a brushgear housing. The brushes are electrically connected to direct current input terminals housed in an excitation terminal box mounted on the outside of the brushgear housing. The terminal box also houses capacitors connected between the terminals and earth, to suppress interference which may affect, for example, the reception of radio signals. The rotor shaft is splined at the drive end, and supported in a roller bearing fitted in the main housing. An oil seal is provided to prevent the entry of oil from the driving source into the main housing. The stator windings are star-connected, and an end frame clamps the whole assembly in the main housing, which has an integral

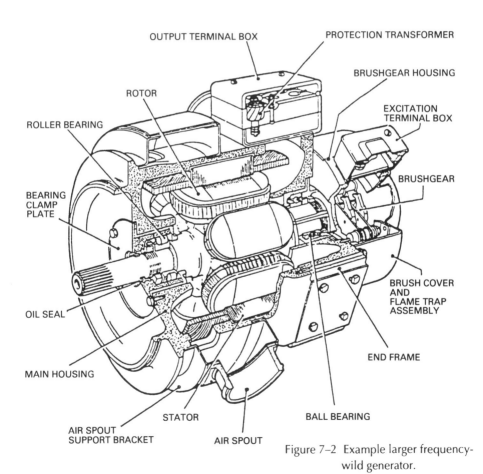

Figure 7–2 Example larger frequency-wild generator.

flange for mounting the generator at the corresponding drive shaft outlet of the engine accessory gearbox. The ends of the stator windings are brought to a three-way output terminal box mounted on the end frame. The generator is cooled by ram air passing into the main housing via an inlet spout; the air escapes from the main housing through ventilation slots at the drive end, from where it is usually ducted overboard.

Direct current for the initial excitation of the rotor field windings is provided from the main bus-bar, via a 'start' switch in the circuit, to the excitation terminals and brushgear. As the generator rotates, a three-phase alternating voltage is induced in the stator windings which is supplied to the bus-bar distribution. The output voltage is controlled by feeding it to a voltage regulator, and to a three-phase bridge rectifier, which together with other protection circuits, are contained within a separate control unit. At a pre-determined output voltage, the generator is able to run as a self-excited machine, and could operate independently of the direct current supply from the main bus-bar.

7.3 Constant-Speed/Frequency Generators

These generators are utilised in those types of aircraft requiring (i) a much wider application of alternating current, (ii) a considerable amount of electrical power and (iii) generator system load-sharing capability. Generators designed for such applications are currently of the brushless type, and are driven by an engine through the medium of a special constant-speed drive unit. In most applications, the generators may be removed and installed separately and with the drive unit 'in-situ', but for certain types of aircraft, the generators are integrated with the drive unit so that removal and installation as a complete assembly is necessary. Examples of both types are shown in Figs 7-3 and 7-4 respectively. The constant-speed drive is basically a differential gear transmission system which converts variable input speed of an engine to a constant output speed appropriate to the generator rating. The output speed of the generator is controlled by a hydromechanical governor system. The construction of generators varies, but, in general, they consist of three principal components: a pilot exciter, a main exciter and rotating rectifier, and a main generator. All three components are contained within a casing made up of an end bell section and a stator housing section. A mounting flange, which is an integral part of the stator housing section, provides for attachment of the generator to the constant-speed drive unit by means either of studs and retaining nuts, or a quick attach/detach coupling.

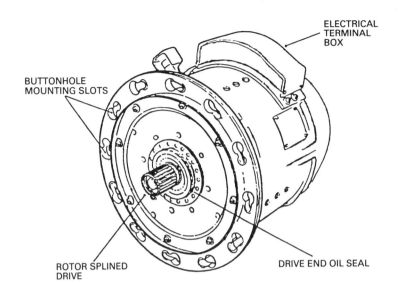

Figure 7–3 Example constant-speed generator.

The purpose of the pilot exciter is to provide the magnetic field necessary for initial excitation of the main exciter. It comprises a stator, and a permanent magnet rotor which is mounted on the same shaft as the main exciter and main generator rotor. The AC output from the pilot exciter is fed to the main exciter field via a control and protection unit.

The rotating rectifier assembly supplies excitation current to the main generator rotor field coils from the main exciter rotor, and eliminates the need for brushes and slip rings. It usually consists of six silicon diodes connected as a three-phase, full-wave bridge rectifier circuit, sometimes contained within a tubular insulator located in the hollow shaft on which both the exciter rotor and main generator rotor are mounted, but can be mounted in any convenient position on the rotor, provided the radius from the centre line is not excessive.

The main generator consists of a three-phase, star-wound stator, a rotor and associated field windings, which are connected to the rotating rectifier assembly. The leads from the three stator phases are connected to a terminal block, which permits connection of the generator to the aircraft power distribution system.

When a generator starts operating, an initial flow of current is provided to the field of the main exciter via the control and protection unit, and a three-phase voltage is produced in the exciter rotor. This voltage is then supplied to the rotating rectifier assembly, the direct current output of which, in turn, is fed to the field coils of the main generator as the required excitation current. A rotating magnetic field is thus produced which induces a three-phase voltage output of 200 volts, at a frequency of 400 Hz, in the main stator windings. The output voltage is sensed at the busbar by the voltage regulator, which controls the amount of excitation current required by the main generator section to maintain the desired AC output.

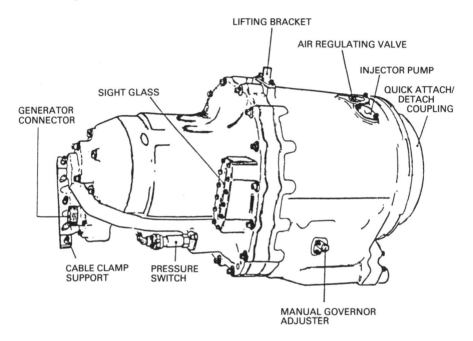

Figure 7–4 Example integrated drive generator.

Generator cooling is normally provided by ram air which enters through the end bell section of the casing, and passes through the windings, the rotor shaft, and the rectifier assembly. The air is exhausted through a perforated screen around the periphery of the casing, at a point adjacent to the main generator stator, then usually ducted overboard. In the case of integrated drive generators, cooling of the windings and rectifier assembly is provided by oil which is also used for the hydraulic speed governing system. The oil is supplied from a reservoir which is integral with the casing of the integrated drive generator, and is circulated by a charge pump driven by the output shaft of the hydraulic transmission system. The oil is passed through a cooler mounted on the engine, and, depending on the installation, the cooling medium for the oil may either be air tapped from a low-pressure stage of the compressor or fuel from the fuel system of the aircraft.

The constant speed drive unit is a hydromechanical device, and as previously stated, the oil for the integrated drive unit is contained in a reservoir which is built into the generator assembly. The CSU is controlled by a governor assembly which is an integral part of the CSU. The output from the generator passes through a Frequency Controller which monitors the frequency of the generator output. Any variation in frequency output beyond set limits causes the frequency controller to send signals to the CSU governor which in turn corrects the frequency output.

A frequency meter is also provided to permit the pilot to monitor the generator frequency in the cockpit. In systems which have more than one generator, only one frequency meter is fitted in the cockpit with a mode switch to select the generator frequency reading required.

There are two warning lights fitted to the CSU. The first will illuminate in the event of excessive temperature within the CSU, the other light illuminates should the oil pressure drop below a certain value. Should either or both of these lights illuminate to indicate a malfunction within the CSU, a manually operated disconnect switch must be operated by the pilot. This will disconnect the CSU drive and can only be re-set on the ground.

When two such AC generators are paralleled or load shared, the Active load sharing is borne by the frequency controllers, and the Reactive load sharing is borne by the Voltage regulators. The reactive load on a generator is measured in kVAR, kilovolts ampere reactance. On some generators kVAR meters are fitted in the field circuit.

7.4 Brushless Alternators

A generator now commonly in use is the brushless type. It is more efficient because there are no brushes to wear down or to arc at high altitudes.

This generator consists of a pilot exciter, an exciter, and the main generator system. The necessity for brushes has been eliminated by using an integral exciter with a rotating armature that has its AC output rectified for the main AC field, which is also of the rotating type. A brushless alternator is illustrated in Fig 7-5.

The pilot exciter is an 8-pole, 8000 rpm, 533 cps, AC generator. The pilot exciter field is mounted on the main generator rotor shaft and is connected in series with the main generator field. The pilot exciter armature is mounted on the main generator stator. The AC output of the pilot exciter is supplied to the voltage regulator, where it is rectified and controlled, and is then impressed on the exciter field winding to furnish excitation for the generator.

The exciter is a small AC generator with its field mounted on the main generator stator and its 3-phase armature mounted on the generator rotor shaft. Included in the exciter field are permanent magnets mounted on the main generator stator between the exciter poles.

The exciter field resistance is temperature compensated by a thermistor. This aids regulation by keeping a nearly constant resistance at the regulator output terminals. The exciter output is rectified and impressed on the main generator field and the pilot exciter field. The exciter stator has a stabilising field, which is used to improve stability and to prevent voltage regulator over-correction for changes in generator output voltage.

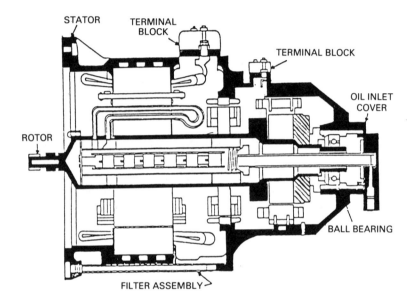

Figure 7–5 A typical brushless alternator.

The AC generator shown in Fig 7-5 is a 6-pole, 8000 rpm unit having a rating of 31.5 kilovolt amperes (KVA), 115/200 volts, 400 cps. This generator is 3-phase, 4-wire, wye-connected with grounded neutrals. By using an integral AC exciter the necessity for brushes within the generator has been eliminated. The AC output of the rotating exciter armature is fed directly into the 3-phase, full-wave, rectifier bridge located inside the rotor shaft, which uses high-temperature silicon rectifiers. The DC output from the rectifier bridge is fed to the main AC generator rotating field.

Voltage regulation is accomplished by varying the strength of the AC exciter stationary fields. Polarity reversals of the AC generator are eliminated and radio noise is minimised by the absence of the brushes. Any existing radio noise is further reduced by a noise filter mounted on the alternator.

The rotating pole structure of the generator is laminated from steel punchings, containing all six poles and a connecting hub section. This provides optimum magnetic and mechanical properties.

Some alternators are cooled by circulating oil through steel tubes. The oil used for cooling is supplied from the constant-speed drive assembly. Oil flow between the constant-speed drive and the generator is made possible by ports located in the flange connecting the generator and drive assemblies.

Voltage is built up by using permanent magnet interpoles in the exciter stator. The permanent magnets assure a voltage build up, precluding the necessity of field flashing. The rotor of the alternator may be removed without causing loss of the alternator's residual magnetism.

7.5 Alternator-Rectifier Unit

The wiring diagram of a type of alternator used in many aircraft weighing less than 5700 kg is shown in Fig 7-6. This type of power source is some-times called a DC generator, since it is used in DC systems. Although its output is a DC voltage, it is in fact an alternator-rectifier unit.

This type of alternator-rectifier is self-excited but does not contain a permanent magnet. The excitation for starting is obtained from the battery, and immediately after starting, the unit is self-exciting. Cooling air for the alternator is conducted into the unit by a blast air tube on the air inlet cover.

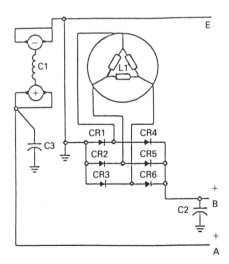

Figure 7–6 Wiring diagram of alternator-rectifier unit.

The alternator is directly coupled to the aircraft engine by means of a flexible drive coupling. The DC output voltage may be regulated by a carbon pile voltage regulator. The output of the alternator portion of the unit is three-phase alternating current, derived from a three-phase, delta-connected system incorporating a three-phase full-wave bridge rectifier (Fig 7-7).

This unit operates in a speed range from 2100 to 9000 rpm, with a DC output of 26–29 volts and 125 amperes.

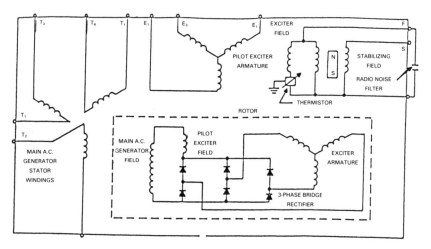

Figure 7–7 Three-phase, full-wave bridge rectifier.

7.6 Combined AC and DC Electrical Systems

Many aircraft, especially those of more than 5700 kg, employ both a DC and an AC electrical system. Often the DC system is the basic electrical system and consists of paralleled DC generators with output of, for example, 300 amperes each.

The AC system on such aircraft may include both a fixed frequency and a variable frequency system. The fixed frequency system may consist of three or four inverters and associated controls, protective and indicating components to provide single-phase, AC power for frequency sensitive AC equipment. The variable frequency system may consist of two or more engine-driven alternators, with associated control, protective, and indicating components, to provide three-phase, AC power for such purposes as resistive heating on propellers, engine ducts and windshields.

Such combined DC and AC electrical systems normally include an auxiliary source of DC power to back up the main system. This generator is often driven by a separate piston engine or turbine-powered unit.

Section 7   Test Yourself Questions

AC Generators

1. A frequency wild generator:
    (a)   is always used as a DC generator.
    (b)   produces constant frequency but at a variable rpm.
    (c)   maintains constant rpm but has a variable frequency.
    (d)   has a variable frequency output.

    Ref 7.2.

2. In order to load share:
    (a)   constant speed generators are normally used.
    (b)   constant speed frequency-wild generators are used.
    (c)   any type of generator may be used.
    (d)   frequency-wild generators with TRUs may be used.

    Ref 7.3.

3. The constant speed unit of a constant speed generator is controlled by:
    (a)   a governor unit.
    (b)   a centrifugal clutch mechanism.
    (c)   a disconnect switching device.
    (d)   a hydraulic pump.

    Ref 7.3.

4. Oil for the operation of the CSU of a constant speed generator is supplied:
    (a)   by the engine lubrication system.
    (b)   by a self-contained system within the generator.
    (c)   by the aircraft hydraulic system.
    (d)   by the gearbox drive system.

    Ref 7.3.

5. Constant speed AC generators are normally:
    (a)   self-exciting.
    (b)   excited by the battery bus-bar.
    (c)   excited by the DC supply.
    (d)   excited by a separate frequency-wild generator.

    Ref 7.3.

8

Control and Regulation of AC Generators

8.1 Introduction

Alternators are classified in several ways in order to distinguish properly the various types. One means of classification is by the type of excitation system used. In alternators used on aircraft, excitation can be effected by one of the following methods:

(a) A direct-connected, direct-current generator. This system consists of a DC generator mounted on the same shaft as the AC generator. A variation of this system is a type of alternator which uses DC from the battery for excitation, after which the alternator is self-excited.

(b) By transformation and rectification from the AC system. This method depends on residual magnetism for initial AC voltage build-up, after which the field is supplied with rectified voltage from the AC generator.

(c) Integrated brushless type. This arrangement has a direct-current generator on the same shaft with an alternating-current generator. The excitation circuit is completed through silicon rectifiers rather than a commutator and brushes. The rectifiers are mounted on the generator shaft and their output is fed directly to the alternating-current generator's main rotating field.

Another method of classification is by the number of phases of output voltage. Alternating-current generators may be single-phase, two-phase, three-phase, or even six-phase and more. In aircraft the three-phase alternator is by far the most common.

Still another means of classification is by the type of stator and rotor used. From this standpoint, there are two types of alternators: the revolving-armature type and the revolving-field type. The revolving-armature alternator is similar in construction to the DC generator, in that the armature rotates through a stationary magnetic field. The revolving-armature alternator is found only in alternators of low power rating and generally is not used. In the DC generator, the emf generated in the armature windings is converted into a uni-directional voltage (DC) by means of the commutator. In the revolving-armature type of alternator, the generated DC voltage is applied unchanged to the load by means of slip rings and brushes.

The revolving-field type of alternator (Fig 8-1) has a stationary armature winding (stator) and a rotating-field winding (rotor). The advantage of having a stationary armature winding is that the armature can be connected directly to the load without having sliding contacts in the load circuit. A rotating armature would require slip rings and brushes to conduct the load current from the armature to the external circuit. Slip rings have a relatively short service life and arc-over is a continual hazard; high-voltage alternators are therefore usually of the stationary-armature, rotating-field type. The voltage and current supplied to the rotating field are relatively small, and slip rings and brushes for this circuit are adequate. The direct connection to the armature circuit makes possible the use of large cross-section conductors, adequately insulated for high voltage.

Since the rotating-field alternator is used almost universally in aircraft systems, this type will be explained in detail, as a single-phase, two-phase, and three-phase alternator.

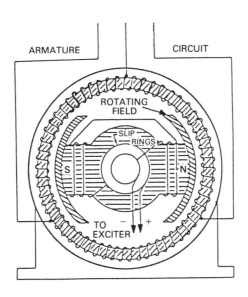

Figure 8–1 Alternator with stationary armature and rotating field.

8.2 Single-Phase Alternator

Since the emf induced in the armature of a generator is alternating, the same sort of winding can be used on an alternator as on a DC generator. This type of alternator is known as a single-phase alternator, but since the power delivered by a single-phase circuit is pulsating, this type of circuit is objectionable in many applications.

A single-phase alternator has a stator made up of a number of windings in series, forming a single circuit in which an output voltage is generated. Figure 8-2 illustrates a schematic diagram of a single-phase alternator having four poles. The stator has four polar groups evenly spaced around the stator frame. The rotor has four poles, with adjacent poles of opposite polarity. As the rotor revolves, AC voltages are induced in the stator windings. Since one rotor pole is in the same position relative to a stator winding as any other rotor pole, all stator polar groups are cut by equal numbers of magnetic lines of force at any time. As a result the voltages induced in all the windings have the same amplitude, or value, at any given instant. The four stator windings are connected to each other so that the AC voltages are in phase, or 'series adding'. Assume that rotor pole 1, a south pole, induces a voltage in the direction indicated by the arrow in stator winding 1. Since rotor pole 2 is a north pole, it will induce a voltage in the opposite direction in stator coil 2, with respect to that in coil 1.

For the two induced voltages to be in series addition, the two coils are connected as shown in the diagram. Applying the same reasoning, the voltage induced in stator coil 3 (clockwise rotation of the field) is the same direction (counterclockwise) as the voltage induced in coil 1. Similarly, the direction of the voltage induced in winding 4 is opposite to the direction of the voltage induced in coil 1. All four stator coil groups are connected in series so that the voltages induced in each winding add to give a total voltage that is four times the voltage in any one winding.

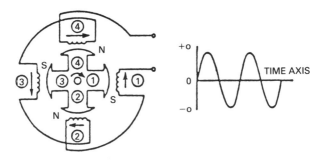

Figure 8–2 Single-phase alternator.

8.3 Two-Phase Alternator

Two-phase alternators have two or more single-phase windings spaced symmetrically around the stator. In a two-phase alternator there are two single-phase windings spaced physically so that the AC voltage induced in one is 90° out of phase with the voltage induced in the other. The windings are electrically separate from each other. When one winding is being cut by maximum flux, the other is being cut by no flux. This condition establishes a 90° relation between the two phases.

8.4 Three-Phase Alternator

A three-phase, or polyphase circuit, is used in most aircraft alternators, instead of a single or two-phase alternator. The three-phase alternator has three single-phase windings spaced so that the voltage induced in each winding is 120° out of phase with the voltages in the other two windings. A schematic diagram of a three-phase stator showing all the coils becomes complex and makes it difficult to see what is actually happening.

A simplified schematic diagram, showing each of three phases, is illustrated in Fig 8-3. The rotor is omitted for simplicity. The waveforms of voltage are shown to the right of the schematic. The three voltages are 120° apart and are similar to the voltages which would be generated by three single-phase alternators whose voltages are out of phase by angles of 120°. The three phases are independent of each other.

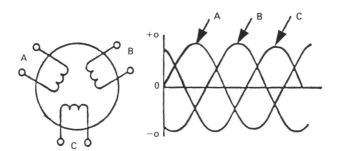

Figure 8–3 Simplified schematic of three-phase alternator with output waveforms.

Rather than have six leads from the three-phase alternator, one of the leads from each phase may be connected to form a common junction. The stator is then called star-connected. The common lead may or may not be brought out of the alternator. If it is brought out, it is called the neutral lead. The simplified schematic (A of Fig 8-4) shows a star-connected stator with the common lead not brought out. Each load is connected across two phases in series. Thus, R_{AB} is connected across phases A and B in series; R_{AC} is connected across phases A and C in series; and R_{BC} is connected across phases B and C in series.

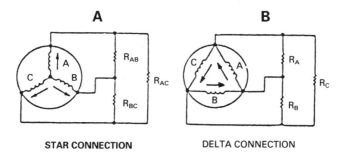

Figure 8–4 Star and delta-connected alternators.

The voltage across each load is therefore larger than the voltage across a single phase. The total voltage, or line voltage, across any two phases is the vector sum of the individual phase voltages. For balanced conditions, the line voltage is 1.73 times the phase voltage. Since there is only one path for current in a line wire and the phase to which it is connected, the line current is equal to the phase current.

A three phase stator can also be connected so that the phases are connected end-to-end as shown in (b) of Fig 8-4. This arrangement is called delta connection. In a delta connection, the voltages are equal to the phase voltages; the line currents are equal to the vector sum of the phase currents, and the line current is equal to 1.73 times the phase current when the loads are balanced.

For equal loads (equal kW output), the delta connection supplies increased line current at a value of line voltage equal to phase voltage, and the star connection supplies increased line voltage at a value of line current equal to phase current.

8.5 Load-Sharing or Paralleling of AC Generators

(a) Frequency-wild Systems

In systems of this type, the AC output is supplied to independent consumer equipment and since the frequency is allowed to go uncontrolled, then paralleling or sharing of the AC load is not possible. In most applications this is by design; for example, in electrical de-icing equipment employing resistance type heaters, a variable frequency has no effect on system operation; therefore reliance is placed more on generator dependability and on the simplicity of the generating system. In rectified AC systems frequency is also uncontrolled, but as most of the output is utilised for supplying DC consumer equipment, load sharing is more easily accomplished by paralleling the rectified output through equalising circuits in a similar manner to that adopted for DC generating systems.

(b) Constant-Frequency Systems

These systems are designed for operation under load-sharing or paralleling conditions and in this connection regulation of the two parameters, real load and reactive load, is required. Real load is the actual working load output in kilowatts (kW) available for supplying the various electrical services, and the reactive load is the so-called 'wattless load' which is in fact the vector sum of the inductive and capacitive currents and voltage in the system expressed in kilovolt-amperes reactive (kVAR).

Since the real load is directly related to the input power from the prime mover, ie the aircraft engine, real load-sharing control must be on the engine. There are, however, certain practical difficulties, but as it is possible to refer back any real load unbalance to the constant-speed drive unit between engine and generator, real load-sharing control is effected at this unit by adjusting torque at the output drive shaft.

Reactive load unbalances are corrected by controlling the exciter field current delivered by the voltage regulators in accordance with signals from a reactive load-sharing circuit.

8.6 Voltage Regulation of Alternators

The problem of voltage regulation in an AC system does not differ basically from that in a DC system. In each case the function of the regulator system is to control voltage, maintain a balance of circulating current throughout the system and eliminate sudden changes in voltage (anti-hunting) when a load is applied to the system. However, there is one important difference between the regulator system of DC generators and alternators operated in a parallel configuration. The load carried by any particular DC generator in either a two- or a four-generator system depends on its voltage as compared with the bus voltage, whereas the division of load between alternators depends upon the adjustments of their speed governors, which are controlled by the frequency and droop circuits.

When AC generators are operated in parallel, frequency and voltage must be equal. Where a synchronising force is required to equalise only the voltage between DC generators, synchronising forces are required to equalise both voltage and speed (frequency) between AC generators. On a comparative basis, the synchronising forces for AC generators are much greater than for DC generators. Where AC generators are of sufficient size and are operating at unequal frequencies and terminal voltages, serious damage may result if they are suddenly connected to each other through a common bus. To avoid this, the generators must be synchronised as closely as possible before connecting them together.

The output voltage of an alternator is best controlled by regulating the voltage output of the DC exciter, which supplies current to the alternator rotor field. This is accomplished as shown in Fig 8-5 by a carbon-pile regulator of a 28-volt system connected in the field circuit of the exciter. The carbon-pile regulator controls the exciter field current and thus regulates the exciter output voltage applied to the alternator field. The only difference between the DC system and the AC system is that the voltage coil receives its voltage from the alternator line instead of from the DC generator. In this arrangement, a three-phase step-down transformer connected to the alternator voltage supplies power to a three-phase, full-wave rectifier. The 28-volt DC output of the rectifier is then applied to the voltage coil of the carbon-pile regulator. Changes in alternator voltage are transferred through the transformer rectifier unit to the voltage coil of the regulator and vary the pressure on the carbon disks. This controls the exciter field current and the exciter output voltage. The exciter voltage anti-hunting or damping transformer is similar to those in DC systems and performs the same functions.

The alternator equalising circuit is similar to that of the DC system in that the regulator is affected when the circulating current supplied by one alternator differs from that supplied by the others.

8.7 Alternator Constant-Speed Drive

Alternators are not always connected directly to the aircraft engine like DC generators. Since the various electrical devices operating on AC supplied by alternators are designed to operate at a certain voltage and at a specified frequency, the speed of the alternators must be constant; however, the speed of an aircraft engine varies. Therefore, some alternators are driven by the engine through a constant-speed drive installed between the engine and the alternator. The following discussion of a constant-speed drive system will be based on such a drive, found on large multi-engined aircraft.

The constant-speed drive is a hydraulic transmission which may be controlled either electrically or mechanically.

The constant-speed drive assembly is designed to deliver an output of 6000 rpm, provided the input remains between 2800 and 9000 rpm. If the

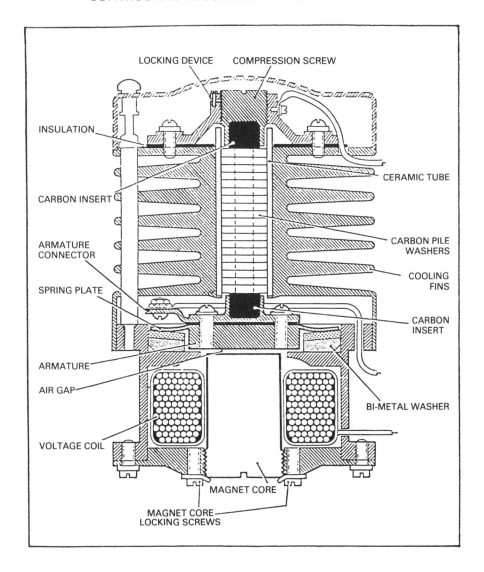

Figure 8–5 Carbon-pile voltage regulator construction.

input, which is determined by engine speed, is below 6000 rpm, the drive increases the speed in order to furnish the desired output. This stepping up of speed is known as overdrive.

In overdrive, a car engine will operate at about the same rpm at 60 mph as it does in conventional drive at 49 mph. In aircraft, this principle is applied in the same manner. The constant-speed drive enables the alternator to produce the same frequency at slightly above engine-idle rpm as it would at take-off or cruising rpm.

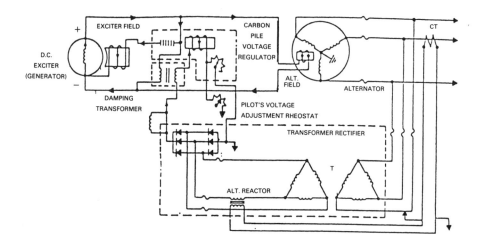

Figure 8–6 Carbon-pile voltage regulator circuit for an alternator.

Section 8   Test Yourself Questions

Control and Regulation of AC Generators

1. In a three-phase generator, or alternator, the phases are:
   (a) spaced 90 degrees apart.
   (b) spaced at 45 degree intervals.
   (c) spaced 120 degrees apart.
   (d) may be spaced at any interval provided they are insulated from each other.

   Ref 8.4.

2. In a three-phase star-connected generator:
   (a) phase current is greater than line current.
   (b) line current is equal to phase current.
   (c) line voltage is equal to phase voltage.
   (d) line voltage is less than phase voltage.

   Ref 8.4.

3. In a star-connected three-phase generator, if one phase becomes disconnected:
   (a) only that phase will be affected.
   (b) the current on the neutral will remain constant.
   (c) all three phases will be affected.
   (d) the generator will immediately stop.

   Ref 8.4.

4. In a star-connected three-phase generator, if one phase becomes disconnected:
   (a) line voltage will increase.
   (b) the generator will stop.
   (c) voltage on the neutral will remain constant.
   (d) a large voltage will be thrown on the neutral.

   Ref 8.4.

5. In a delta-connected three-phase generator:
   (a) line voltage is greater than phase voltage.
   (b) phase current is equal to line current.
   (c) phase voltage is equal to line voltage.
   (d) line voltage is less than phase voltage.

   Ref 8.4.

9

AC Motors and Conversion Equipment

9.1 AC Motors

Because of its advantages, many types of aircraft motor are designed to operate on alternating current. In general, AC motors are less expensive than comparable DC motors. In many instances, AC motors do not use brushes and commutators and, therefore, sparking at the brushes is avoided. They are very reliable and very little maintenance is needed. Also, they are well suited for constant-speed applications and certain types are manufactured that have, within limits, variable-speed characteristics. Alternating-current motors are designed to operate on poly-phase or single-phase lines and at several voltage ratings.

The subject of AC motors is very extensive, and no attempt has been made to cover the entire field. Only the types of AC motors most common to aircraft systems are discussed in detail.

The speed of rotation of an AC motor depends upon the number of poles and the frequency of the electrical source of power:

$$\text{rpm} = \frac{120 \times \text{Frequency}}{\text{Number of Poles}}$$

Since aircraft electrical systems typically operate at 400 cycles, an electric motor at this frequency operates at about seven times the speed of a 60-cycle commercial motor with the same number of poles. Because of this high speed of rotation, 400-cycle AC motors are suitable for operating small high-speed rotors, through reduction gears, in lifting and moving heavy loads, such as the wing flaps, the retractable landing gear, and the starting of engines. The 400-cycle induction type motor operates at speeds ranging from 6000 rpm to 24,000 rpm.

Alternating-current motors are rated in horsepower output, operating voltage, full load current, speed, number of phases, and frequency. Whether the motors operate continuously or intermittently (for short intervals) is also considered in the rating.

9.2 Types of AC Motors

There are two general types of AC motor used in aircraft systems: induction motors and synchronous motors. Either type may be single-phase, two-phase or three-phase.

Three-phase induction motors are used where large amounts of power are required. They operate such devices as starters, flaps, landing gears, and hydraulic pumps.

Single-phase induction motors are used to operate devices such as surface locks, intercooler shutters, and oil shutoff valves in which the power requirement is low.

Three-phase synchronous motors operate at constant synchronous speeds and are commonly used to operate flux gate compasses and propeller synchroniser systems.

Single-phase synchronous motors are common sources of power to operate electric clocks and other small precision equipment. They require some auxiliary method to bring them up to synchronous speeds; that is to start them. Usually the starting winding consists of an auxiliary stator winding.

9.3 Three-Phase Induction Motor

The three-phase AC induction motor is also called a squirrel-cage motor. Both single-phase and three-phase motors operate on the principle of a rotating magnetic field. A horseshoe magnet held over a compass needle is a simple illustration of the principle of the rotating field. The needle will take a position parallel to the magnetic flux passing between the two poles of the magnet. If the magnet is rotated, the compass needle will follow. A rotating magnetic field can be produced by a two- or three-phase current flowing through two or more groups of coils wound on inwardly projecting poles of an iron frame. The coils on each group of poles are wound alternately in opposite directions to produce opposite polarity, and each group is connected to a separate phase of voltage. The operating principle depends on a revolving, or rotating, magnetic field to produce torque. The key to understanding the induction motor is a thorough understanding of the rotating magnetic field.

9.4 Rotating Magnetic Field

The field structure shown at A in Fig 9-1 has poles whose windings are energised by three AC voltages, a, b and c. These voltages have equal magnitude but differ in phase, as shown at B of Fig 9-1.

At the instant of time shown as 0 in B of Fig 9-1 the resultant magnetic field produced by the application of the three voltages has its greatest intensity in a direction extending from pole 1 to pole 4. Under this condition, pole 1 can be considered as a north pole and pole 4 as a south pole.

At the instant of time shown as 1, the resultant magnetic field will have its greatest intensity in the direction extending from pole 2 to pole 5; in this case, pole 2 can be considered as a north pole and pole 5 as a south pole. Thus, between instant 0 and instant 1, the magnetic field has rotated clockwise.

At instant 2, the resultant magnetic field has its greatest intensity in the direction from pole 3 to pole 6, and the resultant magnetic field has continued to rotate clockwise.

At instant 3, poles 4 and 1 can be considered as north and south poles, respectively, and the field has rotated still further.

At later instants of time, the resultant magnetic field rotates to other

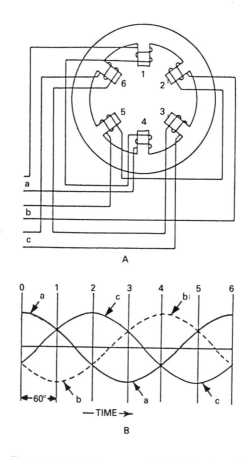

Figure 9-1 Rotating magnetic field developed by
application of three-phase voltages.

positions while travelling in a clockwise direction, a single revolution of the field occurring in one cycle. If the exciting voltages have a frequency of 60 cps, the magnetic field makes 60 revolutions per second, or 3600 rpm. This speed is known as the synchronous speed of the rotating field.

9.5 Rotary Converting Equipment

The most commonly used item to be included under this heading is the machine which converts DC into AC and is variously called a 'rotary converter', 'motor-generator' or an 'inverter'. All three terms can, understandably, cause some confusion regarding their definition, with the result that they tend to be loosely applied to machines which, although performing the same function, have quite different constructional and electrical circuit features. It is not the intention here to justify terminology and applications but the following details may serve to clarify the position.

Rotary Converter
This is, by definition, a 'synchronous machine with a single armature winding having a commutator and slip rings for converting AC into DC or vice versa'. These machines are not used in aircraft and where the term 'rotary converter' is applied, reference to an inverter is more often than not intended.

Motor-generators
These are a 'combination of one or more generators directly coupled to one or more generators directly coupled to one or more motors'. Thus a unit essentially comprises two electrically separate machines mechanically coupled. A DC to AC type of unit is employed in one or two types of aircraft for the supply of secondary AC power, and in such an application is sometimes referred to as a motor alternator and also as an 'inverter'.

Inverter
This term is generally accepted as referring to a DC to AC type of rotary converter having separate DC armature and AC rotor windings, located in the same slots and sharing the same field system. The AC output is derived from the rotor via slip rings.

An inverter is used in some aircraft systems to convert a portion of the aircraft's DC power to AC. This AC is used mainly for instruments, radio, radar, lighting and other accessories. These inverters are usually built to supply current at a frequency of 400 cps, but some are designed to provide more than one voltage: for example, 26-volt AC in one winding and 115 volts in another.

There are two basic types of inverters: the rotary and the static. Either type can be single-phase or multiphase. The multiphase inverter is lighter for the same power rating than the single-phase, but there are complications in distributing multiphase power and in keeping the loads balanced.

9.6 Rotary Inverters

There are many sizes, types and configurations of rotary inverters. Such inverters are essentially AC generators and DC motors in one housing. The generator field, or armature, and the motor field, or armature, are mounted on a common shaft which will rotate within the housing. One common type of rotary inverter is the permanent magnet inverter.

9.7 Static Conversion Equipment

Transformers
A transformer is a device for converting AC at one frequency and voltage to AC at the same frequency but at another voltage. It consists of three main parts: (i) an iron core which provides a circuit of low reluctance for an alternating magnetic field created by, (ii) a primary winding which is connected to the main power source and (iii) a secondary winding which receives electrical energy by mutual induction from the primary winding and delivers it to the secondary circuit. There are two classes of transformers: voltage or power transformers and current transformers.

Principle
The three main parts are shown schematically in Fig 9-2. When an alternating voltage is applied to the primary winding an alternating current will flow and by self-induction will establish a voltage in the primary winding which is opposite and almost equal to the applied voltage. The difference between these two voltages will allow just enough current (excitation current) to flow in the primary winding to set up an alternating magnetic flux in the core. The flux cuts across the secondary winding and by mutual induction (in practice both windings are wound one on the other) a voltage is established in the secondary winding.

When a load is connected to the secondary winding terminals, the secondary voltage causes current to flow through the winding and a magnetic flux is produced which tends to neutralise the magnetic flux produced by the primary current. This, in turn, reduces the self-induced, or opposition, voltage in the primary winding, and allows more current to flow in it to restore the core flux to a value which is only very slightly less than the no-load value.

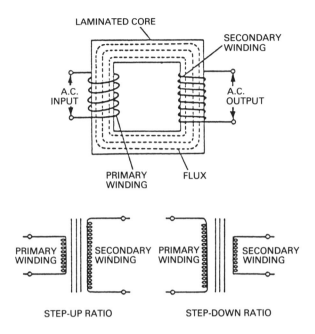

Figure 9–2 Transformer Principle.

The primary current increases as the secondary load current increases, and decreases as the secondary load current decreases. When the load is disconnected, the primary winding current is again reduced to the small excitation current sufficient only to magnetise the core.

To accomplish the function of changing voltage from one value to another, one winding is wound with more turns than the other. For example, if the primary winding has 200 turns and the secondary 1000 turns, the voltage available at the secondary terminals will be $\frac{1000}{200}$, or 5 times as great as the voltage applied to the primary winding. This ratio of turns (N_2) in the secondary to the number of turns (N_1) in the primary is called the turns or transformation ratio (r) and it is expressed by the equation:

$$r = \frac{N_2}{N_1} = \frac{E_2}{E_1}$$

where E_1 and E_2 are the respective voltages of the two windings.

When the transformation ratio is such that the transformer delivers a higher secondary voltage than the primary voltage it is said to be of the 'step-up' type. Conversely, a 'step-down' transformer is one which lowers the secondary voltage. The circuit arrangements for both types are also shown in Fig 9-2.

9.8 Auto-Transformers

In circuit applications normally requiring only a small step-up or step-down of voltage, a special variant of transformer design is employed and this is known as an auto-transformer. Its circuit arrangement is shown in Fig 3 and from this it will be noted that its most notable feature is that it consists of a single winding tapped to form primary and secondary parts. In the example illustrated the tappings provide a stepped-up voltage output, since the number of primary turns is less than that of the secondary turns.

When a voltage is applied to the primary terminals current will flow through the portion of the winding spanned by these terminals. The magnetic flux due to this current will flow through the core and will, therefore, link with the whole of the winding. Those turns between the primary terminals act in the same way as the primary winding of a conventional transformer, and so they produce a self-induction voltage in opposition to the applied voltage. The voltage induced in the remaining turns of the winding will be additive, thereby giving a secondary output voltage greater than the applied voltage. When a load circuit is connected to the secondary terminals, a current due to the induced voltage will flow through the whole winding and will be in opposition to the primary current from the input terminals. Since the turns between the primary terminals are common to input and output circuits alike they carry the difference between the induced current and primary current, and they may therefore be wound with smaller gauge wire than the remainder of the winding. Auto-transformers may also be designed for use in consumer circuits requiring three-phase voltage at varying levels.

9.9 Transformer-Rectifier Units

Transformer-rectifier units (TRUs) are combinations of static transformers and rectifiers, and are employed in some AC systems as secondary supply units; and also as the main conversion units in aircraft having rectified AC power systems.

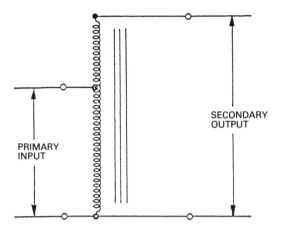

Figure 9–3 Circuit arrangements of an
auto-transformer.

9.10 Static Inverters

In many applications where continuous DC voltage must be converted to alternating voltage, static inverters are used in place of rotary inverters or motor generator sets. The rapid progress being made by the semiconductor industry is extending the range of applications of such equipment into voltage and power ranges which would have been impractical a few years ago. Some such applications are power supplies for frequency-sensitive military and commercial AC equipment, aircraft emergency AC systems, and conversion of wide frequency range power to precise frequency power.

The use of static inverters in small aircraft also has increased rapidly in the last few years, and the technology has advanced to the point that static inverters are available for any requirement filled by rotary inverters. For example, 250 VA emergency AC supplies operated from aircraft batteries are in production, as are 2500 VA main AC supplies operated from a varying frequency generator supply. This type of equipment has certain advantages for aircraft applications, particularly the absence of moving parts and the adaptability to conduction cooling.

Static inverters, referred to as solid-state inverters, are manufactured in a wide range of types and models, which can be classified by the shape of the AC output waveform and the power output capabilities.

Since static inverters use solid-state components, they are considerably smaller, more compact and much lighter in weight than rotary inverters. Depending on the output power rating required, static inverters that are no larger than a typical airspeed indicator can be used in aircraft systems. Some of the features of static inverters are:

1   High efficiency.

2   Low maintenance, long life.

3   No warm up period required.

4   Capable of starting under load.

5   Extremely quiet operation.

6   Fast response to load changes.

Static inverters are commonly used to provide power for such frequency-sensitive instruments as the attitude gyro and directional gyro. They also provide power for autosyn and magnesyn indicators and transmitters, rate gyros, radar and other airborne applications.

9.11 Magnetic Amplifiers

The magnetic amplifier is a control device which is being increasingly employed in many aircraft electrical and electronic systems. This is because of its ruggedness, stability, and safety in comparison to vacuum tubes.

The principles on which the magnetic amplifier operates can best be explained by reviewing the operation of a simple transformer. If an AC voltage is applied to the primary of an iron core transformer, the iron core will be magnetised and demagnetised at the same frequency as that of the applied voltage. This, in turn, will induce a voltage in the transformer secondary. The output voltage across the terminals of the secondary will depend on the relationship of the number of turns in the primary and the secondary of the transformer.

The iron core of the transformer has a saturation point after which the application of a greater magnetic force will produce no change in the intensity of magnetisation. Hence, there will be no change in transformer output, even if the input is greatly increased.

The magnetic amplifier circuit in Fig 9-4 will be used to explain how a simple magnetic amplifier functions. Assume that there is 1 ampere of current in coil A, which has 10 turns of wire. If coil B has 10 turns of wire, an output of 1 ampere will be obtained if coil B is properly loaded. By applying direct current to coil C, the core of the magnetic amplifier coil can be further magnetised. Assume that coil C has the proper number of turns and, upon the application of 30 milliamperes, that the core is magnetised to the point where 1 ampere on coil A results in only 0.24 amperes output from coil B.

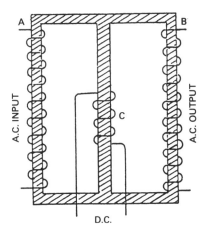

Figure 9-4 Magnetic amplifier circuit.

By making the DC input to coil C continuously variable from 0 to 30 milliamperes and maintaining an input of 1 ampere on coil A, it is possible to control the output of coil B to any point between 0.24 amperes and 1 ampere in this example. The term 'amplifier' is used for this arrangement because, by use of a few milliamperes, control of an output of 1 or more amperes is obtained.

The same procedure can be used with the circuit shown in Fig 9-5.

By controlling the extent of magnetisation of the iron ring, it is possible to control the amount of current flowing to the load, since the amount of magnetisation controls the impedance of the AC input winding. This type of magnetic amplifier is called a simple saturable reactor circuit.

Adding a rectifier to such a circuit would remove half the cycle of the AC input and permit a direct current to flow to the load. The amount of DC flowing in the load circuit is controlled by a DC control winding (sometimes referred to as bias). This type of magnetic amplifier is referred to as being self-saturating.

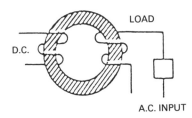

Figure 9–5 Saturable reactor circuit.

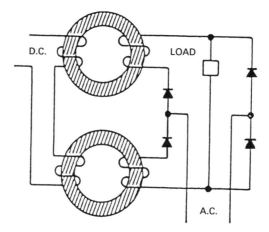

Figure 9–6 Self-saturating, full-wave magnetic amplifier.

In order to use the full AC input power, a circuit such as that shown in Fig 9-6 may be used. This circuit uses a full-wave bridge rectifier. The load will receive a controlled direct current by using the full AC input. This type of circuit is known as a self-saturating, full-wave magnetic amplifier.

Key Points to Remember

Generators and Motors

1. In a DC generator the current flowing in a conductor on the armature is AC.

2. ELECTRO-MAGNETIC INDUCTION means obtaining an electric current by rotating a loop of wire in a magnetic field.

3. In a DC generator the current in the armature is controlled by an equalising current which, in conjunction with the voltage regulator, varies the field excitation current.

4. A COMPOUND-WOUND GENERATOR is one in which the voltage remains constant with increase in load.

5. A Compound-wound generator has its field winding connected in parallel, with a few turns in series.

6. A shunt-wound generator has its field windings in parallel with the main circuit.

7. The output of a Shunt-wound generator will fall gradually as load is applied.

8. The armature of a DC generator receives its initial excitation from permanent magnetism.

9. The generator voltage is regulated in the field coil.

10. Two DC generators in parallel have constant voltage.

11. Two generators in line are controlled by Voltage Regulators.

12. When the generator field is supplied through the Battery master switch and the switch is selected OFF while the engine is running, the generator will be de-excited and cease producing power.

13. When the nominal voltage of the aircraft electrical system is quoted as 24 volts, the generator is usually regulated to 28 volts.

14. A twin-engined aircraft with a generator on each engine has them connected in parallel with independent voltage control.

15. In a generator circuit, the circulating current is the current flowing between two unbalanced generators.

16. If, during cruise flight, one of the generators fails, the pilot should switch off unnecessary electrical loads (load shedding).

17. Generator failure is indicated by a decrease or discharge in ammeter reading and generator warning light ON.

18. On a multi-engined aircraft with a generator on each engine, there will usually be one ammeter per generator.

19. On an aircraft provided with an ammeter which is not of the centre reading type, this instrument will indicate current passing from the generator to the aircraft loads and batteries.

20.
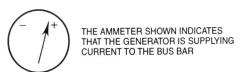
THE AMMETER SHOWN INDICATES THAT THE GENERATOR IS SUPPLYING CURRENT TO THE BUS BAR

21. A 'press to test' warning light in the generator circuit is used by the pilot to test the warning light filament.

22. A device for changing AC to DC current is a RECTIFIER.

23. A device for changing DC to AC current is an INVERTER at 400 Hz.

24. The back emf of a DC motor will increase with increase in speed.

25. Permanent magnet motors can be of the split field series-wound type, and are used in linear actuators. The travel of an actuator can be limited by interrupting the power supply to the motor by the use of limit switches, the contacts of which are closed whilst the motor is travelling and open when the limit of travel is reached.

Batteries

1. A lead-acid battery contains sulphuric acid and distilled water.

2. The number of cells in a 12 Volt battery is six.

3. The specific gravity of the electrolyte of a lead-acid battery will give the state of charge of the battery.

4. To check the state of charge of a lead-acid battery, the terminal voltage of the battery ON LOAD is ascertained.

5. If two 12 volt batteries are connected in parallel, the voltage will be 12 volts.

6. Two 12V 40 Ampere hour batteries connected in parallel will produce 12V 80 Ampere hours.

7. If an aircraft has three batteries, each 12 volts with a 40 Amp/hour capacity, when connected in series they will give a voltage of 36 volts and a capacity of 40 Amp/hours.

8. A battery, which is assumed to be 100% efficient, having a capacity of 40 amp/hours, at the 10 hour rate will deliver 4 amps for 10 hours.

9. If a battery is gassing excessively on charging, this is due to over-charging, causing overheating and buckling of the battery plates.

10. Spillage from a lead-acid battery may be neutralised by washing with a dilute solution of sodium bicarbonate.

11. As an installed battery becomes fully charged by the aircraft generator, the battery voltage nears its nominal level and the charging current decreases.

12. In an AC circuit a battery cannot be used, because it needs a DC current for charging.

13. On an aircraft fitted with a Ni-Cad (Alkaline) battery, if the Ammeter indicates a high state of charge after initial start-up, it is quite normal and no cause for alarm.

14. If an aircraft is fitted with a Ni-Cad battery showing a high temperature after engine start, it could be an indication of thermal runaway.

Voltage Regulators and Cut-outs

1. In a DC generating system, the voltage regulator controls the system voltage within prescribed limits, regardless of varying rpm and electrical load, by inserting a variable resistance in the generator field winding.

2. A generator/battery cut-out is fitted to prevent the battery feeding back into the generator when its voltage exceeds the generator voltage.

3. A generator is brought ON-LINE via the battery cut-out by an increase in the generator voltage.

4. Generator cut-out contacts are kept open by spring tension.

5. The generator cut-out switch contacts will close when circuit loads are equal to generator output.

6. To prevent a battery from discharging back through a non-current producing generator, a reverse current cut-out switch is included in the circuit.

Circuits, Bonding and Screening

1. An electrical system known as an EARTH RETURN circuit is one where the negative returns from electrical components are connected to the aircraft structure.

2. Bonding is used to protect the aircraft against fire due to arcing of static electricity, by ensuring the same electrical potential of all metal components in the aircraft structure.

3. Static wick dischargers are fitted to dissipate the static electricity from the aircraft to atmosphere and minimise radio interference.

4. During refuelling, the aircraft MUST be bonded to earth and the refuelling nozzle MUST be bonded to the fuel tank.

5. To prevent electrical components from interfering with radio receivers, they must be screened with suitable insulating material.

Section 9   Test Yourself Questions

AC Motors and Conversion Equipment

1. A three-phase induction motor is sometimes called a:
    (a)   squirrel cage motor.
    (b)   stepa motor.
    (c)   synchronous motor.
    (d)   beta motor.

Ref 9.3.

2. An inverter is used:
    (a)   to convert AC to DC.
    (b)   to increase or decrease the speed of an electric motor.
    (c)   to convert DC to AC.
    (d)   to step up or step down the voltage of an AC generator.

Ref 9.5.

3. A TRU may be used:
    (a)   in an AC circuit to step down, or up, voltage and rectify the current.
    (b)   in a DC circuit to step up, or step down voltage and rectify the current.
    (c)   in a DC circuit to convert DC to AC.
    (d)   in an AC circuit to produce constant frequency current.

Ref 9.9.

4. Static inverters may be used to supply:
    (a)   frequency-wild AC from aircraft batteries.
    (b)   constant frequency DC from aircraft batteries.
    (c)   constant frequency AC from aircraft batteries.
    (d)   frequency-wild DC from aircraft batteries.

Ref 9.10.

5. Three-phase induction motors are used:
    (a)   to provide small amounts of power to operate clocks etc.
    (b)   to operate devices requiring large amounts of power.
    (c)   only as inverters.
    (d)   as a form of auto transformer.

Ref 9.3.

10

General Information

10.1 General

To prevent problems which arise from brush wear, constant frequency AC (CFAC) generating systems are fitted with rotating rectifier brushless machines. The generator may be self-excited under the influence of a rotating magnet pilot exciter or externally excited from the aircraft DC bus bar on initial start-up, after which excitation is through monitored generator output.

Generator output is controlled 3 phase 200/115 volt 400 Hz and rated in Kilo-volt Amperes (KVA).

Generator cooling can be by Ram Air, Bleed Air or Oil. Ram air in use after take-off with augmentation of bleed air during flight at low speeds. Bleed air cooling in use on ground. Oil cooling by pressure or spray. Generator temperatures are monitored on main electrical panel. Power output of the generator is indicated by an ammeter.

10.2 Voltage Regulator

The voltage regulator maintains the output voltage of the generator constant irrespective of the load current. This is achieved by continual adjustments to the generator field current.

Two basic types of regulator in use: Variable impedance in the form of a magnetic amplifier used to control the current input to the main generator exciter, pulse control regulation using thyristor or transistors to control the current into the main exciter. A voltmeter on the electrical panel indicates the generator voltage output.

10.3 Frequency Controller

The frequency controller provides small adjustment signals to the CSDU governor so that the generator output frequency is maintained at 400 Hz. Utilises magnetic amplifier or transistored frequency discriminator circuits, to supply signals to the CSDU governor.

10.4 Fault Protection Unit

In order to achieve the necessary degree of safety required, a CFAC generating system must include certain protection circuits to continually monitor system performance. Within the protection unit are transistor logic circuits and controls for the opening or closing of the Generator Control Relay (GCR) and the Generator Control Breaker (GCB) depending on the integrity of the circuit.

In a single channel system protection is provided for:
Over voltage
Under voltage
Generator overspeed
Generator underspeed
Generator temperature
Line to line bus-bar faults
Line to earth bus-bar faults.

10.5 Generator Control Relay (GCR switches)

When the generator control relay is closed, the generator field excitation circuit from the voltage regulator is completed. When tripped (open) the generator is de-excited and the generator circuit breaker (GCB) will also trip (open). A signal from the fault protection unit will trip the GCR.

10.6 Generator Circuit Breaker (G.C.B.)

Closing a generator circuit breaker connects the generator output to the generator bus-bar. Under paralleled conditions the GCB will not close unless voltage, frequency and phase sequence are correct. Closing of the GCB is usually indicated on the control panel by a magnetic in-line indicator or lights. The closure of the GCB bringing a generator 'on line' will automatically disconnect any external power supplies connected.

10.7 Generator Failure Warning Light

A generator failure warning light which comes 'on' when the associated generator circuit breaker (GCB) is tripped; the centralised warning system (CWS) light will show and audio systems will operate.

10.8 System Components (Multi-channel)

When more than one source of Constant Frequency Alternating Current is used and the systems are operated in parallel, then other requirements become necessary.

10.9 Bus Tie Breakers (BTB)

A bus tie breaker connects a generator to its synchronising bus-bar. Control of a BTB is automatic and in its normal position it is closed, but trips open under fault conditions. Visual indications by means of magnetic line indicators on the control panel, centralised warning systems and audio. If a fault on the generator system causes the GCB to trip the BTB will reset.

10.10 Reactive Load Sharing Control

This is necessary to ensure that once systems are paralleled the reactive load KVAR on the bus-bars is shared equally between systems. Reactive load sharing is carried out by the voltage regulator.

10.11 Active Load Sharing

This is necessary to ensure that once systems are paralleled the real load kW on the bus-bars is shared equally between systems. Active load sharing is carried out by the frequency controller.

Reactive and active load sharing circuits are not made until the generator control breakers and the generator bus tie breakers are closed, ie systems are paralleled.

10.12 Protection Devices

When the systems are paralleled, discrimination circuits are required to ensure that only the faulty system is disconnected from the bus-bar in event of a generator failure.

Interconnections are made between the individual protective units when the generator control breakers and the bus tie breakers are made, ie systems are paralleled.

10.13 Synchronising Unit

Before two generating systems are paralleled the generators must be 'In Phase'. The synchronising unit ensures that the bus tie breaker cannot be closed until the generators are 'In Phase'. Two methods in use:

(a) **Manual (Lamp Dark Method)**
A synchronising lamp on the panel will be out or 'dark' when synchronism is achieved. Operation of the Sync push switch, closes the bus tie breaker.

(b) Automatic Control

The circuit is so designed that the Sync push switch can be pressed but the bus tie breaker will not close until the systems are 'In Phase'.

10.14 Meters kW/KVAR

The kW/KVAR meters are employed in parallel generating systems to indicate the kW (Real Power) or KVAR (Reactive Power) output of the machine. Normally the meters will indicate kW output until a selector switch is pressed when they will indicate KVAR.

(a) kW. Real Load

The real load borne by a generator is the power that is consumed doing useful work, ie wattful current.

(b) KVAR Reactive Load

The reactive load borne by a generator is the power which is used to produce electro-magnetic fields. As in each half cycle electric power is converted into electro-magnetic fields and back again to electric power, no useful work is accomplished. This is the wattless current component of the load.

10.15 Voltmeters and Frequency Meters

One voltmeter and one frequency meter only is provided for a CFAC system. Selection of a particular generating system by means of a multi position rotary switch enables the voltage and frequency for the selected generator to be observed.

10.16 Emergency Supplies

Unlike the DC system, batteries cannot be used as emergency AC power. Therefore other means have to be supplied. These take the form of small AC generator system separate from the primary generation systems driven from either a Ram Air Turbine (RAT) or an Auxiliary Power Unit (APU), or Static Inverters.

10.17 Ram Air Turbine (RAT)

A 200/115 volt 3-phase ram air driven turbo/generator controlled at a nominal 400 Hz, lowered into the slipstream to ensure that there is an emergency source of AC power for the limited operation of flight and radio services in the event of a total main generator failure.

Once lowered into the slipstream retraction can only be carried out on the ground.

10.18 Auxiliary Power Unit (APU)

A constant speed gas turbine engine, usually mounted in the fuselage tail cone, driving a 200/115 volt 3-phase generator which can be used for ground servicing supplies or emergency supplies in the air. In some aircraft the APU is on during take off and landing.

10.19 Static Inverter

A transistorised (solid state) device which will provide 115 volts 400 Hz AC power for the limited operation of flight and radio services in the event of total electrical power generation failure. It is powered with DC from the aircraft battery which, if fully charged, should supply power for approximately 30 minutes.

10.20 Ground Power CFAC Systems

The standard ground power unit requirement is for a 3-phase 200/115 volt 400 Hz AC supply. This supply can be plugged into the aircraft to maintain all electrical services.

A constant frequency aircraft power supply embodies automatic protection circuits which ensure that:

Ground power cannot be connected to the aircraft distribution system if the system is already being supplied from its own generating system.

Ground power cannot be connected if the phase sequence of the supply is incorrect.

Ground power is rejected and switched off at source if over voltage occurs.

10.21 Conclusion

Because of the problems of parallel operation and the higher voltages involved CFAC generating systems are more complex than DC systems. Therefore CFAC systems are only used on aircraft where the AC power requirements are much greater than the DC requirements, and hence a DC system would be uneconomical to use. CFAC multi channel systems are often operated as independent non-paralleled systems to reduce system complexity and to increase system safety.

ELECTRICAL AND MAGNETIC QUANTITIES, DEFINITIONS AND UNITS

Quantity	Definition	Name of Unit	Unit symbol	Unit definition
Electric potential	That measured by the energy of a unit positive charge at a point, expressed relative to zero potential, or earth.			Difference of electric potential between two points of a conductor carrying constant current of 1 ampere, when the power dissipated between these points is equal to 1 watt.
Potential difference (pd)	That between two points when maintained by an emf, or by a current flowing through a resistance.	Volt	V	
Electromotive force (emf)	Difference of potential produced by sources of electrical energy which can be used to drive currents through external circuits.			
Current	The rate of flow of electric charge at a point in a circuit.	Ampere Milliampere $(A \times 10^{-3})$ Microampere $(A \times 10^{-6})$	A mA μA	The ampere is that constant current which, if maintained in two straight parallel conductors of infinite length, of negligible cross section, and placed 1 metre apart in vacuum, would produce between the conductors a force equal to $2 \times 10\text{-}7$ newton per metre of length.

Quantity	Description	Unit	Symbol	Definition
Resistance	The tendency of a conductor to oppose the flow of current and to convert electrical energy into heat. Its magnitude depends on such factors as: nature of conductor material, its physical state, dimensions, temperature and thermal properties; frequency of current and its magnitude.	Ohm, Megohm ($\Omega \times 10^6$)	Ω, MΩ	The ohm is the electrical resistance between two points of a conductor when a constant pd of 1 volt, applied to these points, produces in the conductor a current of 1 ampere, the conductor not being the seat of any emf.
Power	The rate of doing work or transforming energy.	Watt, Kilowatt (W $\times 10^3$)	W, kW	Is the power which in 1 second gives rise to energy of 1 joule.
Frequency	The number of cycles in unit time.	Hertz	Hz	The definition of frequency also applies with the unit of time being taken as 1 second.
Inductance	The property of an element or circuit which, when carrying a current, is characterized by the formation of a magnetic field and the storage of magnetic energy.	Henry	H	The inductance of a closed circuit in which an emf of 1 volt is produced when the current in the circuit varies at the rate of 1 ampere per second.
Capacitance	The property of a system of conductors and insulators (a system known as a capacitor) which allows the storage of an electric charge when a pd exists between the conductors. In a capacitor, the conductors are known as electrodes or plates, and the insulator, which may be solid, liquid or gaseous is known as the dielectric.	Farad, Microfarad (F $\times 10^{-6}$), Picofarad (F $\times 10^{-12}$)	F, μF, pF	The capacitance of a capacitor between the plates of which there appears a pd of 1 volt when it is charged by a quantity of electricity of 1 coulomb.

ELECTRICAL AND MAGNETIC QUANTITIES, DEFINITIONS AND UNITS (CONTINUED)

Quantity	Definition	Name of Unit	Unit symbol	Unit definition
Electric charge	The quantity of electricity on an electrically charged body, or passing at a point in an electric circuit during a given time.	Coulomb	C	The quantity of electricity carried in 1 second by a current of 1 ampere.
Energy	The capacity for doing work.	Joule	J	The work done when the point of application of a force of 1 newton is displaced through a distance of 1 metre in the direction of the force.
Impedance	The extent to which the flow of alternating current at a given frequency is restricted, and represented by the ratio of rms values of voltage and current. Combines resistance, capacitive and inductive reactance.	Ohm	Z	
Reactance	That part of the impedance which is due to inductance or capacitance, or both, and which stores energy rather than dissipates it.	Ohm	X	

Term	Definition	Unit	Symbol	Notes
Magnetic flux	A phenomenon produced in the medium surrounding electric currents or magnets. The amount of flux through any area is measured by the quantity of electricity caused by flow in a circuit of given resistance bounding the area when this circuit is removed from the magnetic field.	Weber (Volt-second)	Wb	The magnetic flux which, linking a circuit of 1 turn, would produce in it an emf of 1 volt if it were reduced to zero at a uniform rate in 1 second.
Magnetic flux density (Magnetic induction)	The amount of magnetic flux per square centimetre, over a small area at a point in a magnetic field. The direction of the magnetic flux is at right angles to the area.	Tesla	T	Equal to 1 weber per square metre of circuit area.
Magnetic field strength (Magnetizing force	The strength or force which produces or is associated with magnetic flux density. It is equal to the magnetomotive force per centimetre measured along the line of force.	Ampere per metre	A/m	
Magnetomotive force (mmf)	The magnetic analogue of emf. It represents the summated current or equivalent current, including any displacement current, which threads a closed line in a magnetic field and produces a magnetic flux along it. Can also be stated as the work done in moving a unit magnetic pole around a closed magnetic circuit.	Ampere-turns / Gilbert		The product of current and the number of turns of a coil.

ELECTRICAL AND MAGNETIC QUANTITIES, DEFINITIONS AND UNITS (CONTINUED)

Quantity	Definition	Name of Unit	Unit symbol	Unit definition
Reluctance	The ratio of magnetic force to magnetic flux. May be considered as the opposition to the flux established by the force. It is the reciprocal of permeance.	Ampere-turn/Weber/ Gilbert/Maxwell		
Permeability (μ)	The ratio of the magnetic flux density in a medium to the magnetizing force producing it.			
Permeance	The capability of a magnetic circuit to produce a magnetic flux under the influence of an mmf, and which is represented as the quotient of a given magnetic flux in the magnetic circuit and the mmf required to produce it.			

Ohm's Law
This law is fundamental to all direct current circuits, and can in a modified form also be applied to alternating current circuits.

The law may be stated as follows: *When current flows in a conductor, the difference in potential between the ends of the conductor, divided by the current flowing, is a constant provided there is no change in the physical condition of the conductor.*

The constant is called the resistance (R) of the conductor, and is measured in ohms (Ω). In symbols,

$$R = \frac{V}{I} \tag{1}$$

where,

V = potential difference in volts
I = current in amperes.

Calculations involving most conductors, either singly or in a variety of combinations, are easily solved by this law, for if any two of the three quantities (V, I and R) are known, the third can always be found by simple transposition. Thus, from (1)

$$V = IR \text{ volts} \tag{2}$$

$$I = \frac{V}{R} \text{ amperes} \tag{3}$$

Since some of the values used to determine the power delivered to a circuit are the same as those used on Ohm's law, it is possible to substitute Ohm's law values for equivalents in the fundamental formula for power (P) which is:

$$P = V \times I \text{ watts}$$

Thus, if $\frac{V}{R}$ is substituted for I in the power formula,
it becomes:

$$P = V \times \frac{V}{R} \text{ or } P = \frac{V^2}{R}$$

Similarly, if IR is substituted for V in the power formula, then

P = I x I x R or P = I²R

By transposing the formula P = I²R to solve for the current I, we obtain

$$I^2 = \frac{P}{R}$$

from which

$$I = \sqrt{\frac{P}{R}}$$

Other transpositions of the foregoing formulae are as follows:

$$I = \frac{P}{V} \qquad\qquad V = \sqrt{PR}$$

$$R = \frac{P}{I^2}$$

$$V = \frac{P}{I}$$

POWER IN AC CIRCUITS
Real (or average) Power

The power dissipated is P = VI cos θ where

       V = rms voltage across circuit

       I = rms current flowing in circuit

       θ = phase angle between V and I

cos θ = the power factor (PF) of the circuit

(i) For inductors, capacitors, or circuits containing only inductors and capacitors, PF = O, ie no power is dissipated.

(ii) For resistors and resistive circuits, PF = 1 ie power is dissipated.

(iii) For circuits containing resistance and reactance, phase angle θ varies between 0° and 90°.

Real power dissipated in an AC circuit is also equal to

I^2R and $\dfrac{V^2}{R}$ where

 I = rms current flowing in R
 V = rms voltage across R.

Reactive Power

Reactive power P_q = VI sin θ where V, I and θ are the same as for real power.

Also $P_q = I^2X$ and $\dfrac{V^2}{X}$ where

 I = rms current in the reactance
 V = rms voltage across reactance
 X = net reactance.

Pq is measured in volt-amperes reactive (VA1)

Apparent Power

Apparent Power P_a = VI where V and I are the same as for real power.
P_a is measured in volt-amperes (VA)

CAPACITORS

In series
Capacitors in series may be considered as increasing the separation of the outer plates of the combination. Thus, the total capacitance C_T is less than the smallest capacitance of the individual capacitors, and so the relationship for C_T is similar to that for resistors in parallel, ie:

$$\frac{1}{C_T} = \frac{1}{C_1} + \frac{1}{C_2} + \frac{1}{C_3} + \cdots \text{ or } CT = \frac{1}{\dfrac{1}{C_2} + \dfrac{1}{C_2} + \dfrac{1}{C_3} + \cdots}$$

When only two capacitors are in series, then

$$CT = \frac{C_1 \times C_2}{C_1 + C_2}$$

If the capacitors are of equal value C, then
$$CT = \frac{C}{n}$$
where n = the number of capacitors in series.

The total working voltage rating of capacitors in series is equal to the sum of the ratings of the capacitors.

The total charge is $Q_T = Q_1 = Q_2 = Q_3 \ldots$

In Parallel

Capacitors in parallel may be considered as effectively increasing the area of the plates; therefore, since capacitance increases with plate area, the total capacitance C_T is equal to the sum of the individual capacitances. Thus, the relationship for C_T is similar to that for resistors in parallel, ie

$CT = C1 + C2 + C3 = \ldots$

The working voltage of a parallel combination is limited by the smallest working voltage of the individual capacitors.

The total charge is $QT = Q1 + Q2 + Q3 + \ldots$

Energy stored

The energy (eC) stored in a capacitor is

$$e_C = \frac{CV2}{2} \text{ where}$$

> C = capacitance in farads
>
> V = voltage impressed across capacitor.

Inductors

Inductors in series, parallel or in combination circuits act similarly to resistors. Thus:

in series, total inductance $LT = L1 + L2 + L3 + \ldots$

in parallel, $LT = \dfrac{1}{\dfrac{1}{L_1} + \dfrac{1}{L_2} + \dfrac{1}{L_3} + \cdots}$

The energy (eL) stored in an inductor is

$$e_L = \frac{LI^2}{2} \text{ where}$$

> L = inductance in henrys
>
> I = current flow through inductor

APPLICATION OF OHM'S LAW TO SERIES AND PARALLEL CIRCUITS (RESISTANCES)

Circuit	Total Resistance	Total Voltage	Total Current
Series	$R_T = R_1 + R_2 + R_3 + \ldots$ ohms or $R_T = \dfrac{V_T}{I}$ ohms If the resistances are equal of value **R** then: $R_T = n\,R$ ohms	$V_T = (I_1 R_1) + (I_2 R_2) + (I_3 R_3) + \ldots$ volts or $V_T = I R_T$ volts	$I_T = I_1 = I_2 = I_3 = \ldots$ amps or $I_T = \dfrac{V_T}{R_T}$
Parallel	Where n = number of resistors $\dfrac{1}{R_T} = \dfrac{1}{R_1} + \dfrac{1}{R_2} + \dfrac{1}{R_3} + \ldots$ ohms or $R_T = \dfrac{1}{\dfrac{1}{R_1} + \dfrac{1}{R_2} + \dfrac{1}{R_3} \ldots}$ If the resistances are of equal value **R**, then: $R_T = \dfrac{R}{n}$ When only two resistances in parallel, the total resistance is: $R_T = \dfrac{R_1 \times R_2}{R_1 + R_2}$	$V_T = V_1 = V_2 = V_3 = \ldots$ volts	$I_T = I_1 + I_2 + I_3 + \ldots$ amps

167

APPLICATION OF OHM'S LAW TO SERIES AND PARALLEL CIRCUITS (RESISTANCES) (CONT'D.)

Circuit	Total Resistance	Total Voltage	Total Current
Series – parallel	R_T, V_T and I_T are found by first reducing the parallel circuit to a single resistance, and then solving the whole as a simple series circuit.		

FUNDAMENTAL A.C. CIRCUITS AND FORMULAE

Circuit	Inductive reactance (X_L) (ohms)	Impedance (Z) (ohms)	Applied voltage (V_T)	Current (I_T)
	$X_L = 2\pi fL$ Where f= frequency (Hz) L = inductance in henrys	As for Inductive Reactance (X_L)	$V_T = IX_L$	$I = \dfrac{V_T}{X_L}$
	$X_{L\ total} = X_{L_1} + X_{L_2} + \cdots$		$V_T = IX_{L_1} =+ IX_{L_2}$	$I_T = I_{L_1} = I_{L_2}$
	$X_{L\ total} = \dfrac{1}{\dfrac{1}{X_{L_1}} + \dfrac{1}{X_{L_2}} + \cdots}$		$V_T = IX_{L_1} = IX_{L_2}$	$I_T = I_{L_1} + I_{L_2}$

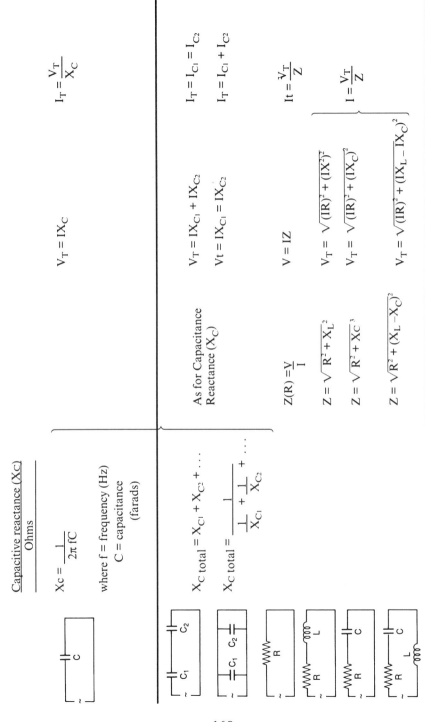

Capacitive reactance (Xc)
Ohms

$X_c = \dfrac{1}{2\pi fC}$

where f = frequency (Hz)
C = capacitance (farads)

$X_{C\ total} = X_{C_1} + X_{C_2} + \cdots$

$X_{C\ total} = \dfrac{1}{\dfrac{1}{X_{C_1}} + \dfrac{1}{X_{C_2}} + \cdots}$

$V_T = IX_C \qquad I_T = \dfrac{V_T}{X_C}$

As for Capacitance Reactance (X_C)

$V_T = IX_{C_1} + IX_{C_2} \qquad I_T = I_{C_1} = I_{C_2}$

$V_t = IX_{C_1} = IX_{C_2} \qquad I_T = I_{C_1} + I_{C_2}$

$Z(R) = \dfrac{V}{I} \qquad V = IZ \qquad It = \dfrac{V_T}{Z}$

$Z = \sqrt{R^2 + X_L^2} \qquad V_T = \sqrt{(IR)^2 + (IX)^2}$

$Z = \sqrt{R^2 + X_C^2} \qquad V_T = \sqrt{(IR)^2 + (IX_C)^2}$

$Z = \sqrt{R^2 + (X_L - X_C)^2} \qquad V_T = \sqrt{(IR)^2 + (IX_L - IX_C)^2}$

$I = \dfrac{V_T}{Z}$

169

Final Practice Paper

AC and DC Electrics

1. The electrical pressure which exists in a conductor is known as:
   (a) the current.
   (b) the resistance.
   (c) the electromotive force.
   (d) the field current.

Ref 2.3.

2. The unit of potential difference in a circuit is the:
   (a) ohm.
   (b) watt.
   (c) emf.
   (d) volt.

Ref 2.4.

3. emf is induced in a conductor:
   (a) as it cuts the lines of magnetic force.
   (b) if it is placed in a magnetic field.
   (c) if the conductor moves parallel to the lines of magnetic force.
   (d) if the conductor has current flowing in it.

Ref 3.2.

4. The magnitude of an induced emf is dependent upon:
   (a) the speed of rotation of the generator.
   (b) the strength of the magnetic field.
   (c) the strength of residual magnetism.
   (d) the number of armature laminations.

Ref 3.4.

5. In a DC generator, sometimes:
   (a) DC is converted to AC by a commutator.
   (b) DC is converted to AC by an inverter.
   (c) initial excitation is provided by current from the field circuit.
   (d) commutation supplies DC to the bus-bar.

Ref 3.6.

6. The state of charge of a battery must be checked:
   (a)   once a year.
   (b)   every seven days.
   (c)   every three months.
   (d)   every six months.

Ref 4.7.

7. The specific gravity of the electrolyte in an individual battery cell is checked with:
   (a)   a voltmeter.
   (b)   an ammeter.
   (c)   a specograph.
   (d)   a hydrometer.

Ref 4.7.

8. When the battery is connected to the bus-bar:
   (a)   the battery ammeter will indicate on the + side.
   (b)   the cut-out switch is open.
   (c)   the generator will stop.
   (d)   the generator warning light is off.

Ref 5.12.

9. An inertia switch:
   (a)   isolates the generator if it excessively overvolts.
   (b)   isolates the batteries when the aircraft crashes.
   (c)   isolates the generator drive if the aircraft crashes.
   (d)   isolates the batteries when the main isolation switch is moved to the OFF position.

Ref 5.14.

10. The failure of a hydraulic system may be indicated by the action of:
   (a)   an inertia switch.
   (b)   a microswitch.
   (c)   a flow switch.
   (d)   a pressure switch.

Ref 5.16.

11. Damage to the motor of a linear actuator, in an overload situation, is prevented by:
   (a)   the electro-magnetic brake, when the coil is energised.
   (b)   the electro-magnetic brake when the coil is de-energised.
   (c)   the limit switches, when both move to the open position.
   (d)   the clutch, which will slip.

Ref 5.28.

12. The strength of a magnetic field around a conductor:
    (a) depends on the current flowing in it.
    (b) depends upon the direction of current flow.
    (c) depends upon the current in volts and the length of the conductor.
    (d) depends upon the current in ohms and the length of the conductor.

Ref 2.10.

13. A battery rated at 12 volts consists of:
    (a) 12 cells in series.
    (b) 6 cells in parallel.
    (c) 6 cells in series.
    (d) 12 cells in parallel.

Ref 4.4.

14. The battery in a DC supply system is prevented from discharging into the generator when the battery is connected to the bus-bar:
    (a) by the battery switch when open.
    (b) by the cut-out switch when open.
    (c) by the voltage coil.
    (d) by the differential switch when it is closed.

Ref 3.24.

15. Initial excitation of a DC generator is achieved through:
    (a) the battery bus-bar.
    (b) the field windings.
    (c) residual magnetism from the field circuit.
    (d) residual magnetism from the magnetic poles.

Ref 3.24.

16. When load shedding takes place:
    (a) voltage decreases at the bus-bar.
    (b) field current increases.
    (c) current at the bus-bar decreases.
    (d) current at the bus-bar increases.

Ref 3.24.

17. In a star-connected three-phase generator:
    (a) phase voltage is less than line voltage.
    (b) line current is greater than phase current.
    (c) phase voltage is greater than line voltage.
    (d) phase voltage is equal to line voltage.

Ref 8.4.

18. Static inverters may be used to supply:
    (a) emergency constant frequency AC.
    (b) emergency constant frequency DC.
    (c) emergency frequency-wild AC.
    (d) emergency frequency-wild DC

Ref 9.10.

19. A pilot exciter is:
    (a) a small separate DC generator used to excite the main AC generator.
    (b) a small DC generator mounted on the same drive shaft as the main AC generator.
    (c) a small battery exciter.
    (d) a generator exciter operated by an impulse mechanism.

Ref 7.3.

20. In a star-connected AC generator, each load is connected:
    (a) to a single phase.
    (b) between two phases.
    (c) across all three phases.
    (d) between the phase and neutral.

Ref 8.4.

Note: When making your choice of answer, choose the most correct answer.

Part 2

1

Advanced Flying Systems

1.1 Introduction General

Modern civil transport aircraft are increasingly fitted with advanced flying control systems which are designed to allow a variety of automatic functions to be carried out in flight and during the landing sequence. Such systems incorporate the use of computers and various other types of electronic devices. Such devices also include the use of advanced instrumentation in what has become known as the 'Glass Cockpit' concept.

In order to understand the operation of such systems, included in this part are chapters explaining such items as Semi-conductors, Logic Circuits, EFIS, EICAS, ECAM, the Automatic Flight Systems, Auto-Land and a variety of items included within such systems.

Chapter One gives an overall general explanation of the basic concepts of automatic flight systems.

It is essential that this part should be read with a good understanding of the Principles of Flight and also in conjunction with the 'Electrics' section of this *The Commercial Pilots Study Manual Series*.

It must be noted that systems do vary from aircraft type to type. The systems within this section are of a general nature and are designed to assist the student in his or her studies for CPL and ATPL levels.

1.2 Automatic Flight and Landing

Introduction

For long periods of flight using manual operation of the flying controls the pilot would become very tired, both physically and mentally. To assist the pilot in this matter, the Automatic Pilot was evolved to take the stress and strain out of the flying. This enables the pilot to concentrate on the other duties associated with flying such as R/T communication, visual scan checks both of the instrumentation and the outside environment. The automatic pilot (more commonly known as the autopilot) has developed, under today's technology into the Automatic Flight and Automatic Landing Systems.

This section is designed to express the basic fundamentals of the autopilot, and its operational facilities. Its emergence into automatic landing will also be discussed, although in-depth knowledge of both should be acquired by the pilot when completing a conversion course onto a specific aircraft type.

1.3 The Autopilot

The automatic pilot discussed in this section is of a basic type from which all other autopilots are derived. A general understanding of the operation and requirements of the autopilot will enable the pilot to understand the aircraft type system more readily.

1.4 Autopilot Requirements

An autopilot is required to fulfil three main functions of aircraft control. These are for aircraft stabilisation, aircraft manoeuvring and facility coupling.

(a) Aircraft Stabilisation:
This is to maintain the aircraft in a stable condition with respect to its selected flight path regardless of fast rate or slow rate disturbances. Fast rate disturbances are associated with turbulence, whereas slow rate disturbances could be due to trim changes affected by fuel consumption.

(b) Aircraft Manoeuvring:
The autopilot must contain a control unit to allow the aircraft to be displaced in pitch or roll and so to be climbed, dived or turned by selection by the pilot.

(c) Facility Coupling:
Certain aircraft navigational facilities or ground facilities (ie ILS, autoland) must be able to be coupled into the system.

1.5 Aircraft Stabilisation

Rate Gyros are used to detect disturbances in the pitch, roll and yaw axes of the aircraft. The axes of rotation are set at 90° to each other. The rate gyros are able to detect disturbances above a certain signal threshold, below which the signal may be too small for detection. To overcome this problem, mercury switch and pendulum monitors are used to detect the finer disturbances. The complete system is designed to be proportional in operation to the initial disturbance. That is to say that a signal output is proportional to the original disturbance, and rate/rate principle is that the rate of control is proportional to the rate of disturbance.

1.6 The Basic Channel

The basic channel comprises four units which are illustrated in Fig 1-1.

(a) Rate Gyro

Comprised of a three-phase hysteresis motor where the rotor is the rotating mass. An 'E' and 'I' bar transformer produces the signal, the signal amplitude being proportional to the rate of disturbance. The 'I' bar is connected to the gimbal assembly, the 'E' bar supplies the signal pick-off, and the phasing will depend upon the direction of the disturbances.

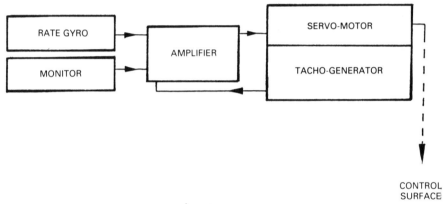

Figure 1–1 Autopilot Basic Channel Circuit.

(b) Monitors

A 'C' and 'Y' bar transformer is used for the roll signal which originates from the aircraft's compass system. A pendulous element provides the originating signal for pitch and yaw. This signal is supplied to a variable inductor which is similar in operation to the 'E' and 'I' bar transformer.

(c) Amplifier

A high gain amplifier is used to amplify and discriminate the disturbance signal, the output of which drives a channel servo-motor.

(d) Servo-motor and Tacho-generator

The control surface is driven by a servo-motor via an electro-magnetic clutch. To provide proportional feedback, a tacho-generator supplies a negative, velocity feedback signal which completes the signal loop.

1.7 Combined Channel Circuit

The combined channel circuit is designed to cover all three primary control surfaces, the rudder, aileron and elevator. Figure 1-2 illustrates the combined channel circuit showing interconnections between rudder to aileron and aileron to rudder. The interconnections of the rudder/aileron and aileron/rudder channel are termed crossfeed.

1.8 Operation in Pitch

If there is an initial disturbance which has the tendency to put the aircraft in a nose down attitude, the pitch gyro displaces the 'E' and 'I' bar causing a signal to be fed to the amplifier unit. After the signal has been amplified, the output is phased according to the direction of the initial disturbance and the resultant is applied to the elevator servo-motor. The servo-motor moves the elevator up and the rotation causes the tachogenerator to give a feedback signal back to the amplifier. This ensures that the rate of correction by the servo-motor is proportional to the initial rate of disturbance.

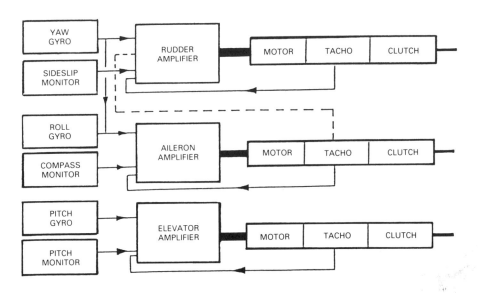

Figure 1–2 Autopilot Combined Channels Circuits.

The elevator movement causes a turning movement to correct the original disturbance. When the opposing torques are equal, the elevator movement will stop. When the original disturbance has ceased, the elevator up position causes a turning movement in the opposite direction creating a disturbance. The pitch gyro detects this change in pitch movement causing a signal to be sent to the servo-motor restoring the neutral position of the elevator. The pendulous element of the monitor detects all the final displacement and adjusts the servo-motor signal to regain level flight in the pitching plane.

1.9 Operation in Yaw

Operation of the autopilot in yaw is similar in operation to the elevator control. A signal is sent from the yaw gyro to the rudder amplifier to move the servo-motor in the correct direction to oppose the initial disturbance. When the opposing torques are equal, further rudder application ceases. Once the initial disturbance has been removed, a signal in the opposite sense causes the servo-motor to remove the rudder deflection to the neutral position.

When a disturbance in yaw is felt and corrective action taken, a disturbance is also felt around the roll axis due to a yaw causing one wing to be leading and one lagging. The changed airflow over both wings induces a lift differential which causes a roll to occur. To overcome this roll tendency and to correct for it, a yaw gyro signal is fed to the aileron channel amplifier which will then oppose the rolling tendency and correct the attitude of the aircraft. This yaw gyro signal is channelled through a rudder/aileron crossfeed and a feedback signal is fed from the tacho-generator on the aileron servo-motor to the rudder amplifier.

1.10 Operation in Roll

This is similar to the yawing condition and an aileron/rudder crossfeed is used in older aircraft which are not fitted with differential ailerons. Final control correction of the roll situation is accomplished by the compass monitor due to the turning effect created by the aileron correction.

1.11 Manoeuvring

With the autopilot engaged it is sometimes required of the pilot to change the heading or the altitude/flight level. To accomplish this a simple turn switch and a pitch switch is incorporated into the autopilot system. These switches cause a signal to be sent to the gyro platforms which apply a false datum. The false datum causes a signal to be sent to the appropriate channel amplifiers and servo-motors which will then turn the aircraft or cause a climb or descent according to the initiating input signal of the switch.

1.12 Manoeuvres in Pitch

Figure 1-3 and the following text describe the sequence of events to obtain a descent using the pitch control on an autopilot. To obtain a climb, the reverse order of the control selections should be initiated.

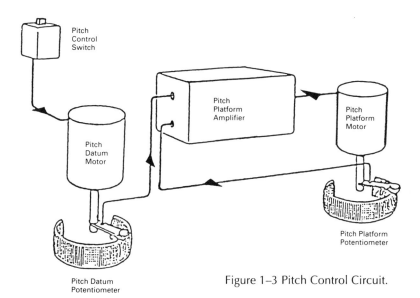

Pitch Control Switch

Pitch Platform Amplifier

Pitch Platform Motor

Pitch Datum Motor

Pitch Platform Potentiometer

Pitch Datum Potentiometer

Figure 1-3 Pitch Control Circuit.

(a) The pitch control switch is pushed forward with the intention of diving the aircraft. Light pressure results in a slow change of attitude, heavy pressure on the switch results in a fast change of attitude.

(b) The control switch operates the pitch datum motor which rotates the pitch datum potentiometer wiper. Differential signals between the datum potentiometer and the pitch platform are applied to the pitch platform amplifier.

(c) The amplifier output is applied to the pitch platform motor, thus rotating the pitch platform in the 'nose up' configuration. Platform movement is detected as a disturbance by the pitch gyro which applies corrective elevator to put the aircraft nose down.

(d) Elevator application ceases when the aircraft is rotating nose down at the same rate as the pitch platform is rotating nose up. The pitch platform is maintained level in space. The aircraft is now rotating nose down, at a constant rate, under the action of the applied elevator.

(e)   When the required angle of dive has been reached, the pitch control switch is released. The pitch datum motor stops.

(f)   The pitch platform potentiometer has been closely following the datum potentiometer and when the misalignment signal is zero, the platform ceases to rotate.

(g)   Further pitching nose down is detected as a disturbance, the applied elevator is removed, and the descent attitude is maintained at that selected when the controller was released.

(h)   Levelling of the aircraft is achieved by operating the pitch control switch in the reverse direction until the rate of descent falls to zero.

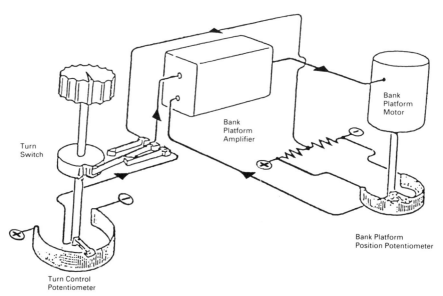

Figure 1–4   Azimuth Control Circuit.

1.13 Manoeuvres in Azimuth

With the aid of Fig 1-4 the following sequence describes a turn to port when selected on the pilot's controller. Maintaining the roll frame level is normally accomplished by the misalignment signal which is developed between the bank platform position potentiometer (BPPP) and the bank datum potentiometer (BDP). By operating the turn switch, a false signal is used on the roll frame which causes an output signal to activate the servo-motor moving the ailerons.

1.14 Turn to Port Selection

(a) Offsetting the turn controller to port initially operates the turn switch, disconnecting the BDP and substituting the turn control potentiometer.

(b) When the controller is turned, a misalignment signal is introduced between the turn control potentiometer and the BPPP. This signal is applied to the bank platform amplifier, and the output drives the bank platform motor, thereby rotating the roll frame.

(c) Rotation of the roll frame is detected by the roll gyro as a disturbance tending to lower the starboard wing. The correction signal causes the starboard aileron to go down raising the starboard wing thereby initiating a turn to port.

(d) When the misalignment signal between the turn control potentiometer and the BPPP are equal the platform rotation ceases.

(e) Whilst the controller is offset the aileron remains applied and the amount by which the controller is offset determines the rate of turn.

(f) Suppression of the yaw gyro and compass monitor signals, which would tend to oppose the turn, is achieved by a 1° microswitch operated by the roll frame. When this is made, the compass monitor signal is short circuited and the electro-magnetic clutch is disengaged at the monitor input. The yaw signal is opposed by the pick-off from a turn demand potentiometer, the output of which is determined by the angle of bank.

(g) The rudder to aileron crossfeed is disconnected by a further microswitch set at 5°, thereby allowing the sideslip monitor to co-ordinate the turn.

(h) When the central controller is returned to the central position to stop the turn, the BDP replaces the turn control potentiometer. The aileron is then removed as the misalignment signal between the BDP and BPPP levels the roll frame.

(i) A manoeuvre in azimuth can only be carried out if the controller was returned to the centre before autopilot engagement.

1.15 System Coupling

Altitude Locks
When the control (labelled ALT) is pulled out on the switch unit, the aircraft is able to be coupled to a pre-selected pressure altitude. The

altitude lock system operation is described below and is shown in Fig 1-5. The sequence of operation described is for an aircraft climbing up to the datum altitude and its subsequent coupling to that altitude.

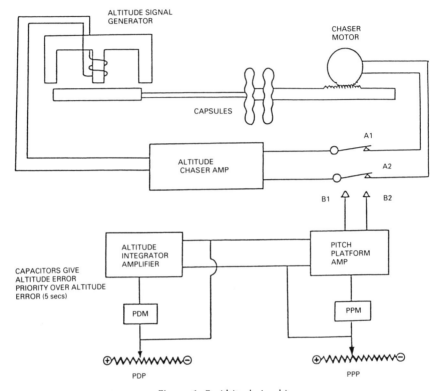

Figure 1–5 Altitude Locking.

(a)   An electromagnetic pick-off remains in the sensitive, 'no signal' position due to the chaser motor when the ALT lock is disengaged. The chase rate is sufficient to cope with an altitude change rate of at least 100 ft/sec.

(b)   The ALT control is pulled out when the aircraft has reached the datum altitude. The chaser motor is disconnected but the aircraft continues to climb through and above the datum altitude therefore giving an error signal which is then applied to the altitude signal amplifier.

(c)   An output is applied to the pitch platform from the altitude signal amplifier causing the platform to be motored 'nose up'. This causes the elevators to be operated which levels the aircraft until the altitude error signal is zero and pitch platform movement ceases.

(d) The altitude control circuit within the Altitude Error Integrating Amplifier, backs off the misalignment signal between the pitch platform potentiometer wiper and the pitch datum potentiometer. A time lag is introduced which enables the aircraft to be locked onto the datum altitude for various conditions of pitch trim altitude.

1.16 Heading Selector

The heading selector incorporates:

(a) Compass monitor

(b) Compass repeater

(c) A pre-select heading facility

All of which are shown in Fig 1-6 and the circuit diagram is illustrated in Fig 1-7.

(a) Compass Monitor
The 'C' and 'Y' type of pick-off is used for developing the compass monitor signal with a change in heading resulting in the 'C' type armature rotating about the 'Y' stator. The error signal resulting from this is applied to the aileron channel. The 'C' bar drive from the synchro is taken via an electromagnetic clutch which is disengaged when the bank platform is rotated by the 1° switch.

(b) Compass Repeater
Synchro heading information is received by a synchro-control transformer stator, a misalignment signal from the rotor is picked off and fed to a chaser amplifier. The output is then fed to a chaser motor, reduction gear train and then to the rotor shaft which backs off the synchro-control transformer output. An indication of heading against a fixed lubber mark on the face of the selector is provided by a compass card attached to, and rotating with, the rotor shaft.

(c) Pre-Select Heading Facility
Friction-loaded to the compass card is a select heading pointer which normally rotates with it. By pressing and turning the select heading knob, the pointer may be rotated independently of the compass card. Rotating the pointer away from the lubber mark also causes the wiper of a heading error potentiometer to be offset. When a new heading is required to be set, pressing of the Set Heading button on the front of the unit feeds the heading error pick-off into the bank platform network. The resultant heading change and synchro-operation

provides the signal to back off the heading error, the 'Alter Heading' button only requires to be momentarily depressed to initiate the heading change.

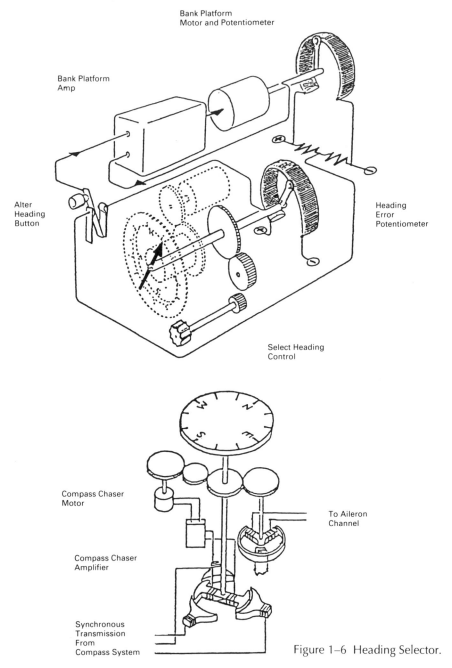

Figure 1–6 Heading Selector.

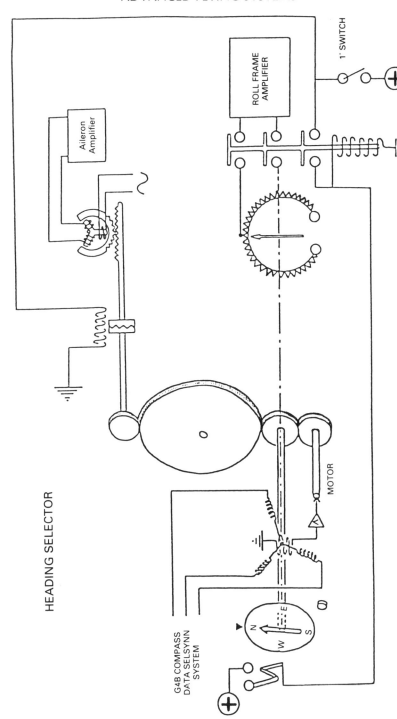

Figure 1–7 Heading Selector Circuits.

1.17 ILS Coupling – Localiser

For a localiser coupling onto the ILS, a smooth join without overshoot is required and this is achieved when the localiser beam is attached at an optimum angle of 60°. When 'TRACK' is selected on the switch unit, a mixing of the heading error and localiser beam displacement signals is permitted giving a resultant output signal. This resultant signal is amplified in the azimuth control amplifier, as illustrated in Fig 1-8, and is then applied to the bank platform amplifier. The ratio of the two signals allows the optimum angle of attack on the localiser beam.

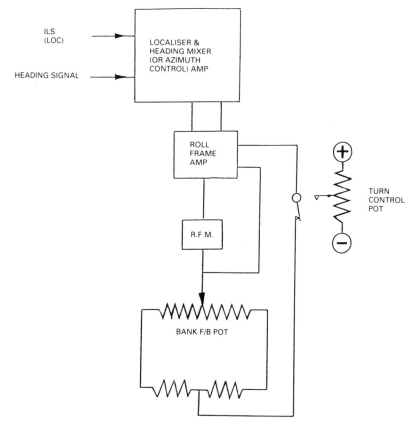

Figure 1–8 Localiser Coupling.

1.18 ILS Coupling – Glidepath

To achieve coupling to the ILS glidepath, an output signal from the glidepath receiver via the glidepath signal amplifier is applied to the pitch platform amplifier as illustrated in Fig 1-9. The present attitude of the aircraft type on an ILS may be superimposed over the glidepath signal and is known as 'GLIDE A'. The adverse effects of the aircraft's pitch changes are overcome with the use of an error integrator amplifier. For the coupling to be achieved, selection of the 'GLIDE' switch must be initiated.

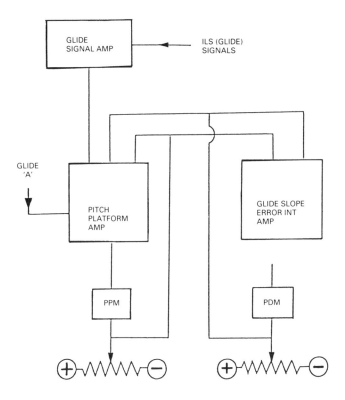

Figure 1–9 Glidepath Coupling.

1.19 Supply and Control

Switch Unit
The switch unit, as illustrated in Fig 1-10, displays several switches to cover TRACK, GLIDE, ALTIMETER as well as the POWER and ENGAGE switches. The power switch supplies power to the autopilot and its associated gyros. The gyros run up to speed and ensure that the platforms are level after 45 to 90 seconds.

The power supplies are 115V 400 Hz 3-phase AC and 28V DC which is routed via a torque switch in the aircraft's control circuit. This ensures that the DC supply is supplied to the autopilot only when the AC is satisfactory.

After the delay switch has operated correctly and the AC and DC supplies are satisfactory the READY flag will appear. When all three channel switches are selected in, the ENGAGE button is pulled and the READY flags disappear from view and the IN flags appear, indicating all three channels are selected in and engaged. If one or two of the channel switches are not selected in when the ENGAGE switch is selected, then the READY flag will still be in view when the IN flag appears. This is an indication that not all three channel switches have been selected.

As maintaining the altitude is a function of elevator control, the DC circuit ensures that the ALT hold-on coil cannot be selected when the elevator servo-motor clutch is de-energised.

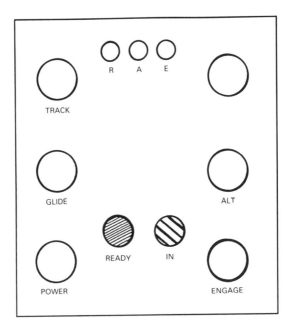

Figure 1–10 Switch Unit..

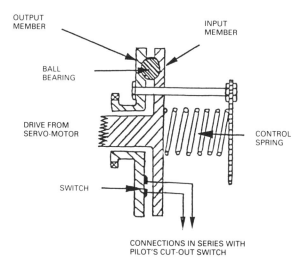

Figure 1–11 Excess Torque Cut-Out.

1.20 Safety Features

(a) Pilot's Instinctive Cut-Out – this is situated on the control column and when selected will ensure instant disengagement.

(b) Roll Error Cut-Out – this cut-out disengages the autopilot if the rate of aileron application is excessive, thereby preventing a dangerous roll attitude in the event of an aileron channel malfunction.

(c) Excess Torque Cut-Out – this is used to limit the torque imparted to the aircraft controls in the event of malfunction, or normal response to a large disturbance of the aircraft. The unit consists of two members, input and output as illustrated in Fig 1-11. The input member is driven by the servo output, the output member drives the control linkage. If the torque level is exceeded, the members move axially as well as radially to each other. This causes the ball bearings to rise up their own cone bush, the axial displacement between members against control spring tension causing contacts in series with the engaging circuit to open.

(d) Shear Linkage – a further safeguard is a weak link in the control linkage from the servos which will shear if the torque exceeds 100lb/ft.

1.21 Interlocks

An autopilot system needs to have an interlock system which allows some conditions to be overridden. The following list indicates some interlocks that are common to autopilots:

(a)   Pilot's Controller overrides Co-pilot's

(b)   Controlled turns override pre-selected turns

(c)   TRACK overrides pre-selected turns

(d)   ALT overrides slow pitch control

(e)   Fast pitch control overrides ALT control

(f)   GLIDE overrides ALT and pitch control

1.22 Miscellaneous Information

Remote Trim Indicator
Provides an indication of sustained loads on the elevator servo-motor associated with an out-of-trim condition. The unit may also incorporate remote Ready and IN flags as illustrated in Fig 1-12.

Engagement
The autopilot may be engaged in a climb or dive, but not in a turn. Whilst the autopilot may be used when flying through turbulence, it is generally recommended that coupling locks (ALT, etc) should not be engaged and that speed is reduced to the turbulence speed for the aircraft type.

Limitations
All altitude and speed limitations must be adhered to, especially the minimum altitude limit.

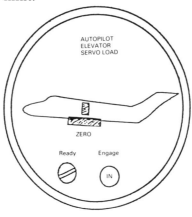

Figure 1–12   Remote Trim
Indicator.

With more and later types of electronic and control sophistication being used on the aircraft, scientists and engineers have perfected the autopilot and navigation systems to enable the aircraft to take-off and land automatically. This later development allows an increased accuracy for landing in bad visibility conditions which would otherwise cause an aircraft to divert, and it is known as the Automatic Landing System.

Test Yourself One   Advanced Flying Systems

1. In a basic autopilot channel circuit the control surface is driven by:
   (a) a mechanical system.
   (b) the servo-motor.
   (c) the monitor.
   (d) the amplifier.

   Ref 1.8.

2. In automatic flight systems the term ALT means:
   (a) aircraft lateral trim.
   (b) aircraft longitudinal trim.
   (c) altitude.
   (d) alert.

   Ref 1.15.

3. Proportional feedback is provided in a servo-motor control system to complete the signal loop by the:
   (a) amplifier.
   (b) motor.
   (c) gyro.
   (d) tacho-generator.

   Ref 1.6.

4. The heading selector permits:
   (a) real time selection.
   (b) pre selection.
   (c) trim heading only.
   (d) roll trim only.

   Ref 1.16.

5. Remove Trim Indication is given in:
   (a) pitch.
   (b) roll.
   (c) yaw.
   (d) roll and pitch.

   Ref 1.14.

2

Semiconductors

2.1 Introduction

Before it is possible to take a more detailed look at Semiconductors, a basic knowledge of Resistors, Rectifiers, Capacitors, Transistors, and some selected definitions is necessary for an understanding of Semiconductor materials and Integrated Circuits, the basis of 'Solid State' components used universally in electronics and computers.

2.2 Electric Charge

The unit of electric charge called the coulomb is the quantity of electricity (or number of electrons) transported in one second by a current of one ampere.

2.3 Resistors

Resistance is that property of an electrical circuit which determines, for a given current, the rate at which electric energy is converted into heat or radiant energy. Generally speaking, resistance is in opposition to current flow in a material, and is one of its physical properties.

The unit of resistance is called the OHM, written as Omega from the Greek alphabet (Ω). The definition of resistance is 'that resistance between two points of a conductor when a constant difference of potential of one volt, applied between these two points, produces in this conductor a current of one ampere' (the conductor NOT being the source of any electromotive force).

2.4 Rectifiers

Semiconductor rectifiers are the most used solid state devices in the electronics industry. (The term semiconductor will be explained later). A rectifier basically allows current flow in one direction, and offers a very high resistance to flow in the opposite direction.

2.5 Capacitors

A capacitor basically consists of two plates separated from each other by a thin layer of insulation material (a dielectric). When a source of DC potential is momentarily applied across these plates, they become charged. If the same two plates are then joined together momentarily by means of a switch, the capacitor will discharge.

When the potential was first applied, electrons immediately flowed from one plate to the other through the source of potential. However, the circuit from plate to plate in the capacitor was incomplete (the two plates being separated by the dielectric) and thus the electron flow ceased, meanwhile establishing a shortage of electrons on one plate and a surplus of electrons on the other.

When a deficiency of electrons exists at one end of a conductor, there is always a tendency for the electrons to move about in such a manner as to re-establish a state of balance. In the case of the capacitor, the surplus quantity of electrons on one of the capacitor plates cannot move to the other plate because the circuit has been broken; that is, the battery or DC potential was removed. This leaves the capacitor in a **charged** condition; the capacitor plate with the electron deficiency is **positively** charged, the other being **negatively** charged.

The charge represents a definite amount of electricity, or a given number of electrons. The potential energy possessed by these electrons depends not only on their number, but also on their potential or voltage. For example, a 1 µ F capacitor charged to 1000 volts possesses twice as much potential energy as does a 2 µ F capacitor charged to 500 volts, although the charge (expressed in coulombs) is the same in each case.

The unit of capacitance is the FARAD and is the capacitance of a capacitor between the plates of which there appears a difference of potential of one volt when charged by a quantity of electricity (or number of electrons) equal to one coulomb.

2.6 Construction of Transistors

One of the earliest detection devices used in radio was the galena crystal, a crude example of a **semiconductor** diode. More modern examples of semiconductors are the silicon rectifier, the germanium diode, and numerous varieties of the transistor and integrated circuit (these last two items will be described).

All of these devices offer the interesting property of greater resistance to the flow of electrical current in one direction than in the opposite direction (Rectification principle). The transistor is a three-terminal device which is made in a special way and consists of several layers of semiconductor materials; it offers current amplification and may be used for a wide variety of control functions including amplification, oscillation and frequency conversion.

2.7 Atomic Structure of Germanium and Silicon

Since the mechanism of conduction of a semiconductor is different from that of a vacuum tube, it is well to review briefly the atomic structure of various materials used in the manufacture of solid state devices.

Electrons in an element having a large atomic number are conveniently pictured as being grouped into rings, each ring having a definite number of electrons. Atoms in which these rings are completely filled are termed **inert gases**, of which helium and argon are examples. All other elements have one or more incomplete rings of electrons.

If the incomplete ring is loosely bound, the electrons may be easily removed, the element is called **metallic** and is a conductor of electric current. Copper and iron are examples of conductors.

If the incomplete ring is tightly bound, with only a few electrons missing, the element is called **nonmetallic** and is an insulator (nonconductor) to electric current.

A group of elements, of which germanium, gallium, and silicon are examples, fall between these two sharply defined groups and exhibit both metallic and nonmetallic characteristics. Pure germanium or silicon may be considered good insulators. The addition of certain impurities in carefully controlled amounts to the pure element will alter the conductivity of the material. In addition, the choice of the impurity can change the direction of conductivity through the element, some impurities increasing conductivity to positive potentials, and others increasing conductivity to negative potentials. More about this aspect later.

Early transistors were mainly made of germanium but most modern transistors arc madc of silicon. Some newer devices are being made of gallium arsenide, which combines some of the desirable features of germanium and silicon, but exhibits faster speed than either.

In consideration of the basic material used in the construction of a diode, namely silicon, this will be described because it is still by far the most popular semiconductor material in use. However, bear in mind that germanium and all other semiconductor materials follow the same general principles.

Like all materials, silicon is made up of atoms. At the centre of the silicon atom is a concentrated mass called the nucleus. The nucleus contains fourteen electrically charged particles called 'protons', plus some neutral particles which can be ignored. Circling the nucleus like little satellites are fourteen other electrically charged particles called 'electrons'.

Protons are positively charged and electrons are negatively charged. Proton and electron charges are not only opposite, but equal. This means that a proton and electron together are electrically neutral, the equal unlike charges neutralize each other. So this combination neither attracts nor repels any other particles. See Fig 2-1.

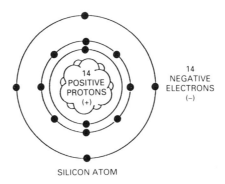

SILICON ATOM

Figure 2–1 Silicon Atom.

Looking at Fig 2-1 we see that ten of the electrons are in the shells close to the nucleus, they are in 'low orbits'. Therefore, counting just the nucleus and the two inner shells, there are ten electrons and fourteen protons, giving a net charge of +4. In the outer shell, there are four electrons, giving that shell a total (negative) charge of –4. So the –4 of the outer shell balances the +4 charge of the core (the nucleus and the inner two shells) leaving the whole atom electrically neutral.

Although the silicon atom has four electrons in its outer orbit, it has what is described as a 'desire' to have eight electrons (this term 'desire' is borrowed from the physicists method of description, and cannot be improved by the author of these notes). This 'desire' is what binds silicon atoms together into a crystal. See Fig 2-2 for a conceptual diagram of a typical section of a silicon crystal.

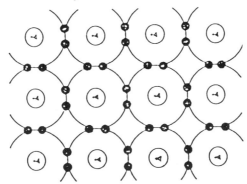

Figure 2–2 Bound Silicon Atoms.

Note that each silicon atom's 'desire' to merge has been satisfied by sharing each of its outer electrons with four neighbours, so the outer orbit of each atom, in effect, interlocks with the outer orbits of four adjoining atoms.

Since the total number of protons now equals the total number of electrons, the crystal is electrically neutral. From an electrical viewpoint, it's not a lot of use in conduction, because in this state, it is a very good insulator. All the electrons are tightly bound in their shared orbits. These electrons cannot flow to carry electrical current.

In the manufacture (or growing) of the silicon crystal, certain impurities are added intentionally. This is called 'doping'. For example the element phosphorus may be added and scattered throughout the silicon lattice. Phosphorus atomic structure is similar to silicon, but has one more proton in its core, and a fifth electron in its outer orbit. This 'spare' electron is free to wander about looking for unfilled orbits.

Doping the silicon raw material with phosphorus provides a means of conduction. Of course the amount of doping will control the degree or ease of conduction, ie, the number of free phosphorus electrons available. Electrons in outer orbits are negative, therefore this process produces 'N' (negative) type semiconductor material.

If this material is used in an electrical circuit, negative electrons being pumped into it will cause the free electrons from the phosphorus atoms to migrate to the other ends of the crystal and out along the wire connection. This is because like charges repel one another. The number of electrons in the **crystal** remains constant; one electron leaves for every one pumped in. This is the concept of electricity flowing in an N-type semiconductor.

If, however, the doping agent is boron, P-type silicon crystals are made. The boron atom has only three electrons in its outer orbit. Instead of donating an extra free electron as the phosphorus did, the boron atom creates a deficiency of one electron in the orbit. This deficiency is called a 'hole'.

Just as the free electrons can wander, so can these holes wander through the crystal lattice. Obviously, a hole is not a physical entity like an electron, but when an electron moves from one place to another, it is just as though the hole it moved to had moved in the **opposite direction**. A hole always represents a positive charge (+1) after it has moved away from the boron atom. So, the hole can be thought of as a freely moving positive charge.

The degree of doping will control the ability of the silicon to conduct. The more boron used creates more holes and therefore the more electrons they can accommodate, the more current the crystal can carry.

Remember: P-Type (positive) conducts electricity only by means of holes, and has **virtually no free electrons**. N-type (negative) conducts **only** by means of free electrons; **it has virtually no holes**.

2.8 Mechanism of Conduction

It has already been stated that there exists in semiconductors both negatively charged electrons and absence of electrons in the lattice (holes), which behave as though they had a positive electrical charge equal in magnitude to the negative charge on the electron. These electrons and holes drift in an electrical field with a velocity which is proportional to the field itself.

In an electric field the holes will drift in a direction opposite to that of the electron, and will have about one-half the velocity, since the hole mobility is about one-half the electron mobility.

A sample of a semiconductor, such as germanium or silicon, which is both chemically pure and mechanically perfect, will contain in it approximately equal number of holes and electrons and is called an **intrinsic** semiconductor.

The intrinsic resistivity of the semiconductor depends strongly on the temperature. As an example, at room temperature germanium is about 50 ohm/cm, and silicon is about 65,000 ohm/cm. Notice this is quoted for cm; actual resistance in the very small component spacing is very much less in a real semiconductor component.

The impurities which contribute electrons are called **donors**. N-type silicon has better conductivity than pure silicon in one direction, and a continuous stream of electrons will flow through the crystal in this direction as long as an external potential of the correct polarity is applied across the crystal.

The impurities which create holes are called acceptors. P-type silicon has better conductivity than pure silicon in one direction. This direction is opposite to that of the N-type material. Either the N-type or the P-type silicon is called **extrinsic** conducting type.

The doped materials have lower resistivities than the pure materials, and doped semiconductor material in the resistivity range of 0.01 to 10 ohm/cm is normally used in the production of transistors. The electrons and holes are called carriers; the electrons are termed majority carriers, and the holes are called minority carriers.

2.9 The PN Junction

The semiconductor diode is a PN junction, or junction diode. This device is one of the simplest semiconductor (solid state) devices and will be described. (A diode is a device which conducts generally in one direction up to a certain current limitation). It has the general electrical character-istic of Fig 2-3.

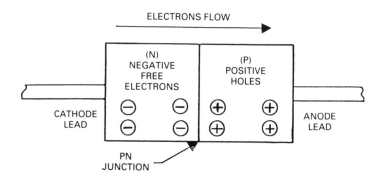

Figure 2–3 PN Junction Diode.

In Fig 2-3, the PN junction diode is made to have N-type material on one side and P-type material on the other. In this example is shown four free electrons in the N material, and four holes in the P material. The dividing line between the two types is called the 'PN junction'. It is the behaviour of the electrons and holes in the vicinity of this junction that gives diodes and other semiconductors their unique properties.

Suppose that in Fig 2-3 electrons are being pumped into the N region from an external generator. These negatively charged electrons repel the free negative electrons already there, forcing them to move towards the PN junction. At the same time, bound electrons are being withdrawn from the P region, creating new holes. The new holes repel the old holes, moving the holes towards the PN junction. So the holes in the P-type silicon and the free electrons in the N-type silicon **are moving towards each other**.

When the holes and free electrons meet at the junction, the free elec-trons fall into the holes. This conduction process continues as long as there are new holes and free electrons being 'pumped in'.

This is how a diode 'conducts' electricity in one direction, so how can it block current in the opposite direction?

In Fig 2-4 is shown a similar PN junction except that electrons are attempting to flow in the opposite direction, from P to N. This is what happens when an AC generator enters the second half of the alternating-current cycle. Since the electrons are attempting to flow away from P to N, the free electrons in the N region migrate **away** from the PN junction.

In the P region, as bound electrons move in the direction of attempted electron flow, the holes move in the opposite direction **away** from the PN junction. The result is that there are no free electrons or holes anywhere

SEMICONDUCTORS

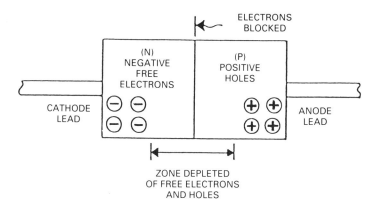

Figure 2–4 PN Junction Diode with Reverse Flow.

near the junction. In effect, this zone is like undoped silicon crystal, which is effectively an insulator **until** the electrons again attempt to flow in the acceptable direction. Electrons can flow from N to P, but not from P to N.

This chip of doped silicon is an electrical conductor under certain conditions, but is an insulator under other conditions – hence the term **'semiconductor'**.

A further definition must be introduced at this point and this is the **avalanche voltage point**. As the applied inverse voltage rises, a potential will be reached at which there will be a breakdown of the current control and a large reverse current and destruction of the diode is more than possible.

Silicon diodes are rated in terms similar to those used for vacuum-tube rectifiers. One of the most important is **Peak Inverse Voltage (PIV)**, which is the maximum reverse voltage that may be applied to a specific diode type before the avalanche breakdown point is reached.

The avalanche voltage point can be used in certain types of diodes as a reference voltage point, or control point as a design feature. In a silicon element operated in the reverse-bias avalanche breakdown region, the breakdown from nonconductance to conductance is very sharp at voltages beyond the breakdown point. The voltage drop across the diode junction becomes essentially constant for a relatively wide range of currents. This is called the zener control region, and diodes which operate utilising the breakdown point are called **zener diodes**. Voltage control in zener diodes is available from 1.8 volts to 200 volts.

2.10 Switching and Amplifying Transistors

Ordinary transistors are **bipolar**, having two PN junctions separated by a very thin layer called the **base**. There are, therefore, three terminals, or connections: the Base, Collector and Emitter, see Fig 2-5.

The word 'transistor' was chosen to describe the function of a three-terminal PN junction device that is able to amplify signal energy (current). The transistor was invented by Shockley, Barden and Brittain at the Bell Laboratories (USA) in 1947 and has become the standard amplifying device in electronic equipment. The action of amplification will be described later.

Some transistors are manufactured so that they operate better as switches, and others are made so they operate better as amplifiers. It is possible that most transistors could be used either to switch or amplify. However, it is not the transistor itself that determines whether it will switch or amplify; rather it is the control circuit, the device that controls the transistor that causes it to function as one or the other. Transistor types are generally classified as amplifiers or switches, but not both.

The study of diode action in semiconductor material will help now in the understanding of other types of semiconductors. In Fig 2-5 is a schematic cross-section of a NPN transistor.

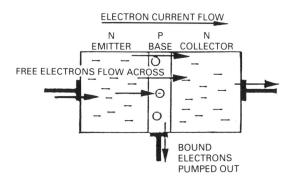

Figure 2–5 Cross-section through an NPN Transistor.

Remember that N-type semiconductor material conducts electricity by means of its supply of free electrons, and that P-type conducts by its supply of positively charged holes. The P region of the transistor is much narrower than the N regions. This P region is much less heavily doped than the N regions; that is, the holes are fewer and farther apart compared to the free electrons in the N regions.

If free electrons from an external generator are pumped from the emitter lead to the collector lead, they continue on their way from the N region of the emitter, across the P region of the base, into the N region of the collector and on down the connecting wire. This process will continue for only a brief instant of time. This may look like a contradiction in the operation of the diode action already discussed, how do the electrons get into the base and pass on to the collector.

It would be expected that these free electrons would be captured in the base area by falling into holes, so that no electrons would pass from base to the collector. In fact the base regions of transistors are very narrow and **lightly doped**, so that the holes are scattered rather sparsely. Most of the electrons (typically 98%) are able to cross the base without falling into a hole.

The few electrons that do fall into holes are stuck there. They accumulate in the base region piling up a negative (repelling) charge in the base. This is what permits the transistor to perform its job of throttling back the emitter-collector working current. The excess bound electrons in the base region repel the free electrons trying to cross through from emitter to collector, making it harder for this current to pass. It does not take long, about 50 nanoseconds for current to be shut off entirely.

Just to recap on this action, as it is the important principle of operation; the nature of the barrier that is shutting off the current, ie the junction between emitter and base, form a PN junction (a diode). In order to get appreciable forward conduction across this diode junction, as with any diode, the electron pressure in the emitter must be greater than the voltage in the base, but the excess electrons that have now accumulated in the base region have **raised** the electron pressure in the base to such a level that the difference becomes less, to the point that no electrons are able to pass on.

The only way to get the working current going again is to withdraw some of the excess bound electrons from the base region. This is done by applying a **lower** voltage pressure of electrons to the base lead which simply allows bound electrons to move out along the path of less electron pressure, ie the control circuit. This creates new holes in the base, tending to restore the proper number of holes.

With this electron pressure barrier lowered, electron current resumes from emitter to collector. For every electron withdrawn from the base, typically 50 electrons cross over from emitter to collector before one falls into a hole. Thus, the small base current proportionally controls the far larger working current. It can now be appreciated how important in manufacture control over the doping levels has to be.

2.11 SCR Devices

Thyristor is a generic term for that family of multilayer semiconductors that comprise **silicon-controlled rectifiers (SCRs), triacs, diacs, four-layer diodes,** and similar devices. The SCR is perhaps the most important member of the family, at least economically, and is used in the control of power. It is the next solid state device in terms of complexity leading to the integrated circuit.

The SCR is a three-terminal, three-junction semiconductor. The SCR will conduct high current in the forward direction with low voltage drop, presenting a high impedance in the reverse direction. The three terminals of an SCR device are **anode, cathode, and gate** (anode is the collector, cathode is the emitter and the gate is the base). Without gate current, the SCR is an open switch in either direction. Sufficient gate current will close the switch in the forward direction only. Forward conduction will continue even with the gate current removed until anode current is reduced below a critical value. At this point the SCR again blocks open. The theory of this action was described earlier, the difference is mainly that SCRs can handle very high current. The SCR is therefore a high speed unidirectional switch capable of being latched in the forward direction.

The gate signal used to trigger an SCR may be an AC wave, and the SCR may be used for dimming lights or speed control of small AC universal series-wound motors, such as those commonly used in power tools.

2.12 Power Amplification

It has already been stated that transistors are used (among other things) for power amplification, and a brief description of how this is achieved follows. The Base, Collector and Emitter can be compared to the Grid, Anode and Cathode of a triode valve.

Because the collector is biased in the back direction, the collector-to-base resistance is high. On the other hand, the emitter and collector currents are substantially equal, so the power in the collector circuit is larger than the power in the emitter circuit. From Ohm's law $P=I^2R$, so the powers are proportional to the respective resistances if the currents are the same. In practical transistors, emitter resistance is in the order of a few Ohms, while the collector resistance is hundreds or thousands of times higher, so power gains of 20 to 40 dB or even higher are possible.

2.13 Transistor Types

The transistor may be one of the types shown in Fig 2-3. The assembly of P- and N-type materials may be reversed, so that PNP and NPN transistors are both possible. The first two letters of the NPN and PNP designations indicate the respective polarities of the voltages applied to the emitter and collector in normal operation. See Fig 2-6 for the symbols used in transistors.

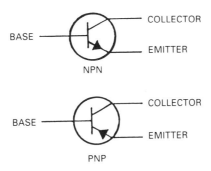

Figure 2–6 Symbols used for NPN and
PNP type transistors.

In a PNP transistor, for example, the emitter is made positive with respect to both the collector and the base, and the collector is made negative with respect to both the emitter and the base.

Most modern transistors are of the junction variety. Various names have been given to the several types, some of which are junction alloy, mesa and planar. Though their characteristics may differ slightly, they are basically of the same family and simply represent different physical properties and manufacturing techniques.

2.14 Bipolar Transistor Switches

Our present day technology includes the use of solid-state switches as practical alternatives to mechanical switches. When a bipolar transistor is used in a switching application it is either in an ON or OFF state. In the ON state a forward bias is applied to the transistor, sufficient in level to saturate the device. The common emitter format is used for nearly all transistor switches.

2.15 Integrated Circuits

There are two general types of integrated circuits (ICs): linear and digital. Dealing first with Linear ICs (sometimes called microcircuits or chips): they respond to continuously variable signals and contain many active and passive components. Some ICs have only a single type of component (diodes or transistors), while others have a combination of capacitors, diodes, resistors and transistors. Modern Linear ICs contain hundreds or thousands of active and passive components.

Digital ICs respond only to ON and OFF states, and are mainly confined to computers. The basic IC is formed on a uniform wafer of N-type or P-type silicon. Circuit designs using linear and digital ICs generally have two advantages over their counterparts made from discrete components. The first is that all similar components on the substrate have nearly identical performance characteristics, a condition impossible to realize without very closely matched discrete components. The second advantage is that equipment designed with ICs does not require as much space on a printed circuit board as one using all discrete components. This leads to more compact equipment.

ICs are available in a variety of packages. The most popular style is the moulded plastic duel inline package (DIP) having 8, 14, 16, 18, 20 or 22 pins. Another style is the TO–5 metal can package having 8, 10 or 12 leads. Use of this style is declining, however, because it does not provide enough leads for many modern ICs. See Fig 3-37 and 3-38 which shows in schematic form 14-pin DIL ICs used in computer logic circuits (the significance of the symbols used is discussed in the next chapter on logic circuits).

Test Yourself Two   Semiconductors

1. A Rectifier is a device which:
    (a) offers equal resistance to electrical current in both directions.
    (b) allows current flow in both directions.
    (c) allows current flow in one direction.
    (d) allows no current flow in either direction.

Ref 2.4.

2. The unit of Capacitance is the:
    (a) Farad.
    (b) Volt.
    (c) Amp.
    (d) Hertz.

Ref 2.5.

3. The two general types of Integrated Circuits are:
    (a) linear and rotary.
    (b) AC and DC.
    (c) linear and digital.
    (d) digital and directional.

Ref 2.15.

4. Within the silicon atom Protons are:
    (a) not changed.
    (b) positively charged.
    (c) negatively charged.
    (d) constantly alternating their state of charge.

Ref 2.8.

5. Digital ICs respond to:
    (a) ON and OFF states.
    (b) circuits not involving computers.
    (c) no variation of voltage input.
    (d) multi input values.

Ref 2.15.

3

Logic Circuit

3.1 Introduction

The study of simple logic circuits will allow the student to understand how computers make decisions. There are basically two types of computer: Digital and Analogue. Information (suitably encoded) can be handled by either, and manipulated, processed and used to display answers on a visual display unit, or to control equipment like opening and shutting a door, or flying an aeroplane.

Dealing firstly with an analogue computer, there is a tremendous variety of electrical systems that use voltage analogue to transmit information. Most old-fashioned car fuel gauges worked this way with a float in a tank controlling a variable resistor. As the level of petrol changes, the voltage going to the petrol gauge changes. Such a gauge is really a voltmeter whose dial is marked from empty to full, instead of in volts.

Another example of voltage analogue computers (where voltage stands for numbers or mathematical functions of numbers) is in telephones, the voltage standing for fluctuating air pressure, which the ear interprets as sound.

Measurements other than voltage can be used to transmit information. Current analogue systems, for example, operate the same way as voltage analogue systems except that they depend on measurements of current, or Amps instead of voltage.

The codes used in this type of computer are continuous waves and are 'modulated' in the same way as that used in radio modulation systems. The two basic systems are Amplitude Modulation (AM) and Frequency Modulation (FM). An AM system would use the height of the waves to indicate the numbers that may be transmitted. With FM systems the frequency, for example, could vary from 5 Hertz to 10 Hertz, then there is a method of transmitting the numbers from 5 to 10.

There are many analogue methods available, but in summary, it can be stated that all analogue methods are based on regulating various properties of electricity. Conversely digital methods are based on switching electricity on and off, and it is the digital system that will be described.

3.2 Electronic Counting

An understanding of the methods of counting must first of all be looked at because computers use more efficient methods than using the base of ten (fingers).

3.3 Computer Arithmetic

We are used to the decimal numbering system, ie that in which we count in powers of ten. This may well have originated from counting on ten fingers. However, for reasons which should become clear later, it is not convenient for electronic digital computers to use the decimal system. We may input information into a computer in this manner, but its process of computation and manipulation is done using other counting methods, and again, the output could well be in terms of decimal to be readily understood by the human operator. Computers can use the decimal system, but the electronics become even more unwieldy and therefore uneconomic.

In computer arithmetic there are three counting systems:

1   The Octal System

2   The Hexadecimal System

3   The Binary System

It is necessary to review the decimal numbering system first of all because the process of analysis is similar. When we write the number 147 as an example, it is the conventional shorthand way of expressing a decimal number. The longhand way of writing the same number is:

$$(1\times10^2) + (4\times10^1) + (7\times10^0) = 147_{10}$$

The ten (printed as a subscript) is known as the BASE, or RADIX, of the system and the indices (printed as superscript) indicate the power to which the base is raised. The base and the particular index to which it is raised are called the WEIGHT; that is, the least significant weight is 10^0 which is 1, the next is 10^1 which is 10 and so on. The numbers by which each weight is multiplied are called digits. In practice, only the digits of the system are written, the weights are implied.

Another way of representing the decimal system follows as we will be able to use the same approach in other systems. Taking a bigger figure of 5738 (decimal) of 5738^{10} it can be written as below:

1000s	100s	10s	1s
5	7	3	8

In other words, we mean:

$$(5\times10^3) + (7\times10^2) + (3\times10^1) + (8\times10^0) = 5738_{10}$$

$$\text{or } (5\times1000) + (7\times100) + (3\times10) + (8\times1) = 5738$$

The OCTAL System of numbering is often used in digital computers to control the input and output units. The digital computer uses the BINARY System for its basic method of computation, but octal is used in certain steps in some devices that are being controlled because it requires far fewer digits than does the binary system.

The octal system of numbers uses the base or radix of eight. This means that each digit position in the octal system represents a power of eight. Octal counting proceeds from 0 to 7 just as the decimal system. The digits 8 and 9 do not exist in octal, and to progress from 7 requires a carry operation. An octal number of 1264, (1264_8) for example, could be written as follows:

8^3	(512s)	8^2	(64s)	8^1	(8s)	8^0	(1s)
1		2		6		4	

Which in decimal is:

$$512 + 128 + 48 + 4 = 692_{10}$$

Therefore the octal number of 1264 = 692 decimal.

Notice the columns are headed by 8 multiplied by the power of 8 the appropriate number of times, for example, the column headed by 512s = $8\times8\times8$, so the next column would be $8\times8\times8\times8 = 4096$s. The column headed by 1s is the same as decimal up to 7. Remember 8 and 9 do not exist in octal.

We know that any decimal number can be represented with ten digits 0, 1, 2, 3, 4, 5, 6, 7, 8, 9. Similarly, any octal number may be represented by the eight digits 0, 1, 2, 3, 4, 5, 6, 7. The highest octal number of 4 digits if 7777_8 or $(7\times512) + (7\times64) + (7\times8) = (7\times1) = 4095_{10}$.

In the HEXADECIMAL system of numbering we require sixteen different digits or symbols (base or radix being sixteen) and we therefore require another six in addition to the digits 0 to 9. To fulfil this requirement we use the letters of the alphabet A, B, C, D, E, F to represent the equivalent numbers 10, 11, 12, 13, 14, 15 respectively. This system is unique in having the ten decimal digits 0 to 9. Furthermore, another feature is that each digit is equal to 4 bits, a term used in the binary system.

A number such as 183 hexadecimal (183_{16}) is

16^2	(256s)	16^1	(16s)	16^0	(1s)
1		8		3	

or (1×256) + (8×16) + (3×1)

256 + 128 + 3 = 387_{10}

To take this a step further, the decimal equivalent of $2A9D_{16}$ is:

16^3	(4096s)	16^2	(256s)	16^1	(16s)	16^0	(1s)
2		A		9		D	

= (2×4096s) + (10×256) + (9×16) + (13×1)

= $10,909_{10}$ (decimal)

(Remember A = 10 and D = 13 in decimal: see Fig 3-1).
The highest hexadecimal number using 4 digits is $FFFF_{16}$

or (15×4096) + (15×256) + (15×16) + (15×1) = $65,535_{10}$

The BINARY System of counting is a digital computer's working language. It is possible to represent very large numbers in binary notation, with just the digits 1 and 0. These binary digits are frequently referred to as bits.

As the binary numbering system uses two symbols only, 1 and 0, it is a convenient system for digital computers to use since electronic logic circuits have two distinct states of operation (these circuits are introduced later) but we see that a binary number may be represented by a row of switches (open or closed) or a row of lamps (on or off).

The binary system of counting has a radix of 2. This means that each digit position of a binary number represents a power of 2. Consequently the only symbols we require to express a number in the binary system are 0 and 1 since the next highest digit we are familiar with, 2, will be carried over to the next column. For example, 1001 (binary) means:

2^3 (8s)	2^2 (4s)	2^1 (2s)	2^0 (1s)
1	0	0	1

or (1x8) + (0x4) + (0x2) + (1x1) = 9_{10}

Remember that writing 1001 (binary) is equivalent to writing 1001_2.
Figure 3-1 lists counting in decimal, octal, hexadecimal and binary.

Decimal	Octal	Hexadecimal	Binary
1	1	1	1
2	2	2	10
3	3	3	11
4	4	4	100
5	5	5	101
6	6	6	110
7	7	7	111
8	10	8	1000
9	11	9	1001
10	12	A	1010
11	13	B	1011
12	14	C	1100
13	15	D	1101
14	16	E	1110
15	17	F	1111
16	20	10	10000
17	21	11	10001
18	22	12	10010
19	23	13	10011
20	24	14	10100
21	25	15	10101
22	26	16	10110
23	27	17	10111
24	30	18	11000
25	31	19	11001
26	32	1A	11010
27	33	1B	11011
28	34	1C	11100
29	35	1D	11101
30	36	1E	11110
31	37	1F	11111
32	40	20	100000

Figure 3–1 Counting in Decimal, Octal, Hexadecimal and Binary.

Although it is quite easy for computers to understand and manipulate binary numbers, it is not so easy for human beings, because of the number of 1s and 0s needed to represent large decimal numbers. Also they are rather awkward to pronounce if we want to communicate them to other people.

Electronic circuits which convert binary numbers to decimal numbers are very complex and so we need an easier way for the computer to express binary numbers so that they are more readily understood. Figure 3-2 shows the powers of 2, 8 and 16 which are implied when we write numbers in the binary, octal and hexadecimal systems respectively.

2^n	Power of 2	Power of 8	Power of 16
1	0	0	0
2	1		
4	2		
8	3	1	
16	4		1
32	5		
64	6	2	
128	7		
256	8		2
512	9	3	
1024	10		
2048	11		
4096	12	4	3
8192	13		
16384	14		
32768	15	5	
65536	16		4

Figure 3–2 Powers of 2, 8 and 16.

3.4 Binary–Octal Conversion

We can see quite clearly from Fig 3-2 that powers of 8 and 16 are also powers of 2. It seems logical therefore that binary numbers can be very easily converted to octal or hexadecimal and vice versa. This is why computers, although working in binary, frequently accept and display numbers in octal or hexadecimal.

The rules for converting binary whole numbers to octal are very simple, eg consider the binary number: 10100111011

(i) Divide the number into groups of 3 bits starting from the least significant figure, ie the right-hand end. The above number is then written as 10 100 111 011

(ii) Now convert each group of three bits to the equivalent decimal number, ie:

	10	100	111	011
becomes:	2	4	7	3

(iii) Put the converted digits together to give the equivalent octal number, ie 2473_8

3.5 Octal–Binary Conversion

To convert octal whole numbers to binary we reverse the rules used above; eg to convert the octal number 3072^8 to binary we write down the binary code for each digit in the octal number, ie:

	3	0	7	2
becomes:	011	000	111	010

We then group these digits together to form the equivalent binary number, ie 11000111010; notice we have dropped the 0 at the most significant figure, ie the left-hand end.

3.6 Binary–Hexadecimal Conversion

The rules for converting binary whole numbers to hexadecimal numbers are very similar to those for converting to octal, the main difference being that the binary number must be divided into groups of four bits rather than three, eg:

To convert binary 110110110011110 to hexadecimal:

(i) Divide the binary number into groups of four bits starting from the least significant end. The above number then becomes:

110	1101	1001	1110

(ii) Next convert each group to the equivalent decimal number. The number in the above example becomes:

110	1101	1001	1110
6	13	9	14

(iii)   The next step is to convert any number greater than 9 resulting from the above step to the equivalent hexadecimal symbol (refer to Fig 3-1), before grouping all the digits together to give the equivalent hexadecimal number. In the above example this becomes $6D9E_{16}$.

3.7 Hexadecimal–Binary Conversion

The reverse of the above applies when converting hexadecimal whole numbers to binary, eg to convert the number $D39A_{16}$ to binary:

(i)   First convert the hexadecimal symbols to decimal so that the number becomes:

D	3	9	A
13	3	9	10

(ii)   Then write the binary equivalents for each of these numbers:

13	3	9	10
1101	0011	1001	1010

(iii)   Finally, group the numbers together to form the binary result, ie: 1101001110011010

These conversions are applicable to whole numbers; the conversion of fractions is beyond the scope of this syllabus.

3.8 Digital Information

It has been shown that the working language of a digital computer is binary, and in this section, it will be shown how intelligence can be sent by digital means. The binary system is a two-state system, and basically digital computers use high speed switches which are either open or closed (two-state).

To see how it is possible for such techniques to be used in computers, consider the simple circuit in Fig 3-3. This is a schematic of a simple old-fashioned telegraph circuit.

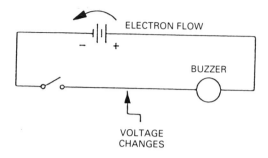

Figure 3–3 Simple Telegraph Circuit.

The power supply is a battery which 'pumps' electrons to a higher voltage on one side of the circuit than the other. The switch in the schematic is the telegrapher's transmitter key, and there is a simple buzzer as a receiver. In the schematic, the switch is in the off (or open) position. Since the voltage on both sides of the buzzer is the same, the receiver is silent. When the key is pressed, turning the switch on, the voltage on the switch side of the receiver goes high, increasing the current flow and causing the buzzer to operate. When the switch is returned to the off position, the current flow stops and the buzzer becomes silent.

It can be said it is the change in voltage in the wire that carries the information and can be visualized as shown in Fig 3-4. The level of the bottom horizontal lines represents zero voltage, meaning that the switch is off.

Figure 3-4 Switched Voltage Curve Showing
an 'A' in Morse Code.

When the switch is turned on, the voltage rises to a higher level indicated by the upper horizontal lines. If the switch is closed for a short time, we get a dot in Morse code. If it's held closed for a longer period we get a dash. The curve shown gives a dot–dash, which is an 'A' in Morse code. This is the simplest digital system, switch on and switch off. A point in passing, the Morse code is one of the very few digital systems that can be decoded by the human brain. It normally decodes analogue inputs.

The Morse code requires a cumbersome five characters for each digit, but computers use a more efficient code, the binary number code. In a digital computer, it is usual to let a low voltage represent a zero, and a higher voltage to represent a one. Figure 3-5 shows the voltage curve.

LOGIC CIRCUIT

Figure 3–5 Voltage Curve in a Two-State
Binary Counting System.

Since all that can be transmitted in a binary code is zeros and ones, how is it possible to extract intelligence from the code? In Fig 3-6 is a five-bit word; each zero or one is called a BIT and a given number of bits makes up a word. This five-bit word will serve as an example, even though typical computers use 32-bit words (and higher). To read this word as a number in binary code, the first bit reading from the right stands for one; the second bit for two; the third bit for four; the fourth for eight; and the fifth for sixteen.

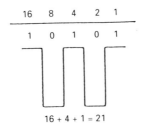

Figure 3–6 A Five-Bit Word
in Binary Code.

Now thinking of zeros as standing for NO and the ones for YES it is possible to read the word from right to left in the following way: YES, we have a one; NO, we don't have a two. YES we have a four; NO we don't have an eight. YES we have a sixteen. Add up the values we do have, as we have done on the bottom line of Fig 3-6, and you get twenty-one. So twenty-one is the number represented by this word: 10101 in the binary code.

It is now easy to see how it is possible to add more bits to the left. The next bit would represent thirty-two, the next would be sixty-four, the next one hundred and twenty-eight, etc. In this way it is possible to send numbers as large as is necessary. It is also possible to encode decimal fractions.

Digital computers use many other codes, such as binary-coded decimal (BCD), Grey code, and for letters, the Hollerith code, but all these codes use just zeros and ones, so they are all binary codes. (Binary means 'two-state', on or off).

This simple principle of transmitting digital information has remained the same from the old-fashioned telegraph system through to today's most modern and powerful digital computers.

3.9 Digital Decisions

As it was possible to see how detailed information can be communicated using only the words YES and NO, or in electrical terms – HIGH or LOW voltages, how is it possible for digital systems to make decisions? Before this can be described, it is first necessary to understand some aspects of Boolean Functions because the analysis of switching circuits (Logic Gates) are universally described by this method, and some practical applications will help in the understanding of how decisions are made.

Boolean algebra was introduced by George Boole, an English mathematician in 1847. The algebra was intended as a shorthand notation for the system of logic originally set forth by Aristotle. Aristotle's system dealt with statements which were considered to be either true or false. Boole's algebra deals with variables which may have two discrete possible states or values (often referred to as true or false).

Until the coming of digital electronics and digital computers, Boolean algebra had very little practical use. Now it is extensively used for handling any digital problem. We have already seen that digital computers use the binary numbering system which has only two states, 0 and 1. Boolean algebra is therefore ideally suited to dealing with problems of binary arithmetic and electronic digital systems.

The binary states of Boolean variables may be conveniently illustrated by referring to a simple switch. Here the two states are switch open and switch closed. Let us say that an open switch is equivalent to a 0 and a closed switch is equivalent to a 1. (See Fig 3-7.)

Figure 3–7 Simple switch (a) open, (b) closed.

In diagram (a) the switch is open and so there is no connection between points X and Y (0 condition). In diagram (b) the switch is closed and so there is a connection between points X and Y (1 condition). Further use of the switch analogy will be made later. It is important to understand the first basic examples of Boolean algebra, these being OR and AND. They are referred to as the 'OR function' and the 'AND function'.

3.10 The OR Function

This is obeyed in a situation with Boolean variables when a desired result will occur after at **least** one of two (or more) conditions are satisfied. A 'Boolean variable' is a variable with just two possible states such as on or off, open or shut, etc.

To examine the Boolean OR function, the following problem will be considered: assume that a burglar alarm system is fitted to a building; the building has one door and one window, each will cause the alarm to sound if opened ie: alarm sounds if door open OR window open

The alarm has two states – on or off

The door has two states – open or closed

The window has two states – open or closed

The door, the window and the alarm have each got two states and are, therefore, Boolean variables. Since all variables in the problem are Boolean, the problem can be expressed in Boolean algebra. In the statement above, the word OR is used to describe the alarm's dependence on the states of the door and window; OR is called a logical connective. The + symbol is used for the OR function. Thus we can write a Boolean equation to represent the alarm system:

(door open) + (window open) = (alarm sounding)

Note that the + sign is used here quite differently from the way it is used in ordinary mathematics. Before being introduced to the Boolean OR function it was possible to interpret the equation as: 'door open and window open equals alarm sounding' – this is not the same thing at all, although it is also true.

Referring to the switch analogy mentioned earlier, the OR function may be represented as shown in Fig 3-8.

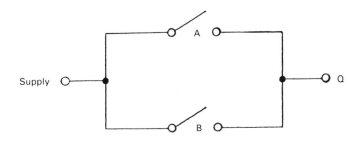

Figure 3–8 The OR function representation.

In Fig 3-8, the switch 'A' could be operated by the door, and switch 'B' could be operated by the window. The Q connection is the burglar alarm.

For a connection to be made between the supply and point Q (the burglar alarm), either switch A (the door) OR switch B (the window) must be closed, ie: Connection (Q) = A+B

It is now possible to construct a table with all possible combinations of states A and B, showing which conditions cause a connection to Q. (Fig 3-9).

A	B	(Q) Connection
Open	Open	No
Open	Closed	Yes
Closed	Open	Yes
Closed	Closed	Yes

Figure 3–9 Basis of a 'Truth Table'.

Reconsider now the case of the two switches represented by the OR function. A closed switch is represented by a 1 and an open switch with a 0. The condition is also represented when a connection (Q) is made with a 1 and the condition when a connection is not made with a 0. The truth table now becomes as in Fig 3-10.

A	B	Q
0	0	0
0	1	1
1	0	1
1	1	1

Figure 3–10 Simple Truth Table.

This is the binary truth table for the Boolean OR function, ie: Q = A=B

The truth table is the same for any OR function of two binary variables and is known as the OR truth table.

Note that Q = 1 if either A = 1 OR B = 1

Taking this a stage further, consider a three-switch circuit as shown in Fig 3-11, and the equivalent truth table in Fig 3-12.

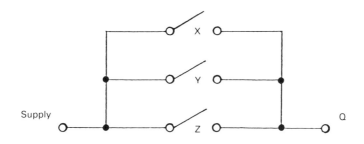

Figure 3–11 A three-switch circuit, X Y and Z.

X	Y	Z	Connection (Q)
0	0	0	0
0	0	1	1
0	1	0	1
0	1	1	1
1	0	0	1
1	0	1	1
1	1	0	1
1	1	1	1

Figure 3–12 Truth table for a three-switch circuit.

This is the connection if switch X or Y or Z is closed, ie: $X+Y+Z = Q$.

3.11 The AND Function

This is the second of the Boolean functions. If a situation which may be described with Boolean variables gives a desired result when all of several external conditions are satisfied, then that situation is said to obey the Boolean AND function.

The following example explains the AND function in simple terms. Consider a gas-fired central heating system in a building. Figure 3-13 illustrates a schematic for such a thermostatically-controlled system.

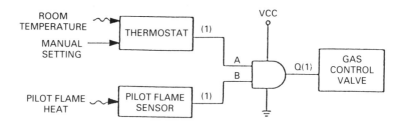

Figure 3–13 Thermostatically-Controlled Gas-Fired
Central Heating System.

The thermostat on the wall compares actual room temperature with the desired temperature setting which was manually set. The output wire from the thermostat carries digital information. A high voltage means 'Yes, the room needs more heat'. A low voltage means 'No, the room does not need heat'. This signal is sufficient to turn the gas valve on or off at the proper time.

However, as a safety factor, the system must incorporate a second stream of information. We need a temperature sensor next to the pilot flame which will determine whether this flame is on or not, because we depend upon it to ignite the main burner. In an all-electronic system, the information from this sensing function would be either a high voltage saying 'Yes, the pilot flame is burning', or a low voltage saying 'No, it is not burning'.

ie, **The main burner will be ignited if the thermostat is on AND the pilot flame sensor is on.**

The main burner has two states – on or off

The thermostat has two states – on or off

The pilot flame sensor has two states – on or off

Referring to the switch analogy mentioned earlier, the AND function may be represented as shown in Fig 3-14 where switch A could be the wall thermostat and switch B could be the pilot flame sensor.

Figure 3–14 The AND switch analogy.

The AND gate has an output which goes to the gas valve control. If the thermostat says 'Yes, we need heat', AND the pilot sensor says 'Yes, the pilot flame is burning', THEN the AND gate decides 'Yes, turn on the gas valve'. On the other hand, if we get a 'No' at EITHER of these inputs, then the output will be 'NO'. Using an AND gate, we get a 'Yes' output ONLY if BOTH inputs are 'Yes'.

Consequently, Boolean algebra may be used to express this situation as: (Thermostat on). (Pilot-flame sensor on) = main gas valve on.

The word AND is the Boolean logical connective for the AND function. In practice the full stop symbol (.) is used for this connective.

The truth table for the thermostatically-controlled gas-fired central heating system is given in Fig 3-15.

Thermostat On	Pilot Flame On	Burner Ignites
No	No	No
No	Yes	No
Yes	No	No
Yes	Yes	Yes

Figure 3–15 The central heating Truth Table.

If we now look at the switch analogy of the AND function and adopt the convention as before, that an open switch is represented by an 0, a closed switch by a 1, a connection (Q) is represented by a 1 and a no connection by a 0, then the truth table is as shown in Fig 3-16.

A	B	C
0	0	0
0	1	0
1	0	0
1	1	1

Figure 3–16 The binary truth table for the Boolean AND function.

The truth table is the same for any AND function of two binary variables and is known as the AND truth table. Note that $Q = 1$ only if $A = 1$ AND $B = 1$. ($Q = A.B$)

To take this a stage further, using the switch circuit in Fig 3-17, we obtain the corresponding truth table set out in Fig 3-18.

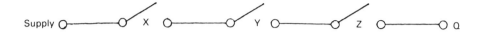

Figure 3–17 The AND switch analogy.

For a connection to be made to Q all three switches X AND Y AND Z must be closed.

X	Y	Z	Q
0	0	0	0
0	0	1	0
0	1	0	0
0	1	1	0
1	0	0	0
1	0	1	0
1	1	0	0
1	1	1	1

Figure 3–18 Connection if switches X, Y and Z are closed, ie Q = X.Y.Z.

3.12 The AND – OR Combination

It is possible to have Boolean algebra expressions which are more complex than just a single AND or OR function. A convenient way of becoming familiar with these is to continue with the switch analogies given in Fig 3-19.

A condition Q is defined where Q = 1, when there is a connection between the supply and Q, Q = 0 where there is no connection. There are two ways of tackling the problem in order to obtain a Boolean equation for Q. The first is to look at the diagram, and see that there is a connection to Q if both A and B are closed or if both A and C are closed, ie:

$$Q = (A \text{ AND } B) \text{ OR } (A \text{ AND } C)$$

$$Q = A.B + A.C$$

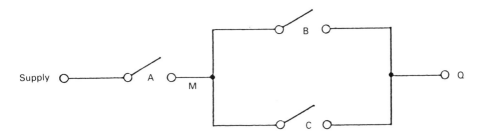

Figure 3–19 AND-OR switch analogy.

With more complex networks it is not so easy to derive an answer by just inspecting the diagram and we must split the network up into parts; eg if we divide the network at point M in Fig 3-19, we can say that we require a connection from the supply to M and a connection M to Q. In Boolean terms this means:

Q = A AND (B OR C)

Q = A.(B+C)

At first sight this may seem to be a different answer from that obtained by the inspection method. However, as with normal algebra, common variables in terms of an expression may be separated out with the introduction of brackets, ie:

A.B + A.C = A.(B+C)

3.13 Logic Gates

Electronic circuits which perform the Boolean function of AND and OR are called logic gates. We have seen the analogy of simple switches in the explanation of logic gates. Switching is achieved electronically by the use of diodes (see under Semiconductors in Section 2).

Figure 3-20 shows a diode built with two input devices (in this example an OR gate). Remember that an OR gate output is '1' (high voltage) if there is a '1' (high voltage) at the input, either 'A' OR 'B'.

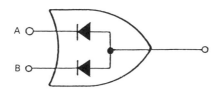

Figure 3–20 OR gate showing the two diode switches.

Electrons at the inputs can move only into the inputs, and not out of them, because of the one-way quality of the diodes. Assume a 1 at input A, and a 0 at input B. Electrons would flow from the high electron voltage at the input to produce a high voltage (1) at the output. The only way to get a 0 at the output is to have 0s at both inputs.

This very simple concept poses the question, why have diodes at all – why not just let the electrons flow through the wires? To answer that, consider what would happen if we had a 1 at input A and a 0 at B. Without the diode on the input path to block outgoing electron current, we would have a short-circuit path, and electrons would run out through this path, rather than through the output. The output voltage would then lie at some indefinite point between high and low. The output would not be a clear cut YES or NO, which is what the computer wants, nor a 'maybe' otherwise the computer will not work. So we need diodes to build this kind of simple logic gate.

If the diodes are turned around so that they block current from coming into the inputs, we would have an AND gate. All the gates described and others later, use a diode matrix arranged in such a manner as to produce the required switching.

There are a number of variations of symbols used for logic gates, and those used in these notes are to MIL standard 806. The basic symbols are shown in Fig 3-21.

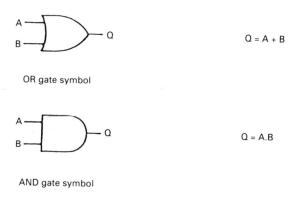

Figure 3–21 Symbols used for logic gates.

We have already seen how to use switches to perform logic functions. In fact the very early computers did actually use electronically controlled electro-magnetic switching, which used coils, a lot of power, and were very slow. Modern computers use thousands of logic gates and although they are associated with circuits that provide power, are becoming very fast indeed.

LOGIC CIRCUIT

The AND or OR gates introduced earlier, may be interconnected to perform a variety of Boolean functions, the binary output voltage patterns of gates being the input information to other gates, as shown at Fig 3-22.

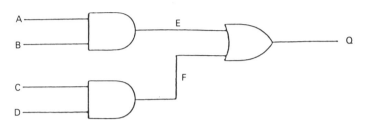

Figure 3–22 Interconnection of AND gates and OR gate to perform more complex logic states.

In Fig 3-22 we see that the logic is:

$$E = A.B$$

and $\quad F = C.D$

also that $\quad Q = E+F$

Therefore $\quad Q = A.B + C.D$

So for the logic diagram shown in Fig 3-22, the Boolean equation for the output Q in terms of the input A, B, C and D is:

$$Q = A.B + C.D$$

When designing logic circuits, the process is generally the reverse of that shown in Fig 3-22, ie we would first have to formulate a Boolean expression which adequately described the problem and then the expression would need to be translated into a logic diagram.

For example, suppose a certain item of machinery is to have an electronic control circuit to switch off the machine or reduce inputs when certain parameters reach critical values. Assume that there are four parameters, their critical values being indicated by electronic signals W, X, Y and Z. The machine must be stopped if W and X become critical at the same time, or if W, Y and Z become critical together.

To check the requirement, the machine must be stopped if **W and X** are critical, or if **W and Y and Z** are critical. This suggests the Boolean expression: W.X + W.Y.Z which may be simplified to W.(X+Y.Z). It now remains to construct a logic diagram, and it is best to start from the output, and also from within the brackets of the expression and working outwards, we then obtain the diagram shown in Fig 3-23.

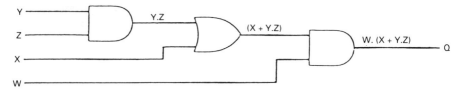

Figure 3–23 A logic diagram.

3.14 The NOT Function

So far there is one important Boolean function which has not been introduced. This is the NOT function.

The NOT function is used, just as it sounds, to describe the INVERSE of an expression, ie:

If A means: switch A is closed

Lock A is secure

point A is at a positive voltage etc

Then NOT A means: switch A is open

Lock A is not secure

point A is at a negative voltage or zero volts etc.

NOT A is written $\bar{A}$ and is pronounced in many ways including NOT A, bar A, A barred, the complement of A, the inverse of A etc.

If the NOT function is applied again, ie to $\bar{A}$, the result is NOT A written $\bar{\bar{A}}$, which is the equivalent of A again, since the inversion becomes the original. The symbol for an electronic NOT gate, more commonly now called an INVERTOR is shown in Fig 3-24.

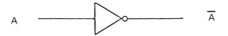

Figure 3–24 Symbol for an Electronic NOT gate (an invertor).

3.15 The Exclusive–OR Function (EX–OR) or (XOR)

The Exclusive–OR function is a Boolean function which differs slightly from the normal OR function already introduced. (The normal OR function is often called the Inclusive-OR function). The differences may be seen from the truth tables in Fig 3-25 and 3-26.

Input A	Input B	Output
0	0	0
0	1	1
1	0	1
1	1	0

Input A	Input B	Output
0	0	0
0	1	1
1	0	1
1	1	1

Figure 3–25 Exclusive-OR truth table.   Figure 3–26 Inclusive-OR truth table.

Notice that whereas the NORMAL OR function (Inclusive–OR) gives a 1 output if any input is a 1, the Exclusive–OR function gives a 1 output if either input is at a 1 but not if both inputs are at 1. A device which performs the Exclusive–OR function is called an Exclusive–OR gate, sometimes referred to as a non-equivalence gate, since if the inputs are not equivalent then the output is a 1. See the appropriate symbol in Fig 3-27.

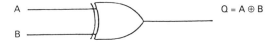

Figure 3–27 The symbol for an Exclusive-OR gate.

There is a new Boolean symbol introduced in Fig 3-27 ($\oplus$). This symbol represents the XOR operation (also it will be seen later in the XNOR) operation. To find the output (Q) of these devices, refer to the truth tables.

More often than not when designing logic circuits we only have the normal OR and AND functions and invertors available. Therefore if we require the Exclusive–OR function we must first know how to implement them with these devices. To do this it must first be expressed in a Boolean algebraic form which is best derived from a study of the truth table. There is a 1 output (Q) when:

A = 1, B = 0 or when A = 0, B = 1

The Boolean representation for the condition A = 1, B = 0 is $A.\bar{B}$ ie, A AND (NOT B).

The Boolean representation for the condition A = 0, B = 1 is $\bar{A}.B$ ie, (NOT A) AND B.

Therefore Q = 1 for $A.\bar{B}$ OR $\bar{A}.B$

ie, $Q = A.\bar{B} + \bar{A}.B$ (written as $Q = A + B$)

This is the Boolean representation of the Exclusive–OR function.

3.16 The NAND Function

This is a Boolean function which is simply a combination of the NOT function (invertor) and the AND function, ie NOT AND is abbreviated to NAND. Consequently the NAND function may be represented as in the circuit in Fig 3-28.

Figure 3–28 The symbol for the NAND circuit.

The NAND of two variables A and B represented in Boolean algebra as A.B, meaning the NOT (or inversion) of A.B. The symbol for the single gate which performs the NAND function is shown in Fig 3-29, and the truth table in Fig 3-30.

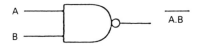

Figure 3–29 The symbol for the NAND function.

As with an invertor, the small circle on the output of the gate indicates an inverted output.

A	B	$\overline{A.B}$
0	0	1
0	1	1
1	0	1
1	1	0

Figure 3–30 Truth table for a two input NAND gate.

3.17 The NOR Function

It has been seen that NAND means the NOT AND function, similarly the NOR function is the NOT OR function and a circuit is shown in Fig 3-31.

Figure 3–31 The symbols for the NOR circuit.

The NOR function of two variables A and B is represented in Boolean algebra as $\overline{A + B}$ meaning the NOT (or inversion) of A + B. The symbol for a gate which performs the NOR function is shown in Fig 3-32, and the truth table in Fig 3-33.

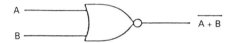

Figure 3–32 The symbol for the NOR function.

As with an invertor, the small circle on the output of the gate indicates an inverted output.

A	B	$\overline{A \oplus B}$
0	0	1
0	1	0
1	0	0
1	1	0

Figure 3–33 Truth table for a two input NOR gate.

3.18 The Exclusive–NOR Function (Ex–NOR)

This is the inverse function of Exclusive–OR (EX–OR). It was pointed out earlier that the EX–OR gate is sometimes called a 'non-equivalence' gate. Consequently the EX–NOR gate may be called an 'Equivalence gate', since the output will be 1 if the inputs are identical (equivalent). The EX–NOR function may be performed by the circuit in Fig 3-34.

Figure 3–34 The symbols for the EX-NOR circuit.

231

The EX–NOR function of the two variables A and B is represented in Boolean algebra as $\overline{A \oplus B}$, meaning the NOT (or inversion) of A + B. The symbol for the gate which performs the EX–NOR function is shown in Fig 3-35 and the truth table in Fig 3-36.

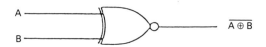

Figure 3–35 The symbol for the EX-NOR function.

As with the invertor, the small circle on the output of the gate indicates an inverted output.

A	B	$\overline{A \oplus B}$
0	0	1
0	1	0
1	0	0
1	1	1

Figure 3–36 Truth table for the Equivalence
gate (EX-NOR gate).

NAND and NOR gates can also perform respectively the AND and OR functions, but in such cases this is achieved by additional inversion (the effect of one inversion is always cancelled by adding a second) at the output. It is also possible for a NAND gate to perform an OR function and a NOR gate to perform an AND function, and this can be done by inverting the inputs and outputs. Thus, any of the three basic logic functions can be performed with either a NAND gate or a NOR gate, permitting some economy to be achieved in applying them to certain digital circuits.

Logic gates are fabricated as Integrated Circuit packs (ICs) either in dual, triple or quadruple circuit arrangements. Figure 3-37 and 3-38 show typical arrangements contained in a dual-in-line (DIL) pack monolithic IC. The numbered squares represent the connecting pins. (TTL means Transistor-Transistor-Logic).

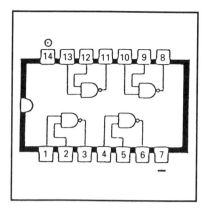

Figure 3–37 DIL type 7400 TTL quadruple
2–input NAND gates.

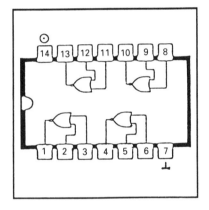

Figure 3–38 DIL type 7402 TTL quadruple
2-input NOR gates.

3.19 Summary of Boolean Functions and Logic Gates

At this point it is useful to summarise the work covered in this chapter. We have seen what is meant by the Boolean functions: AND; OR; EX–OR; NOT; NAND; NOR; EX–NOR. The definitions of these functions are restated below. Also, we have discussed their implementation and use as logic gates. Figure 3-39 shows a summary of Boolean functions, logic gates and truth tables.

the **AND** function gives a 1 only when all inputs (or variables) are 1

The **OR** function gives a 1 when any input is a 1

The **EX–OR** function gives a 1 when any single input is a 1

The **NOT** function gives a 1 when the input is 0, and a 0 when the input is a 1. The NOT function can have only a single input (variable)

The **NAND** function gives a 0 only when all inputs are 1, being the inverse of AND (NOT AND)

The **NOR** function gives a 0 when any input is a 1, being the inverse of OR (NOT OR)

The **EX–NOR** function gives a 0 when any single input only is 1, being the inverse of EX–OR (EX–NOT–OR).

A	B	NOT A $\bar{A}$	NOT B $\bar{B}$	AND $A.B$	OR $A+B$	EX-OR $A \oplus B$	NAND $\overline{A.B}$	NOR $\overline{A+B}$	EX-NOR $\overline{A \oplus B}$
0	0	1	1	0	0	0	1	1	1
0	1	1	0	0	1	1	1	0	0
1	0	0	1	0	1	1	1	0	0
1	1	0	0	1	1	0	0	0	1
SYMBOL		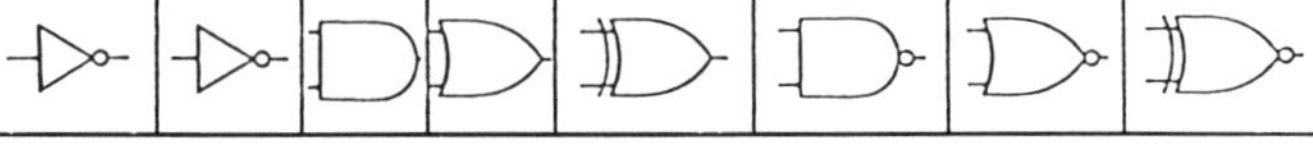							

Figure 3–39 Summary of Boolean functions, logic
gates and truth tables.

Test Yourself Three   Logic Circuits

1. The Output of an AND Gate:
    (a)   has three functions.
    (b)   has only one function.
    (c)   has four functions.
    (d)   has two functions.

Ref 3.11.

2. A NOT gate is more commonly known as:
    (a)   an Invertor.
    (b)   a NAND Gate.
    (c)   a NOR Gate.
    (d)   a Non Gate.

Ref 3.14.

3. The NAND Function is achieved with the use of:
    (a)   a NOT Gate and an OR Gate.
    (b)   a reversed AND Gate.
    (c)   a NOT Gate and an AND Gate.
    (d)   an AND Gate and an OR Gate.

Ref 3.16.

4. The Logic NOR Function employs the use of:
    (a)   an AND and OR Gate.
    (b)   an AND and NAND Gate.
    (c)   a NOT and OR Gate.
    (d)   a NOT and NOR Gate.

Ref 3.17.

5. Switching within logic gates is normally achieved with the use of:
    (a)   Relays.
    (b)   CBs.
    (c)   BTBs.
    (d)   Diodes.

Ref 3.13.

4

Electronic Instrument Display Systems

4.1 Introduction

It is necessary for students to have an understanding of the modern cockpit displays using Cathode Ray Tubes (CRTs) coming into regular use in the airlines. Before looking at particular systems, it will be useful to understand why the technology has moved in this direction, and some background information is given. There are also a number of new abbreviations which are now in common use, and will be seen on the diagrams.

The introduction of CRT technology for the display of flight systems information represented a milestone in the evolution of the flight deck. The so-called glass cockpit provided a release from the many constraints of earlier electro-mechanical displays; it also permitted the integration of displays, a more effective utilization of high priority panel space, and greater flexibility.

The cathode ray tube used in aircraft has been developed to the stage of presenting to the pilot pictorial colour images of the aircraft systems (more later). Valuable development work was carried out in the 1970s by British Aerospace and Smiths Industries at Weybridge in England on what is known as the AFD or Advanced Flight Deck. At the same time, the technology of producing a satisfactory colour CRT was progressing, particularly in Japan.

It was in the early 1980s that the all-digital Airbus A310 and Boeing 757/767 introduced CRT flight displays in civil aviation and this marked the watershed in the evolution of the glass cockpit. While the technology employed in the displays was not significantly different, conceptually the A310 and A300-600 displays were more advanced than those of the Boeing aircraft.

Boeing used an Electronic Attitude Director Indicator (EADI), the display details of which were similar to those of the electro-mechanical ADI which it replaced. On the other hand, Airbus took advantage of the research on the Weybridge AFD and elected to introduce a Primary Flight Display (PFD) which incorporated the main airspeed indication, selected altitude and deviation, full flight mode annunciation and various other items of information. The A310 flight director was conventional but could, on selection, be changed to a flight path vector display.

There was little difference between the CRT Navigation Display (ND) on these aircraft, providing a map mode, a reproduction of the conventional Horizontal Situation Indicator (HSI) and superimposition of weather radar. However, the concept of system display was quite different. The Airbus Electronic Centralised Aircraft Monitoring (ECAM) system employed two CRTs, one for warning displays and the other for systems. The systems display automatically related to phase of flight but had to be manually selected.

Airbus continued to use conventional dial engine indicators. The Engine Indicating and Crew Alerting System (EICAS) of Boeing used the upper of two CRTs for primary engine parameters with secondary information on the lower screen. No systems diagrams or guidance on corrective actions were displayed on these CRTs, as were available on the Airbus ECAM.

The use of CRTs for flight instrument displays is just one of three flight deck functions for the application of this technology. A second is for the display of systems information. This involves engine data as well as other aircraft systems. The flexibility of this time-sharing form of display enables systems information to be presented only when required, either because of the phase of the operation (such as engine starting) or when a system deviates from its normal operating range. This function includes use as part of the warning system.

The third use of CRTs on the flight deck is for the Flight Management System (FMS). These systems are increasingly being installed, particularly to optimise operating efficiency with a primary objective of reducing fuel consumption. The FMS interfaces with the navigation system.

Introduction of the digital FMS is easier on all the new all-digital aircraft. Retro-fitting on earlier analogue aircraft such as the Boeing 747 is expensive, but in certain cases it has proved cost-effective in fuel saving. A distinction should be made between retro-fitting FMS devices to aircraft already in service, and the more complex versions of FMS designed into new aircraft. The latter can typically ensure reduced workload, compile complicated lateral and vertical profiles and supply data for the electronic flight guidance system.

The CRTs used on the flight deck of modern aircraft can display information to the pilot that in former times was impossible. Furthermore, the old style instrumentation cluttered up practically all available areas in the cockpit. The flight engineer had a vast array of instrumentation to monitor during flight, and modern aircraft using a two pilot crew are able to (electronically) monitor not only the navigation and flying conditions, but engine and aircraft systems.

A further very important area, and in some respects because of the design features of glass cockpits, there is the Warning, Advisory and Alerting systems. In early times, a fire bell and a few lights were all that were fitted, but even in the jet age, warnings increased from 172 on the DC-8 to 418 on the DC-10, and from 188 on the Boeing 707 to 455 on the 747. The glass cockpit display is able not only to alert the crew and call for their attention, but report the nature of the condition and **guide the crew in the appropriate corrective procedure**.

4.2 Cathode Ray Tube (CRT)

The cathode ray tube is still currently the preferred method of presenting the information to the pilot as described in the earlier section. However, the modern CRT is more complex than the earlier monochrome CRTs used in weather radar, as apart from being able to generate colour displays, it is also able to present alpha-numeric data, aircraft system line drawings, pictorial instrumentation and moving weather displays.

A CRT is a thermionic device, ie one in which electrons are liberated as a result of heating. Figure 4-1 shows a schematic of a single electron 'gun' CRT. To generate colour, a three-gun CRT is used and this will be described later.

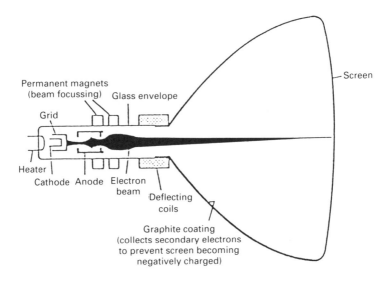

Figure 4–1 Schematic of a single electron 'gun' CRT.

The CRT consists of an evacuated glass envelope, inside which are positioned an electron 'gun' and beam focusing and beam deflection systems. The inside surface of the screen is coated with a phosphor which 'luminesces' when the electron beam strikes it. Control of the electron beam will produce 'pictures' that can be viewed by the pilot.

The electron gun consists of an indirectly heated cathode biased negatively with respect to the screen, a cylindrical grid surrounding the cathode, and two (sometimes three) anodes. When the cathode is heated, negative electrons are liberated and in passing through the anodes they are squeezed to form a beam by negative potential applied to the anodes. Modulation of the beam is also effected by one of the anodes, ie it can be controlled in size (focus) and cut off.

In order to 'trace out' a luminescent display, it is necessary for the spot of light to be deflected about the horizontal and vertical axes, and for this purpose a beam-deflection system is also provided. Deflection systems can be either electrostatic or electro-magnetic, but in aircraft display systems, the electro-magnetic method is used.

An electron beam can be forced to move when subjected to electro-magnetic fields acting across the space within the tube, and coils are therefore mounted around the neck of the tube and are configured so that fields are produced horizontally (X-axis fields) and vertically (Y-axis fields). The coils are connected to the signal sources whose variables are to be displayed, and the electron beam can be deflected to the left or right, up and down, or along some resulting direction depending on the polarities produced by the coils, and on whether one alone is energised, or both are energised simultaneously.

4.3 Colour CRT Displays

Colour CRTs are also used in weather radar display units. In these units, weather data is integrated with the other data displays. The video data received from a radar antenna corresponds to the 'sweeping' movement of the antenna as it is driven by its motor. In a colour display indicator, the scanning of data is somewhat similar to that adopted in the tube of a television receiver, ie 'raster' scanning in horizontal lines, and the data received is converted into an X-Y co-ordinate format. This format also permits the display of other data in areas of the screen where weather data is not displayed. The other scanning technique is called 'stroke' scanning which produces the symbols and alpha-numeric data also presented on the same screen, and this will be described later.

Each time the radar transmitter transmits a pulse, the receiver begins receiving return echoes from 'targets' at varying distances from the transmitter. This data is digitized to provide output levels in binary-coded form, and is supplied to the indicator on two data lines (one data line can supply two states, and two data lines can supply four states).

The binary-coded data can represent four conditions corresponding to the level of return echoes which, in turn, are related to the weather conditions prevailing at the range in nautical miles preselected on the indicator. The data is stored in memories which, on being addressed as the CRT is scanned, will, at the proper time, permit the weather conditions to be displayed. The four conditions are displayed as follows:

Blank screen: Zero, or low-level returns.

Green: Low returns (lowest rainfall rate)

Yellow: Moderate returns (moderate rainfall rate)

Red: Strong returns (high density rainfall rate)

4.4 Colour Generation

A colour CRT has three electron guns, each of which can direct an electron beam at the screen which is coated with different kinds of phosphor
material. The colours are a function of the type of phosphor, the electron
guns are virtually identical and it is the method of control of the three
beams that determines which of the phosphors are energised.

The phosphors luminesce in each of three colours, red, green and blue.
The screen is divided into a large number of small areas or dots, each of
which contains a phosphor of each kind as shown in Fig 4-2. The smaller
the dot size, the better the resolution of the final picture, within the
limitations of manufacturing tolerances.

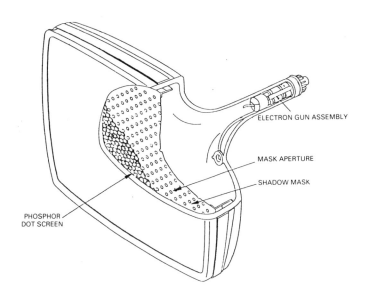

Figure 4–2 A Colour CRT.

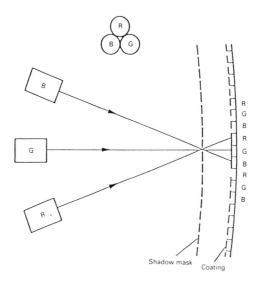

Figure 4–3 Shadow Mask Principle in a Colour CRT.

The beam from a particular gun must be made only to strike screen elements of one colour, and to achieve this in aircraft type CRTs, a perforated steel sheet called a 'shadow mask' is very accurately placed adjacent to the coating of the screen. The perforations are arranged in a regular pattern, and their number depends on the size of the screen; 330,000 is a typical number.

Beams from the three guns pass through the perforations in the mask and they cause the phosphor dots in the coating to luminesce in the appropriate colour, ie the red gun emission will pass through the holes in the shadow mask that are in line with the red phosphor dots, and only red will luminesce. After a full raster sweep of the screen, the eye will perceive a totally red screen as a function of the persistence of vision by the human eye.

For colours other than red, green and blue, control of the electron beams by independent circuitry can effect a kind of 'electronic paint mixing' producing the required colour.

Returning to weather radar displays, the data readout from the memory, apart from being presented at the appropriate location of the CRT screen, must also be displayed in the colours corresponding to the weather conditions prevailing. In order to achieve this, the data is decoded to produce outputs which, after amplification, will turn on the required colour guns.

The output from the memory, which were in two-bit binary, is supplied to a data decoder whose output is three-bit words corresponding to the colours to be displayed, as shown in Fig 4-4.

241

Outputs to guns			
B₁ Green	B₀ Blue	B₂ Red	Resulting Colours
1	1	1	Black (off)
0	0	0	White
0	0	1	Yellow
0	1	1	Red
1	0	0	Light blue
1	0	1	Green

Figure 4–4 Three-bit words determines the colours.

The three-bit word outputs from the data decoder are then applied to a colour decoder and primary decoder circuit, and this in turn provides three outputs, each of which corresponds to one of the colour guns as shown in the data flow in Fig 4-5.

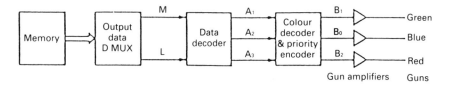

Figure 4–5 Data Flow for Selection of Colour Guns.

The 'Low' state outputs turn on the guns, and it can be seen from Fig 4-4 how simultaneous gun operation produces other colours from a mix of the basic colours. Figure 4-6 shows a typical weather data display together with associated alpha-numeric data, namely ranges in nm, and the operating mode, which in this case is **WX** signifying 'weather' mode.

4.5 Alpha-numeric Displays

The display of data, in alpha-numeric and symbolic form is wide-ranging. For example, in a weather radar indicator is it usually only required for range information and which modes are selected, while in systems designed to perform functions within the realm of flight management, a very much higher proportion of information must be 'written' on the screens of the appropriate display unit.

242

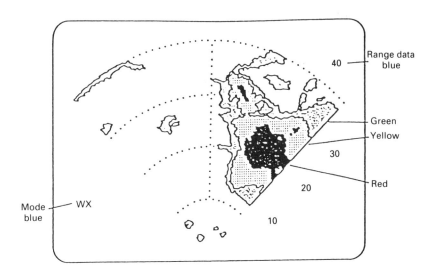

Figure 4–6 Weather Data Display.

This is accomplished in a manner similar to that adopted for the display of weather data, but additional memory circuits, decoders, character and symbol generator circuits are required.

Raster scanning is also used, but where datum marks, arcs (eg engine instrument scales) are to be displayed, a 'stroke pulse' method of scanning is used. The position of each character on the screen is predetermined and stored in a memory.

Figure 4-7 illustrates how the letters WX and the number 40 are formed on the screen of the weather radar display in Fig 4-6. One line of dots is written at a time for the area in which the characters are to be displayed, and it can be seen in Fig 4-7 that seven image lines are required to write the complete characters and/or row of characters, and they have a three dot spacing.

It will be noted also from Fig 4-6 that the mode indication (WX) is displayed in blue, so only the blue electron gun is active in producing these letters.

This particular CRT permits the display of 12 rows each of 32 characters. The CRT display units of more comprehensive electronic instrument systems operate on the same fundamental principles as those just described, but in applying them, more extensive microprocessor circuitry is required in order to process and display far greater amounts of data.

There are symbol generators which supply signals to the beam deflection and colour gun circuits of the CRT, such that its beams are raster and stroke scanned to present the data at the relevant parts of the screen, and in the required colour.

243

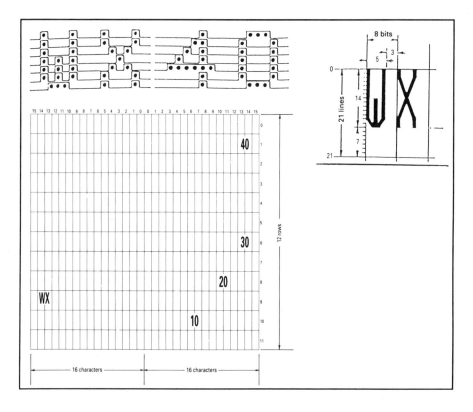

Figure 4–7 Alpha-numeric Display.

The displayed data is in two basic forms: fixed and moving. Fixed data relate in particular to such presentations as symbols, scale markings, names of systems, datum marks, names of parameters being measured, etc. Moving data are in the majority, as they measure changes occurring in the measurement of all parameters essential for in-flight management. The changes are indicated by the movement of symbolic pointers, index marks, digital counter presentations, and system status messages and there are, of course, more.

4.6 Flight Deck Displays

The flight deck displays as shown by the CRTs, are displays necessary for the in-flight operation of the aircraft and its systems, and also for their maintenance. The data is processed by high storage capacity computers, and originates as signals (analogue and/or digital) generated by sensors associated with each individual major system in the aircraft.

The information passed from sensors to displays, falls into two main areas:

(a) Flight Path and Navigational.

(b) Engine and Airframe systems operation.

Appropriate electronic display systems are therefore designed for each of these areas and are known respectively as an Electronic Flight Instrument System (EFIS) and either an Electronic Centralized Aircraft Monitor (ECAM) system, or an Engine Indicating and Crew Alerting System (EICAS). See Fig 4-8 for a flight deck layout of the CRTs, in this example, the Airbus A320.

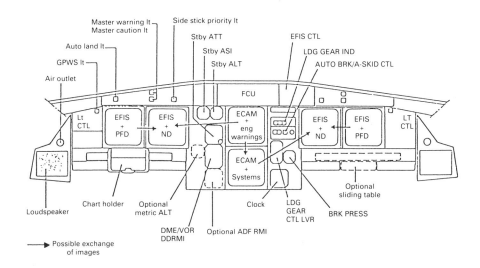

Figure 4–8 EFIS and ECAM CRTs on the Flight Deck of the Airbus A320.

The EFIS installation is made up of left (Captain) and right (First Officer) systems. Each system is made up of two display units. There are certain differences in the terminology used in some modern all glass cockpits; some displays are called Electronic Attitude Director Indicator (EADI) and Electronic Horizontal Situation Indicator (EHSI) whilst the Airbus A320 display (Fig 4-8) is labelled PFD (Primary Flight Display) and ND (Navigation Display).

The flight deck display system also has a control panel, a symbol generator (SG) and a remote light sensor unit. A third (centre) SG is also incorporated so that drive signals may be switched either to the left or the right display units in the event of failure of the corresponding SGs. In

Fig 4-8, the arrows drawn between the EFIS and ECAM displays show how these displays may be switched.

As far as electrical systems are concerned, the operational monitoring is handled either by an ECAM system or by EICAS.

The main presentations of ECAM, EICAS and EFIS will now be described.

4.7 The ECAM and EICAS Systems

The ECAM system (Electronic Centralized Aircraft Monitoring) was introduced in the Airbus A310, and the EICAS system (Engine Indicating and Crew Alerting System) was introduced in Boeing 757 and 767 aircraft.

In respect of EICAS, engine operating data is displayed on its CRT units, thereby eliminating the need for conventional instruments. The data, as well as those relevant to other systems, are not necessarily always on display, but in the event of malfunctions occurring at any time, the flight crew's attention is drawn to them by the automatic display of messages in colours appropriate to the degree of urgency.

The ECAM system on the other hand, displays systems' operation in CHECKLIST and SCHEMATIC form, and as this was a concept based on the view that engine data needs to be displayed during the whole of a flight, traditional instruments were retained in the Airbus A310. In later aircraft, ie, A320, the ECAM system displays engine data also on one of the CRT display units. Figure 4-9 shows a schematic of the ECAM system.

4.8 The CRT Display Units

Units are mounted side by side so that the left-hand unit is dedicated to information in message form on systems' status, warnings and corrective action required, while the right-hand unit is dedicated to associated information in diagrammatic form (sometimes referred to as synoptic format).

There are four modes of display, three of which are automatically selected and referred to as: Flight Phase-Related, Advisory and Failure Related. The fourth mode is manual and permits the selection of diagrams relating to any of the aircraft's systems for routine checking and also the selection of status messages. The selections are made on the ECAM control panel. (See Fig 4-10.)

ELECTRONIC INSTRUMENT DISPLAY SYSTEMS

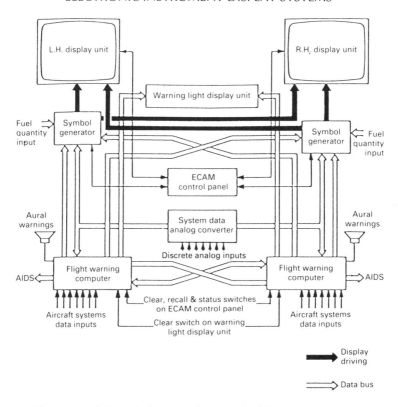

Figure 4-9 Schematic Functional Diagram of the ECAM system.

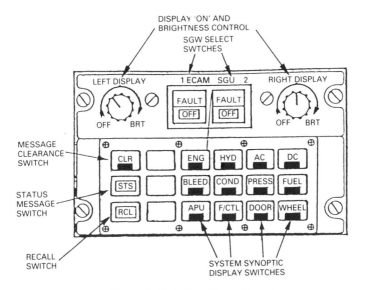

Figure 4-10 ECAM Control Panel.

On the control panel all switches, with the exception of those for display control, are of the push-button, illuminated caption type. Briefly, the functions are:

1 **SGU selector switches**. Control the respective symbol generator units.

2 **Synoptic display switches**. Permit individual selection of synoptic diagrams corresponding to each of the 12 systems.

3 **CLR switch**. Light illuminated white whenever a warning or status message is displayed on the left-hand display unit. Pressed to clear messages.

4 **STS switch**. Permits manual selection of an aircraft status message if no warning is displayed. Status message is suppressed if a warning occurs or if the CLR switch is pressed.

5 **RCL switch**. Enables previously cleared warning messages to be recalled provided the failure conditions which initiated them still exist. If a failure no longer exists the message 'NO WARNING PRESENT' is displayed on the left-hand display unit.

In normal operation the automatic flight phase-related mode is used, and in this case the displays are appropriate to the current phase of aircraft operation, ie pre-flight, take-off, climb, cruise, descent, approach, and after landing.

An example of a pre-flight phase is shown in Fig 4-11; the left-hand display unit shows an advisory memo mode, and the right-hand unit shows a diagram of the aircraft's fuselage doors and arming of the escape slides deployment system.

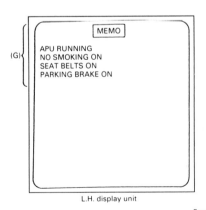
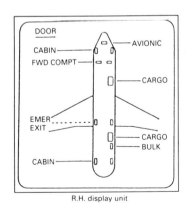

L.H. display unit   R.H. display unit

Examples: Doors locked. Door symbols green and name of door white.
Doors unlocked: Door symbols and name of door amber

Figure 4–11 Pre-flight phase-related mode display.

The failure-related mode takes precedence over the other two modes and the manual mode. An example of a failure-related mode is shown in Fig 4-12. In this case there is problem associated with the number one generator. The left-hand display unit shows the affected system in message form, and in red or amber depending on the degree of urgency, and also the corrective action required in blue.

At the same time, a diagram is displayed on the right-hand display unit. When the number one generator has been switched off, the light in the relevant push-button switch on the flight deck overhead panel is illuminated, and simultaneously, the blue instruction on the left-hand display unit changes to white.

The diagram on the right-hand display unit is also 'redrawn' to depict by means of an amber line that the number one generator is no longer available, and that number two generator is supplying the busbar system.

This is displayed in green, which is the normal operating colour of the displays. After corrective action has been taken, the message on the left-hand unit can be removed by operating a 'clear' button switch located on the ECAM control panel.

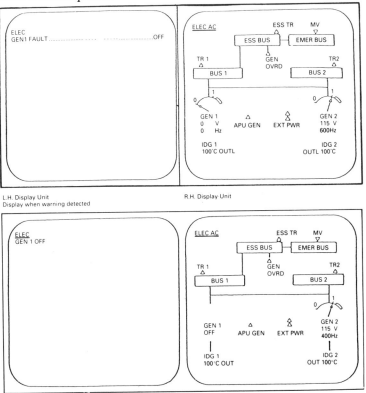

Figure 4–12 ECAM Displays showing number one generator fault.

In the event of a single system malfunction, by convention such warnings are signified by under-lining the system title displayed. In Fig 4-11, the fault is electrical in the AC generator and ELEC is shown underlined in the left-hand display and ELEC AC is shown underlined in the right-hand display.

In cases where a failure can affect other sub-systems, the title of the sub-system is shown 'boxed', as shown in Fig 4-13. Warnings and the associated lights are cleared by means of CLEAR push-button switches either on the ECAM control panel or the warning light display panel.

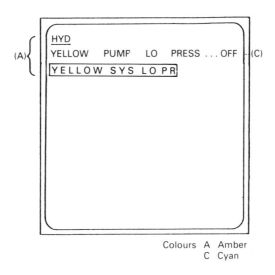

Colours A Amber
C Cyan

Figure 4–13 Display of Failure Affecting a sub-system.

Status messages, which are also displayed on the left-hand display unit, provide the flight crew with an operational summary of the aircraft's condition, possible downgrading of autoland capability, and as far as possible, indications of the aircraft status following all failures except those that do not affect the flight. An example display is shown in Fig 4-14.

System testing. Each flight warning computer of the system is equipped with a monitoring module which automatically checks data acquisition and processing modules, memories, and internal power supplies as soon as the aircraft's main power supply is applied to the system. A power-on test routine is also carried out for correct operation of the symbol generator units. During the test, the display units remain blank.

In the event of failure of the data acquisition and processing modules, or of any of the warning light display panel, a FAILURE WARNING

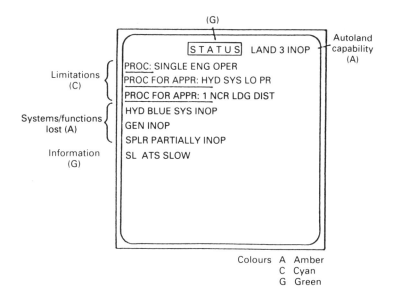

Figure 4–14 Example of a Status Display.

SYSTEM LIGHT on the panel is illuminated. Failure of a computer causes a corresponding annunciator light on the maintenance panel captioned FWC FAULT to illuminate. An SG unit failure causes a FAULT caption on the appropriate push-button switch on the system control panel to illuminate.

4.9 The EICAS System comprises two display units, a control panel, and two computers supplied with analog and digital signals from engine and system sensors as shown in the schematic in Fig 4-15.

Operating in conjunction with the system are discrete caution and warning lights, standby engine indicators and a remotely-located panel for selecting maintenance data displays. The system provides the flight crew with information on primary engine parameters (full-time), with secondary engine parameters and advisory/caution/warning alert messages displayed as required.

4.10 Display units provide a wide variety of information relevant to engine operation, and the operation of other automated systems. The display units are mounted one above the other, as in Fig 4-16.

The upper unit displays the primary engine parameters N_1, speed, EGT, and warning and caution messages. In some cases this unit can also display EPR depending on the type of engines installed. The lower unit

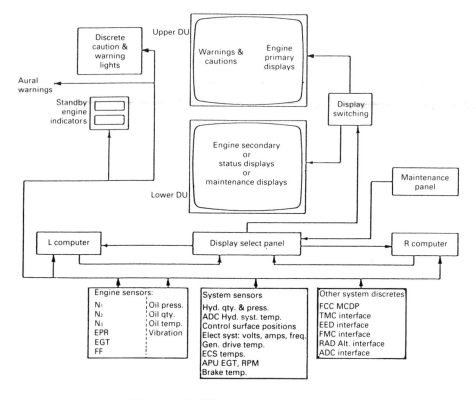

Figure 4–15 EICAS functional schematic.

displays secondary engine parameters, ie N_2 speed, fuel flow, oil quantity, pressure and temperature, and engine vibration. In addition, the status of non-engine systems, ie flight control surface position, hydraulic system, APU, etc. It can also be displayed together with aircraft configuration and maintenance data.

Referring to Fig 4-16, the row of 'V's shown on the upper display unit only appear when secondary information is being displayed on the lower unit.

Seven colours are produced by the CRTs and they are used as follows:

White   All scales, normal operating range of pointers, digital readouts.

Red   Warning messages, maximum operating limit marks on scales, digital readouts.

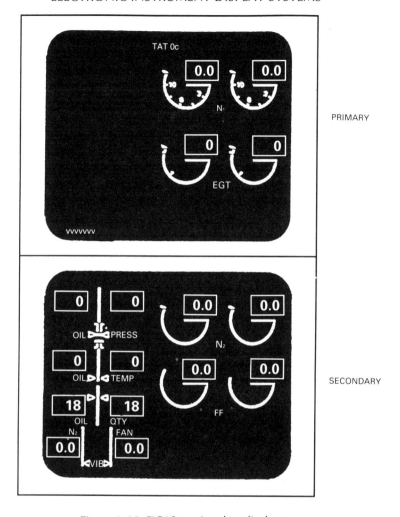

Figure 4–16 EICAS: engine data displays.

Green	Thrust mode readout and selected EPR/N_1 speed marks or target cursors.
Blue	Testing of system only.
Yellow	Caution and advisory messages, caution limit marks on scales, digital readouts.
Magenta	During in-flight engine starting, and for cross-bleed messages.
Cyan	Names of all parameters being measured (eg N_1 oil pressure, TAT, etc) and status marks or cues.

The displays are selected according to an appropriate display selection mode.

Display Modes. EICAS is designed to categorize displays and alerts according to function and usage, for this purpose there are three modes of displaying information:

1. Operational
2. Status
3. Maintenance.

Modes 1 and 2 are selected by the flight crew on the display select panel, while mode 3 is selected on the maintenance panel which is used by engineers only.

4.11 Operational mode. This mode displays the engine operating information and any alerts required to be actioned by the crew in flight. Normally only the upper display unit presents information, the lower one remains blank and can be selected to display secondary information as and when required.

4.12 Status mode. When selected this mode displays data to determine the dispatch readiness of the aircraft. The display (Fig 4-17) shows

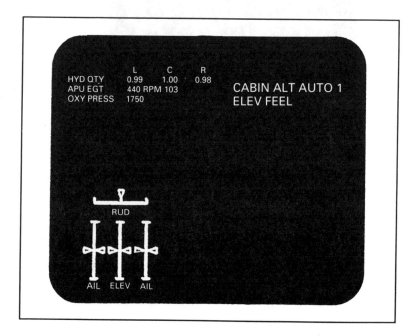

Figure 4–17 Status Mode Display.

position of flight control surfaces against vertical scales (rudder against a horizontal scale). Other items are shown such as selected sub-systems and equipment status. Selection is normally done on the ground as part of the pre-flight checks, or just before shut-down to help the crew complete the aircraft technical log.

4.13 Maintenance mode. This mode provides maintenance engineers with information in five different display formats to aid them in trouble-shooting and verification testing of major sub systems. The displays are presented on the lower display unit. They are NOT available in flight.

4.14 Display select panel. This permits control of EICAS functions and displays and can be used both in flight and on the ground. It is normally located on the centre pedestal of an aircraft's flight deck. See Fig 4-18. Display select panel controls are as follows:

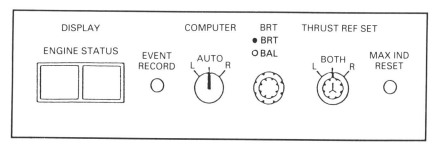

Figure 4–18 EICAS display select panel.

1. **Engine display switch.** This is of the momentary-push type for removing or presenting the display of secondary information on the lower display unit.

2. **Status display switch.** Also of the momentary-push type, this is used to display the status mode information as already described, see Fig 4-14 for an example.

3. **Event record switch.** This is a momentary-push type and is used in the air, or on the ground, to activate the recording of fault data relevant to the environmental control system, electrical power, hydraulic system, performance of APU. Normally, if any malfunction occurs in a system, it is recorded automatically (called an '**auto event**') and stored in memory of the EICAS computer. The push switch also enables the flight crew to record a suspect malfunction for storage, and is called a '**manual event**'. The relevant data can only be retrieved from memory and displayed when the aircraft is on the ground and by operating switches on the maintenance control panel.

4. **Computer select switch.** In the AUTO position it selects the left, or primary, computer and automatically switches to the other computer in the event of failure. The other positions are for the manual selection of left or right computers.

5. **Display brightness control.** The inner knob controls the intensity of the two displays, and the outer knob controls the brightness balance between the two displays.

6. **Thrust reference set switch.** Pulling and rotating the inner knob positions the reference cursor on the thrust indicator display (either EPR or N_1) for the engine(s) selected by the cursor.

7. **Maximum indicator reset switch.** If any one of the measured parameters, eg oil pressure, EGT, should exceed normal operating limits, this will be automatically alerted on the display units. The purpose of the reset switch is to clear the alerts from the display when the excess limits no longer exist.

4.15 Alert messages. The system continuously monitors a large number of inputs from engine and airframe system sensors (over 400) and will detect any malfunctioning of systems. If this should occur, then appropriate messages are generated and displayed on the UPPER display unit in a sequence corresponding to the level of urgency of action that has to be taken; up to eleven messages can be displayed, and at the following levels:

Level A   Warning requiring immediate corrective action. Displayed in red. Master warning lights are also illuminated, and an aural warning (eg fire bell) from a central warning system is given.

Level B   Cautions requiring immediate crew awareness and possible action. Displayed in amber, and also by message caution lights. An aural tone is also repeated twice.

Level C   Advisories requiring crew awareness, also displayed in amber. No caution lights or aural tones are associated with this level.

The messages appear on the top line at the left of the display screen as shown in Fig 4-19. In order to differentiate between a caution and an advisory, an advisory message is indented one space to the right.

The master warning and caution lights are located adjacent to the display units together with a Cancel switch and a Recall switch. Pushing the Cancel switch removes only the caution and advisory messages from the display. Warning messages cannot be cancelled. The Recall switch is used to bring back the caution and advisory messages into the display, at the same time, the word RECALL appears at the bottom of the display.

Figure 4–19 Alert Message Levels.

A message is automatically removed from the display when the associated condition no longer exists. In this case, messages which appear below the deleted one each move up a line.

When a new fault occurs, its associated message is inserted on the appropriate line of the display. This may cause 'older' messages to move down one line.

If there are more messages than can be displayed at one time, the whole list forms a 'page', and the lowest message is removed and a page number appears in white on the lower right side of the list. If there is an additional page of messages it can be displayed by pushing the Cancel switch. Warning messages are carried over from the previous page.

4.16 Display unit failure. If the lower display unit should fail when secondary information is being displayed on it, an amber alert message appears at the top left of the upper display unit, and the information is transferred to it as shown in Fig 4-20. The format of this display is referred to as COMPACT, and may be removed by pressing the ENGINE switch on the display select panel. (Fig 4-16). Failure of a display unit causes the function of the display select panel STATUS switch to be inhibited so that the status page format cannot be displayed.

4.17 Display select panel failure. If this panel fails the advisory message 'EICAS CONTROL PANEL' appears at the top left of the upper display unit together with the primary information, and the secondary information automatically appears on the lower display unit. The cancel/recall switches do not operate in this failure condition.

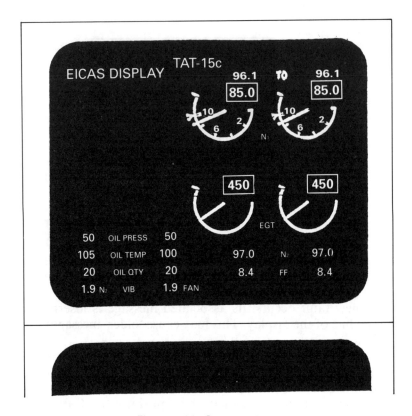

Figure 4–20 Compact Format.

4.18 Standby engine indicator. This indicator provides primary engine information in the event that a total loss of the EICAS displays occurs (see Fig 4-21). The information relates to N_1 and N_2 speeds and EGT, the displays are of the LCD type. Operating limit values are also displayed.

The display control switch has two positions ON and AUTO. In the ON position, the displays are permanently on. In the AUTO position the internal circuits are functional, but the displays will automatically be presented when the EICAS displays are lost due to failure of both displays, or failure of both computers. There is a test switch which selects either of two power supplies.

4.19 Maintenance control panel. This panel is used by maintenance engineers for the purpose of displaying data stored in system computer memories during flight or ground operations. (See Fig 4-22).

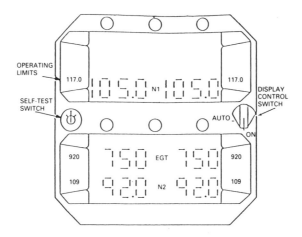

Figure 4–21 Standby Engine Indicator.

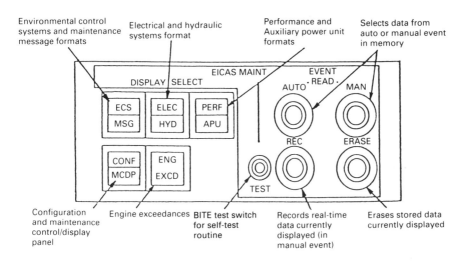

Figure 4–22 Maintenance control panel.

When a switch is activated, a corresponding maintenance display page appears on the lower display unit screen. The pages are listed together with two example displays in Fig 4-23. The upper display unit displays data in the compact format (see Fig 4-20) and has the message PARKING BRAKE at the top of the screen.

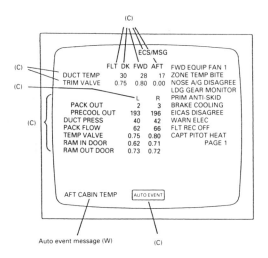

Figure 4–23 Examples of maintenance mode displays.

System failures which have occurred in flight and have been automatically recorded (auto event) in computer memory, and also data entered as a 'manual event', can be retrieved for display by means of the 'event record' switch on the maintenance control panel (Fig 4-23).

A self test of the system can be done only when the aircraft is on the ground and the parking brake on. During the test, the master caution and warning lights and aural devices are activated, and the standby engine indicator is turned on if its control switch is at AUTO.

The message TEST IN PROGRESS appears at the top of left of the display unit screens and remains in view while the test is in progress. On satisfactory completion of the test, the message TEST OK will appear. If a computer or display unit failure has occurred, the message TEST FAIL will appear followed by messages indicating which of the units has failed.

A test may be terminated by pressing the TEST switch a second time or, **if it's safe to do so**, by releasing the parking brake. The display units revert to their normal primary and secondary information displays.

4.20 The EFIS System

The EFIS system (Electronic Flight Instrument System) is fully integrated with digital computer-based navigation systems, and utilizes colour CRT type of EADI (Electronic Attitude Director Indicator) and EHSI (Electronic Horizontal Situation Indicator). The system is far more sophisticated than former flight director systems, not only in terms of physical construction, but also in the extent to which it can present attitude and navigational data to the flight crew.

As in the case of conventional flight director systems, a complete EFIS installation is made up of left (Captain) and right (First Officer) systems (see Fig 4-8). Each system in turn comprises two display units: an EADI and EHSI, a control panel, a symbol generator (SG) and remote light sensor unit. A third (centre) SG is also incorporated so that it drive signals may be switched to either left or right display units in the event of failure of the corresponding SGs.

The signal switching is accomplished within the left and right SGs, using electro-mechanical relays powered from the aircraft's DC power supply via pilot-controlled switches. The interface between the EFIS units and data busses and other systems is shown in Fig 4-24 with the acronyms and abbreviations at Fig 4-25.

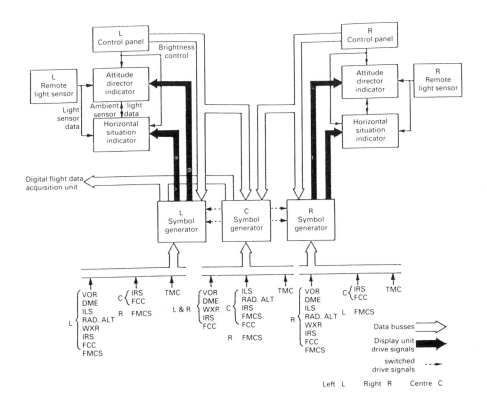

Figure 4–24 EFIS units and signal interfacing.

VOR	Very high frequency Omnidirectional Range
DME	Distance Measuring Equipment
ILS	Instrument Landing System
RAD.ALT	Radio Altimeter
WXR	Weather Radar transceiver
IRS	Inertial Reference System
FCC	Flight Control Computer
FMCS	Flight Management Computer System
TMC	Thrust Management Computer

Figure 4–25 Inputs to data busses: Acronyms and Abbreviations.

In a typical EFIS system, six colours are assigned for the display of the many symbols, failure annunciators, messages and other alpha-numeric information and are as follows: (Note: there are 7 colours in the EICAS system).

White   Display of present situation information.

Green   Display of present situation information where contrast with white symbols is required, or for data having lower priority than the white symbols.

Magenta   All 'Fly to' information such as flight director commands, deviation pointers, active flight path lines.

Cyan   Sky shading on an EADI and for low-priority information such as non-active flight plan map data.

Yellow   Ground shading on an EADI, caution information display such as failure warning flags, limit and alert annunciators and fault messages.

Red   For display of heaviest precipitation levels as detected by weather radar.

Symbol generators (SGs). Provide the analog, discrete and digital signal interfaces between an aircraft's systems, the display units and the control panel, and they also perform symbol generation, system monitoring, power control and the main control functions of the EFIS overall. The interfacing between the computer card modules of an SG is shown in Fig 4-26.

4.21 Remote Light Sensor. There is a photodiode which responds to flight deck ambient light conditions and automatically adjusts the brightness of the CRT displays to a compatible level.

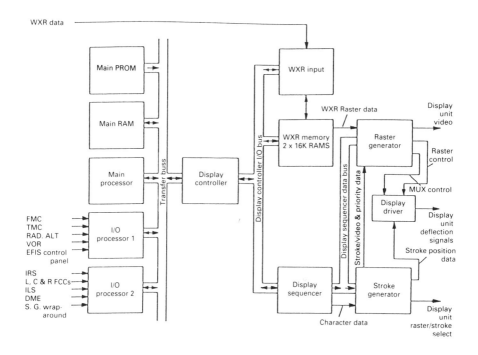

Figure 4–26 Symbol Generator and Computer Card Interfacing.

4.22 The Electronic Attitude Director Indicator (EADI) (Boeing system, but similar to the Airbus A310 Primary Flight Display PFD) displays traditional pitch and roll attitude indications against a raster-scanned background, and as indicated in Fig 4-27, the upper half is in cyan and the lower half in yellow.

Attitude data is provided by an Inertia Reference System (IRS). Also displayed are flight director commands, localizer and glide-slope deviation, selected airspeed, ground speed, Automatic Flight Control System (AFCS) and auto-throttle system modes. Also radio altitude and decision height.

Figure 4-27 shows a representation of an automatically controlled approach-to-land situation, together with the colours of the symbols and alpha-numeric data produced via the EFIS control panel and SGs.

263

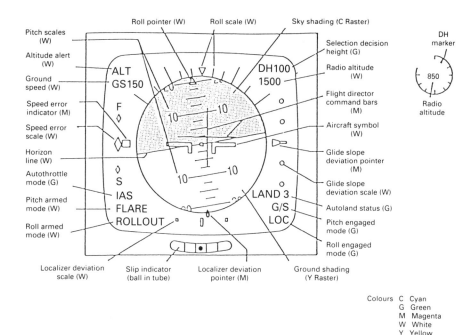

Figure 4–27 EADI Display showing an automatically controlled approach.

The auto-land status, pitch, roll-armed and engage modes are selected on the AFCS control panel, and the decision height is selected on the EFIS control panels. Radio altitude is digitally displayed during an approach when the aircraft is between 2500 and 1000 feet above the ground. When the aircraft is below 1000 feet, the display automatically changes to a white circular scale calibrated in increments of 100 feet, and the selected decision height is then displayed as a magenta-coloured marker on the outer scale.

The radio altitude also appears within the scale as a digital readout. As the aircraft descends, segments of the altitude scale are simultaneously erased so that the scale continuously diminishes in length in an anti-clockwise direction.

At the selected decision height plus 50 feet, an aural alert chime sounds at an increasing rate until decision height is reached. At the decision height, the circular scale changes from white to amber, and the marker changes from magenta to amber, both the scale and the marker also flash for several seconds.

A reset button is provided on the control panel and when pressed, it stops the flashing and causes the scale and marker to change from amber back to their normal colour. The EFIS control panel is shown in Fig 4-28.

If during the approach the aircraft deviates beyond the normal ILS glide slope and/or localizer limits (and when below 500 feet above the ground), the flight crew are alerted by the respective deviation pointers changing colour from white to amber, the pointers also start flashing. This alert condition ceases when the deviations return to within their normal limits.

4.23 The Electronic Horizontal Situation Indicator (EHSI) (Boeing system) (Similar to the ND – Navigation display – Airbus system), presents a selectable, moving (dynamic) colour display of flight progress and plan view orientation. Four principle display modes may be selected on the EFIS control panel, see Fig 4-28.

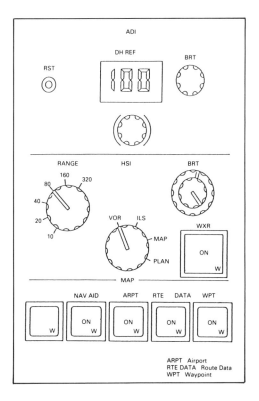

Figure 4–28 EFIS Control Panel.

Referring to Fig 4-28, the following list identifies the switch functions for both sections, EADI and EHSI:

Switch	Function
EADI section:	
BRT	Controls levels of display brightness.
DH SET	Setting of decision height.
RST	Manually resets decision height circuits after aircraft has passed through decision height.
EHSI section:	
RANGE	Selects range for displayed Weather Radar display.
MODE SELECT	Selects display appropriate to mode required.
BRT	Outer knob controls main display brightness: inner knob controls Weather Radar display.
WXR	When pushed in, Weather radar data displayed during all modes except PLAN.
MAP switches	Used in MAP mode, and when pushed in they cause their placarded data to be displayed. (Illuminates in white).

The four modes available for display by the EHSI are MAP, PLAN, ILS, and VOR. In Fig 4-29 is shown the normally used MAP mode display which in conjunction with the flight plan data programmed into a flight management computer, displays information against a moving map background with all elements positioned to a common scale.

The symbol representing the aircraft is at the lower part of the display and an arc of the compass scale, or rose, covering 30° on either side of the instantaneous track is at the upper part of the display.

Heading information is supplied by the appropriate Inertia Reference System (IRS) and compass rose is automatically referenced to Magnetic North (via a crew-operated MAG/TRUE selector switch) when between the latitudes 73°N and 65°S, and True North when outside these latitudes. When the selector switch is set at TRUE, the compass rose is referenced to True North regardless of latitude.

Tuned VOR/DME stations, airports and their identification letters, and the flight plan entered into the flight management system computer are all correctly orientated with respect to the positions and track of the aircraft, and to the range scale (nm/in) selected on the EFIS control panel. Weather radar 'returns' may also be selected and displayed when required, at the *same scale* and orientation as the map.

Indications of other data such as wind speed and direction, lateral and

ELECTRONIC INSTRUMENT DISPLAY SYSTEMS

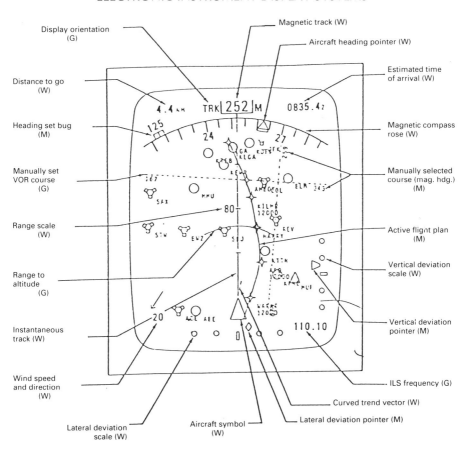

Display orientation (G)

Magnetic track (W)

Aircraft heading pointer (W)

Estimated time of arrival (W)

Distance to go (W)

Heading set bug (M)

Magnetic compass rose (W)

Manually set VOR course (G)

Manually selected course (mag. hdg.) (M)

Range scale (W)

Active flight plan (M)

Range to altitude (G)

Vertical deviation scale (W)

Instantaneous track (W)

Vertical deviation pointer (M)

Wind speed and direction (W)

ILS frequency (G)

Curved trend vector (W)

Lateral deviation scale (W)

Aircraft symbol (W)

Lateral deviation pointer (M)

Symbols:

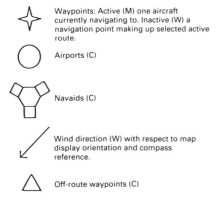

Waypoints: Active (M) one aircraft currently navigating to. Inactive (W) a navigation point making up selected active route.

Airports (C)

Navaids (C)

Wind direction (W) with respect to map display orientation and compass reference.

Off-route waypoints (C)

Colours C Cyan
         G Green
         M Magenta
         W White

Figure 4–29 EHSI in MAP Mode.

vertical deviations from the selected flight profile, distance to waypoint, etc, are also displayed.

The MAP display also provides two types of predictive information. One combines current ground speed and lateral acceleration into a prediction of the path over the ground to be followed over the following 30, 60 and 90 seconds. This is displayed by a curved track vector, and since a time cue is included, the flight crew are able to judge distance in terms of TIME.

The second prediction, which is displayed by a range to altitude arc, shows where the aircraft will be when a selected target altitude is reached.

In the PLAN mode, a static map background with active route data orientated to True North is displayed in the lower part of the EHSI display, together with the display of track and heading information as shown in Fig 4-30.

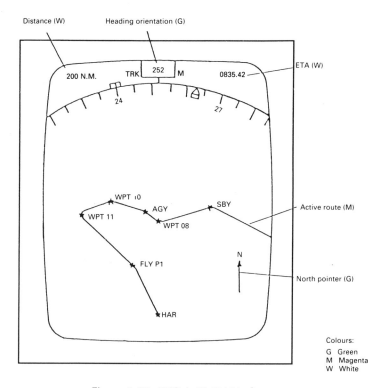

Figure 4–30 EHSI in PLAN Mode.

Any changes to the route are selected at the keyboard of the flight management system display unit, and appear on the EHSI display so that they can be checked by the flight crew before they are entered into the flight management computer.

The VOR and ILS modes present a compass rose (either expanded or full) with heading orientation display as shown in Fig 4-29. Selected range, wind information and system source annunciation are also displayed. If selected on the EFIS control panel, weather radar returns may also be displayed, although only when the mode selected presents an expanded compass rose, see Fig 4-31.

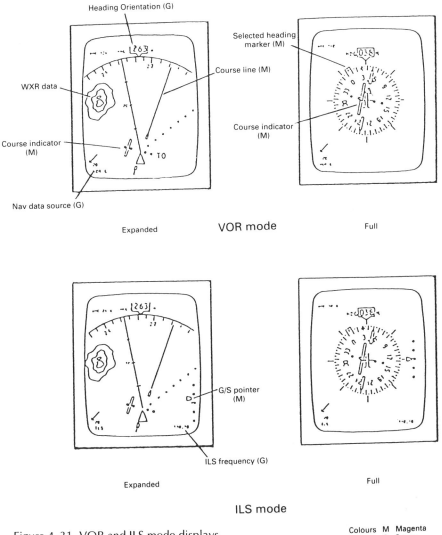

Figure 4–31 VOR and ILS mode displays.
Weather returns are only available when the compass rose is in expanded format.

Colours M Magenta
G Green
All other symbols white

Failure annunciation: Failure of data signals from such systems as the ILS and radio altimeter are displayed on each EADI and EHSI in the form of yellow flags 'painted' at specific matrix locations on the CRT screens. In addition, fault messages may also be displayed: for example, if the associated flight management computer and weather radar range disagree with the control panel range data, the discrepancy message –

'WXR/MAP RANGE DISAGREE' appears on the EHSI.

Data source selection: In the type of system described, means are provided whereby the pilots can, independently of each other, connect their respective display units to alternative sources of input data, eg left or right Air Data Computers (ADCs) flight management computers, flight control computers, and standby Inertia Reference System (IRS).

Each pilot has a panel of selector switches arranged as shown in Fig 4-32. The upper rotary type switch connects either the left, centre or right flight control computer to the EADI as a source of attitude data. The other switches are illuminated push type and are guarded to prevent accidental switching. In the normal operating configuration of systems they remain blank, and when activated they are illuminated white.

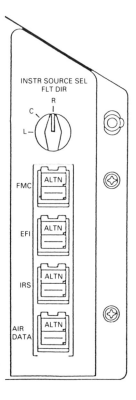

Figure 4–32 Source selector switch panel, normally blank, but when activated are illuminated white.

Display of air data: In a number of EFIS applications, the display of such air data as altitude, airspeed and vertical speed is provided in the conventional manner, ie separate indicators servo-operated from ADCs are mounted adjacent to the EFIS display units in the former basic 'T' arrangement. With continued development of display technology, however, CRTs with much bigger screen areas have already been produced and fitted to Boeing 747–400 aircraft, such displays make it unnecessary to provide conventional primary air data instruments for each pilot.

Flight Management System

Introduction

The Flight Management System (FMS) combines the data from various aircraft navigation systems with inputs from the Air Data Computers to provide a centralised control for navigation and performance management. This chapter is intended only to give you an overview of the system and its capabilities, by far the best way to learn to operate the system is in the aircraft.

FMS data can be used purely as advisory information or can be directed to the autopilot to steer the aircraft. A large database of navigational facilities and routes is stored and processed in the Flight Management Computer (FMC). Data is entered and displayed in the cockpit on a CDU.

The FMS CDU

The CDU consists of a monochrome CRT screen and a keyboard for data entry. The central part of the screen is used to display selected data. Below the data block is a 'scratchpad area' where data that has been keyed in but not entered is displayed and messages can be shown.

FMS Inputs

The FMS continuously computes the aircraft position from data from the Inertial Reference System (IN platforms), VOR, DME and localiser information. When AUTO is selected on the VHF nav controller, the system will tune its own DME frequencies according to the information in the navigational database and will place most reliance on a DME/DME crosscut. DME/VOR is the next most reliable followed by VOR/VOR. When out of range of radio facilities, inertial information is used to determine the position.

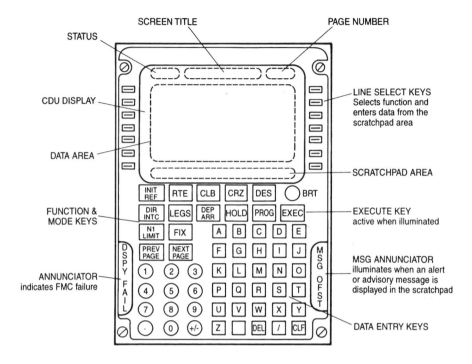

Figure 4–33 Flight Management Computer Cockpit
Display Unit.

LNAV and VNAV

Pre-determined or custom-made routes in the database can be selected
and flown. This is known as LNAV, short for Lateral Navigation. LNAV
is available from take-off to localiser capture. Vertical Navigation or
VNAV controls the altitude of the aircraft and the climb and descent
profiles. A stored company route will contain a complete lateral and
vertical flight profile, this can be amended by the crew, or left untouched.
Standard instrument departure and arrival procedures are also stored in
the database. The RTE key leads into the route selection procedure and
the DEP ARR key into the SIDs and STARs. Figure 4-34 shows the
display indicating a route from Heathrow (EGLL) to Hannover (EDVV).
Runway 09R has been selected for Heathrow with a Dover 3K departure
to Detling then via airway G1 to Dover.

Once the aircraft is airborne the FMS screen shows the active
waypoint, that is to say the next one, in reverse video and gives course and
distance between waypoints together with the speed and altitude at the
waypoints. Speed and altitude may be restrictions built in to the route in

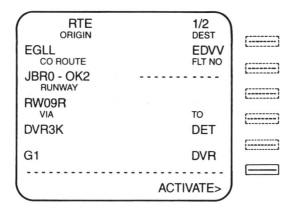

Figure 4–34 A
Route Selected.

which case they are shown in large characters, or they may be computed figures. Legs that require a heading rather than a course to be flown are suffixed HDG or H. Figure 4-35 shows the FMS display for the early part of the departure with the SID itself.

Performance Management

Once the route is loaded the FMS invites the pilot to feed in performance data, temperature and winds so that power settings and speeds can be calculated and the vertical profile can be assessed correctly. Performance management will optimise speeds for the minimum cost taking into account factors such as the price of fuel at departure and destination. This is collectively known as the cost index for a route and is part of stored company routes.

The following entries are required:

1 Either gross weight or zero fuel weight
2 Fuel reserves
3 Cost Index, if not using or overriding a stored route
4 Cruise altitude
5 Transition altitude
6 ISA deviation
7 Winds at height

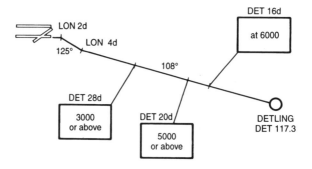

ACT RTE LEGS		1/6
096° HDG	0.4 NM	
LON02	162/	910
125° H	2.0 NM	
LON04	210/	4100
108°	18 NM	
DET28	250/	3000A
108°	8 NM	
DET20	250/	5000A
108°	4 NM	
DET16	250/	6000
- - - - - - - - - - - - - - - -		EXTENDED
		DATA >

Figure 4–35 FMS Display for Early
Parts of Departure.

If the transition altitude is not entered it will default to 18,000ft. If winds are not entered the route will be calculated with observed wind to the next waypoint and for zero wind subsequently. In addition to the above the pilot may also enter low or high speed restrictions for any phase of flight.

Advanced FMS computers will provide take-off information to the pilots. The runway in use is known from the route selection page. Extra data required is the OAT, the surface wind, runway direction, runway condition (dry or wet), slope and C of G position. The FMS will compute trim setting, V1, Vr, V2 and take-off thrust and can provide reduced thrust settings for take-off if performance is not limiting.

Test Yourself Four   Electronic Instrument Display Systems

1. A CRT is a:
    (a) Cathode Ray Tube.
    (b) Cathode Relay Tube.
    (c) Compilation Relay Tube.
    (d) Component Rectifier Tube.

    Ref 4.1.

2. EICAS is the:
    (a) Engine Indicating and Central Alerting System.
    (b) Engine Indicating and Crew Alerting System.
    (c) Electronic Indication and Central Alerting System.
    (d) Electronic Indicating and Central Alternating System.

    Ref 4.1.

3. ECAM is the:
    (a) Electronic Central Aircraft Management system.
    (b) Electronic Central Aircraft Manager.
    (c) Electronic Centralised Aircraft Monitoring.
    (d) Electric Controlled Aircraft Mandate.

    Ref 4.1.

4. The EFIS Display primarily consists of the:
    (a) ADI and HSI.
    (b) EICAS and ECAM.
    (c) EICAS and HSI.
    (d) ECAM, ADI and HSI.

    Ref 4.6.

5. The Upper Display Unit of the EICAS system indicates:
    (a) primary engine functions.
    (b) primary and secondary engine functions.
    (c) secondary and alert status information.
    (d) primary and secondary engine functions.

    Ref 4.9.

5

Automatic Flight

5.1 Fly-by-Wire System

The fly-by-wire control system, although not a new concept in aviation, has had to be re-developed in recent years to control ever more sophisticated types of aeroplanes coming into service. The problems of such sophistication has introduced even more complexity into the mechanical control linkages to operate the flight control system. The fly-by-wire system, as the description suggests, is therefore, where the mechanical linkages are dispensed with, and control wires carrying electrical signals from the pilot's controls replace them. Electrical or hydraulic servo-actuators do the actual movement of control surfaces, but the signals are electrical.

The pilot's controls are connected to electrical transducers which essentially measure the forces applied by the pilot; these forces are then translated in terms of electrical signals, which are amplified and relayed to the appropriate hydraulic servo-actuator directly connected to the flight control surface. In Fig 5-1 the system used by the Boeing 767 spoiler control panel is illustrated.

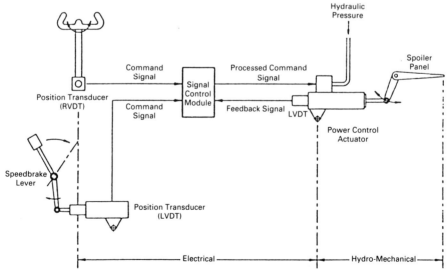

Figure 5–1 Fly-by-Wire System (Boeing 767) Spoiler Control Panel.

276

In considering lateral control, the deployment of the panels is initiated by the pilot moving the control wheel to the left or right. This movement operates position transducers, called Rotary Variable Differential Transformers (RVDTs) through mechanical gear drives from the control wheel. The RVDTs produce command voltage signals proportional to control wheel position and these signals are fed into a spoiler control module for processing and channel selection.

The spoiler control module output signals are then supplied to a solenoid valve forming an integral part of a hydraulic power control actuator. The valve directs hydraulic fluid under pressure to one or other side of the actuator piston which then raises or lowers the spoiler panel.

As the actuator rod moves, it also actuates a position transducer of the Linear Variable Differential Transformer (LVDT) type, and this produces a voltage feedback signal proportional to the spoiler panel position. When the feedback signal equals the command signal, a null condition is reached and the spoiler panel movement stops.

Deployment of spoiler panels for the purpose of acting as speedbrakes is initiated by movement of a speedbrake lever. The lever operates an LVDT type of transducer which produces a command voltage signal for processing by the signal control module. The output signal operates the actuator in the same way as for lateral control except that the spoiler panels are deployed to their fullest extent. Nulling of the command signal is also produced in the same way. Lateral control and speedbrake signals are mixed in the signal control module to provide the proper ratio of simultaneous operation.

A further advance in the fly-by-wire concept, is the use of fibre optic cables for conveying the flight commands to control surfaces. The great advantage of fibre optic cables is the enormous potential of signal carrying, and immunity to electro-magnetic interference, which means it is not necessary to use heavy shielding as in normal signal wires.

With fibre optics, only the commands are transmitted by light through the glass fibres of the conductor; the signal processing is done electronically after passing through a light to electronic transducer. All signal processing is done electronically within the aircraft's control system computers.

5.2 Servo-Mechanisms and Automatic Control Fundamentals

Introduction

With manual controlled flight, the pilot and the flight control system of his aircraft together comprise what may be termed a **closed-loop servo system**. Should the pilot wish to change heading or altitude the controls are manually moved in a way such as to produce the change. Looking closer at a change of altitude, say a descent, the pilot would move the control column forward to apply downward movement to the elevators, thus causing a nose-down attitude of the aircraft and initiate the descent.

Since the descent must be made at a certain angle and rate of change, the pilot will also monitor his primary flight instruments which detect and indicate attitude changes, namely gyro horizon, vertical speed indicator, altimeter and airspeed indicator, and then start returning the elevators to their neutral position by pulling back on the control column.

In order to level out at the new altitude, the control column will first be pulled farther back, thereby applying upward movement of the elevators to produce a nose-up attitude of the aircraft, and then moved forward again to position the elevators in neutral, to fly into the new level flight attitude.

This is a simplified explanation of how an attitude change is effected, and the particular point to be noted is that a pilot must always 'follow-up' his initial control input by applying secondary opposing inputs, thereby progressively removing control so that the attitude changes are made as smoothly and as accurately as possible, and without exceeding those changes commanded by the input.

Such a closed-loop servo-mechanism technique is applied to automatic flight control systems, and the 'follow-up' action in this connection is referred to as **feedback**.

5.3 Servo-Mechanisms

A servo-mechanism may be described in broad terms as a closed-loop system whereby a small powered input controls a much larger powered output while still retaining the proportional movements. In the application of such a system in an aircraft's automatic control, the system must be capable of continuous operation and have the ability to:

(1) Detect the difference between an input and an output (error detection).

(2) Amplify the error signals.

(3) Control the closing of the servo loop by providing **feedback**.

There are two main classes of servo-mechanism:

(a) Position control.

(b) Speed control.

Both classes may be independently applied to automatic flight control systems depending respectively on whether they are of the **displacement** type or the **rate-sensing** type. Some control systems use both types in conjunction.

Position type control mechanisms often utilize potentiometers to register angular position. The input controlling shaft also moves the wiper arm of a potentiometer whose output is fed to a servo-motor after amplification. A second potentiometer is used to measure the output angle whose wiper arm is mechanically coupled to the output shaft. The potentiometers are electrically coupled such that when both wiper arms are in the same angular position, a null or zero signal condition exists.

When it is required to move the load to a particular angular position, the controlling shaft is rotated through the appropriate number of degrees. As there is now a signal generated because of the difference in angular position of the potentiometers, ie they have moved away from null or equal position state, a signal is generated, and also the direction of movement is represented by signal polarity. The servo-motor is energised to move the load shaft in the direction of the new position set by the controlling shaft. The error signal is fed back to the amplifier, thereby reducing the input error signal. When both the load shaft and input shaft are in the same angular position, both potentiometers register a null, or zero signal, and the servo-motor is de-energised.

The **Speed control servo-mechanism** is a method of controlling the output speed of a system by simple comparison of voltages corresponding to input and output speeds. The signals are used to control the speed of the servo-motor and load. The difference between this system and that of the position control system is that the servo-motor also drives a device called a **tachogenerator**.

A tachogenerator, sometimes called a velodyne, produces a voltage which is proportional to the speed of rotation. A voltage setting at the input is compared to the voltage generated by the tachogenerator, any difference producing an error signal which is used to allow the load (the output) to speed up (or slow down) depending on the sign of the error signal compared to the input signal. When the load tachogenerator output voltage matches the input setting, a null or zero voltage exists, and the servo-motor will run at a constant speed. Speed control of the servo-motor is maintained by differences in voltages, and will speed up or slow down until the difference is zero.

5.4 Automatic Control Fundamentals

The closed-loop servo technique is applied in the automatic flight control system of an aircraft. In Fig 5-2 is shown a functional diagram of a closed-loop system which is the basis of all classes of automatic flight control systems. There are four principle elements which together are allocated the task of coping with what is generally termed 'inner-loop' stabilization, the individual functions of the elements are as follows:

(a)   Sensing of attitude changes of the aircraft about its principle axes by means of stable reference devices: eg gyroscopes and/or accelerometers.

(b)   Sensing of attitude changes in terms of error signals and the transmission of such signals.

(c)   Processing of error signals and their conversion into a form suitable for operation of the servo-motors forming the output stage.

(d)   Conversion of processed signals into movement of the aircraft's flight control surfaces.

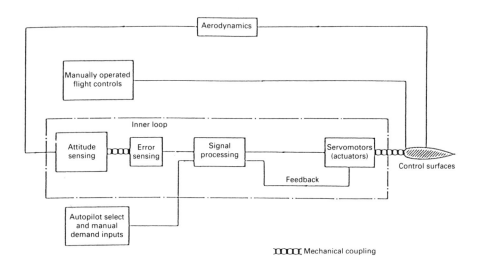

Figure 5–2 Inner-loop Stabilisation.

The number of control loops, or channels, comprising an automatic control system is dependent on the number of axes about which control is to be effected.

5.5 Classification of systems is done on the basis of the number of axes that require control, and are:

(a)   **Single-axis** in which attitude control is normally about the roll axis only. The control surfaces forming part of the one and only control loop are, therefore, the ailerons. Such a control system is the most basic type, and is used in a number of types of small fixed-wing aircraft for lateral stabilization, or wing-levelling as it's often called. The pilot can inject command signals into the control loop thereby enabling him to turn the aircraft automatically. In some cases, signals from a compass system and from radio navigation equipment are also injected into the loop so that magnetic headings, and tracking capability can be automatically maintained. Such operating modes are known as heading-hold and radio-coupling respectively, and form part of the **outer-loop control**.

(b) **Two-axis** in which attitude control is, in most cases, about the roll and pitch axes; the control surfaces forming parts of the two loops are, therefore, the ailerons and elevators. Manual turn control, heading-hold and radio-coupling facilities are normally standard features in any one design with, in some cases, an additional facility for selecting and holding a specific altitude. The two-axis automatic control system consists of: Directional gyro, Attitude gyro, Computer amplifier, Pitch and Roll actuators which are integrated with an attitude director indicator (ADI) and horizontal situation indicator (HSI) of a flight director system.

Such integration permits the sharing of common basic attitude and navigation data, and servo-mechanism loops, and by virtue of the indicators' display presentations, it enables a flight crew to initiate precise flight guidance commands to the automatic control system.

Note: Rudder control is carried out by means of a yaw damper system and does not imply that the automatic control system should therefore be classified as a three-axis system, and not a two-axis system as already described. The reason for this is that a yaw damper system is always separate, and can be operated to apply rudder control regardless of whether or not the automatic control system is engaged.

(c) **Three-axis** in which attitude control about all three axes is carried out by specifically related control channels of an automatic flight control system (AFCS).

5.6 Trimming and Synchronisation

It must be ensured that when the automatic control system is engaged, the system takes over without 'snatching' of the aircraft's control system, ie it must be effected smoothly. This means that the aircraft must be trimmed for the desired flight attitude before engagement, and the automatic control system must be synchronised to maintain that attitude when engaged. Auto-trim is normally a function of pitch only.

When power is applied to the automatic control system, the attitude sensing elements are in operation so will always detect the aircraft's attitude and, therefore, supply any necessary control command signals to the servo-motors. At the same time, any signals will be supplied to the appropriate channels of a trim indicating system, or out-of-trim light system.

As an example, if before control system engagement the aircraft is in a climb, or has been trimmed to fly in a nose-up attitude, the pitch attitude sensing element will detect this, and will supply a signal to the elevator servo-motor commanding it to rotate in a direction corresponding to 'elevator down', such as would be shown on the trim indicator.

Because the signal in this case is a standing one, assuming for the moment that it has no opposition, the servo-motor will continue to rotate, and if the clutch were engaged at any one movement the elevators would be snatched from the trimmed position and so cause a nose-down attitude change.

The aerodynamic load acting on the elevators would be felt by the servo-motor, thereby helping to retard its rotation. As soon as the sensing element of the pitch attitude detector responded to the attitude change, the opposing signal produced would then eventually stop the motor and rotate it in the opposite direction. Thus, control would be of an oscillatory nature and the aircraft would take up the pitch attitude determined by the attitude detector and not that which it was desired the control system should maintain, ie in the example considered, a climb or nose-up trim condition.

It is therefore necessary to oppose the standing signal and reduce it to zero before engaging the control system, thereby stopping the servo-motor in a position which is synchronised with the datum attitude detected by the sensing element, such position being indicated by the return of the trim indicator pointer to its central position.

The manner in which synchronising is effected depends on the type of automatic control system and the signal processing circuit arrangements adopted.

5.7 Gain and Gain Programming

Different aircraft respond at different rates to displacement of their flight control surfaces. In particular they vary with altitude, speed, aircraft load, configuration and rate of manoeuvre. It is because of these differing basic handling characteristics that 'gearing' is incorporated in flight control systems and thereby reduce the effects which variations in flight parameters can have on handling characteristics.

Similarly, in applying particular types of automatic flight control systems to individual aircraft control systems, it is necessary to provide facilities for altering the response of an automatic system to any given level of input signal, thereby obtaining a signal ratio best suited to the operation of the systems when working in combination. Such a ratio is known as **gain** and may be considered as having a function similar to the changing gear ratios in a mechanical gearing system.

Figure 5-3 shows a closed-loop control system in simple form. The signal path from error to response, measured amplification ratio, is the **loop gain**.

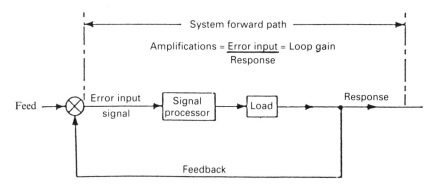

Figure 5–3 Simplified closed-loop system.

Within limits, increased gain improves performance in two ways:

(a) Residual error in steady state is reduced and so improves long-term accuracy.

(b) Initial response to a given command is more rapid.

The limit on these improvements arises from the need for adequate dynamic stability of the system. If, for example, loop gain is increased to some excessive value, then dynamic instability will be produced so that response is grossly oscillatory and never settles to a steady state.

Even before instability is reached, excessive loop gain reduces dynamic stability to an extent that it would take too long for a response to settle at a steady rate: furthermore, it would initially overshoot and then hunt about a steady-state value.

Satisfactory closed-loop performance depends on determining a loop gain which compromises between long-term accuracy plus initial response, and acceptable settling time plus limited overshoot. These factors, in turn, require sufficient inherent damping in the load.

Certain adjustments of command and feedback signals can be pre-set within amplifier and/or computer units in order to produce gain factors which establish a basic 'match' between an automatic control system and the aircraft's characteristics.

Adjustments are based on the variation of electrical resistance at appropriate sections of signal circuits, and as in several types of control system, this is accomplished by means of potentiometers located on a calibration panel that forms an integral part of an amplifier or computer unit.

Further to this, it is also necessary, particularly when the control system is operating in any of the outer-loop control modes, for the gain factor to be altered automatically to offset variations in handling characteristics resulting from changing flight conditions. This process is called **gain programming or scheduling**, and is part of a technique referred to as **adaptive control**.

An example of gain programming relates to an approach to an airport runway when the automatic control system is coupled to the Instrument Landing System (ILS) that is, coupled to the Localiser and Glide Slope modes. The purpose of gain programming in this case is to reduce the gain of beam deviation signals and thereby allow for convergence of the LOC and GS beams.

5.8 Outer-Loop Control

Over and above the primary task of stabilisation performed by an automatic flight control system, it can also be developed to perform the tasks of modifying the stabilised attitude of an aircraft by computing the necessary manoeuvres from inputs such as airspeed, altitude, magnetic heading, interception of radio beams from ground based aids, etc. Such data inputs constitute **outer-loop control**. See Fig 5-4.

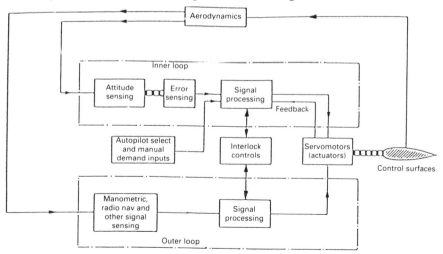

Figure 5–4 Inner-loop stabilisation and outer-loop control.

The provision of raw data inputs relevant to a particular flight-path is referred to as **coupling** or as a **mode of operation**, the selection of each mode being made by the pilot via appropriate control panel switching devices.

Other terms commonly used in connection with operating modes are: **Hold, Lock and Capture**. For example, an aircraft flying automatically at a selected altitude is said to be in the **altitude hold** or **height lock mode**. The term **capture** relates principally to modes associated with the selection and interception of beams from ground-based radio navigation aids, for example, **glide-slope capture**.

In some cases, mode switching is automatic, therefore to switch from intercepting a beam or a heading to tracking the beam on reaching it, a beam sensor is installed. This device senses beam deviation and switches modes automatically when the aircraft flies into the beam. Glide-slope capture can also take place automatically, in this case the pitch control channel is switched from 'altitude hold' mode to glide-slope track when the aircraft flies into the glide-slope beam.

The raw data is supplied from sensors which convert the data into appropriate electrical signals that can be mixed in with inner-loop signal data to produce the changes to the aircraft's flight path. The traditional raw data instrument displays are used by the pilot for monitoring, and programming management. The outer-loop control modes that can be incorporated into a control system are listed in Fig 5-5. Modes actually used are dependent on the type of aircraft and its control system.

In a single-engine light aircraft having a basic wing-levelling control system for example, only altitude and heading modes might comprise the outer-loop control, whereas in a more complex larger type of passenger-carrying aircraft using a flight guidance system, and having automatic landing capability, the outer-loop comprises all the modes listed in Fig 5-5.

5.9 Manometric or Air Data

Raw data inputs which come under this heading are those associated with **altitude, airspeed, vertical speed, and speed in terms of Mach number**, each providing outer-loop control about the pitch axis of an aircraft. Sensing may be carried out either by independent sensor units, or by a central air data computer.

The sensors operate on the same fundamental principles as the basic pilot-static flight instruments, the measuring elements being coupled to appropriate types of electrical pick-off elements in lieu of indicating pointer mechanisms.

Pitch Axis	Roll Axis
Manometric or air data: Altitude select and hold Vertical speed Airspeed select and hold Mach hold	Heading select and hold Bank hold Radio navigation VOR
Pitch hold	Back Beam
Pitch trim	Area navigation: Doppler
Turbulence penetration Vertical navigation	Inertial
Instrument Landing System	
Glide-Slope	Localiser
Autoland	
Approach Flare	Runway align Roll-out
Control wheel steering Touch control steering	

Figure 5–5 Outer-loop control modes.

5.10 Altitude Hold

Any change of aircraft attitude about its pitch axis while in straight and level flight, will be detected by the pitch attitude sensing element of the automatic control system, and the changes will be accordingly corrected; however, after correction the aircraft could be at a new altitude, either above or below that which is desired. Attitude sensing on its own cannot detect altitude changes, and neither can it maintain a required altitude. What is necessary is a means of locking on the altitude selected; also, a means of levelling off at any desired altitude.

An altitude hold, or lock sensor is employed. An altitude hold system employs its own pressure-sensitive capsule, which measures static pressure changes. Any deviations from a selected altitude will result in a signal being applied to the pitch servo-motor to return the aircraft to the selected altitude.

5.11 Airspeed Hold

In an airspeed hold or lock sensor, there is also a capsule, but measurements are taken from the differences in dynamic and static pressure. The assembly expands or contracts under the influence of a pressure differential created by a change of airspeed. The electronics used to pick-off the pressure differential are similar to the electronics used in the altitude hold sensor, the signal then being applied to the pitch servo-control channel. The capsule assembly is usually housed in the same chamber as the altitude capsule assembly.

5.12 Mach Hold

There is a requirement in high performance aircraft to fly at given Mach Numbers at high speed and high altitude, so that both airspeed hold and Mach hold modes are required under automatically controlled flight. The airspeed hold is the more commonly used during the low altitude cruise phase of flight, and Mach hold during the high altitude phase.

Since Mach Number varies with airspeed and altitude, the signal outputs from independent sensors can be integrated to provide required Mach Number signal output. This is accomplished by incorporating all sensors in a unit called a Central Air Data Computer (CADC).

5.13 Vertical Speed Selection and Hold

After taking-off, it is necessary to climb at a particular rate, or at a particular speed in automatic flight, therefore, a vertical speed reference must be incorporated into the system. The rate signal is originated by a tacho-generator driven by the altitude sensor of a central air data computer, and is supplied to the pitch channel of the control system through a vertical speed mode select circuit which forms part of the pilot's control unit.

Signals from this unit are fed to the pitch servo-amplifier and servo-motor to displace the pitch control surfaces in the appropriate direction for restoring the aircraft attitude and vertical speed to that prevailing at the time of engagement of the control system.

5.14 Heading Hold

This system will hold the aircraft in automatic flight on a pre-selected magnetic heading. Since turning the aircraft is carried out by displacement of the ailerons, the heading hold mode relates to control about the roll axis, and heading error signals are applied to the roll control channel of the flight control system.

In most aircraft, heading data is supplied either from a remote-indicating compass or from a flight director system. Since the 'heading select' facility of the compass system provides automatic turn control, it is comparable in function to the turn control provided on a pilot's control panel. It is necessary, therefore to incorporate an interlock circuit between the two to prevent their signals from opposing each other.

5.15 Turbulence Penetration

When flying in turbulent air conditions, varying loads are imposed on the aircraft structure. It is normal for the pilot to adjust the power and the speed and to operate the flight control system in a manner compatible with the flight conditions prevailing.

In an aeroplane under automatic flight control, the control system senses the turbulence as disturbances to aircraft attitude, but in applying corrective control it is possible for additional structural loads to be imposed. The reason for this is that the rate of control system response tends to get out of phase with the rate at which the disturbances occur, the result being that control responses tend to become 'stiffer'.

In turbulent conditions, it is normal to disengage the automatic flight control system. In some current systems, however, turbulence penetration may be an optional selection mode. Under this mode of operation, the gain of both pitch and roll channels is reduced thereby 'softening' flight control system response to turbulence.

5.16 Control Wheel Steering

Some automatic flight control systems are fitted with Control Wheel Steering (CWS). The purpose of CWS is to allow the pilot to manoeuvre his aircraft in pitch and roll by applying inputs to the automatic flight control system, this being achieved by operation of the wheel in a similar manner to the operation of the conventional control column. When the control wheel is released, the automatic flying control system maintains the attitude of the aircraft in the newly selected position.

In some aircraft systems limits are imposed as to the degree of manoeuvring that may be carried out by the CWS.

5.17 Touch Control Steering

Touch Control Steering (TCS), in a similar manner to Control Wheel Steering, will permit the pilot to manoeuvre his aircraft. In this system, unlike the CWS system, the appropriate control channels and servos are disengaged while the aircraft is flown to its new attitude and heading. Release of the Touch Control Steering switch will re-engage normal channels and servos.

Test Yourself Five   Automatic Flight

1. In a Fly-by-Wire control system the Pilot's Control inputs are connected to:
    (a) mechanical linkages to the Power Control Actuator.
    (b) transducers.
    (c) transformers.
    (d) servo amplifiers.

    Ref 5.1.

2. A Two-Axis Automatic Control System normally provides attitude control in the:
    (a) roll axis only.
    (b) roll and yaw axis.
    (c) yaw and pitch axis.
    (d) roll and pitch axis.

    Ref 5.5

3. Auto Trim is normally a function of:
    (a) yaw and pitch.
    (b) roll.
    (c) yaw.
    (d) pitch.

    Ref 5.6.

4. Primary Automatic Control Stabilisation is provided by:
    (a) outer loop.
    (b) inner and outer loop.
    (c) inner loop.
    (d) mechanical inputs only.

    Ref 5.8.

5. Vertical Speed is a function of:
    (a) pitch and yaw axis.
    (b) roll axis.
    (c) pitch axis.
    (d) roll and yaw axis.

    Ref 5.8.

6

Automatic Landing

6.1 Central Air Data Computer (CADC)

Pressure from static vents and pitot tubes are transmitted to the primary flight instruments, ie airspeed indicator, altimeter and vertical speed indicator, via pipelines, the length and quantity of which will vary according to the size of the aircraft, and the number of stations within the aircraft at which relevant indications are required.

In order to reduce the 'pressure plumbing' arrangements, the pressures are supplied to a central location from which they can be transmitted to any number of stations, and in the form of synchronous signal data links. This central facility is called a Central Air Data Computer.

6.12 Automatic Landing

Introduction

Automatic landing is one of the most demanding of the automatic control flight phases. In order to achieve a safe landing, the aeroplane has to be controlled in a manner such that its wheels make contact with the runway within a fairly narrow longitudinal limits along it, and at a low sinking rate, something like 1 to 2 feet per second. The speed at touch-down should have been reduced from the approach margin of about 30% above the stall to about half of this value by progressive reduction of engine power during the landing flare.

The wings should have been levelled prior to the actual landing, and the aircraft yawed to bring its longitudinal axis parallel to the runway centre-line to remove any drift angle due to cross-wind, this manoeuvre being known as 'decrabbing', or 'kick-off'.

Control is therefore required about all three axes simultaneously, as well as the control of airspeed through engine power changes. This is a demanding requirement for the pilot in a manually controlled landing. The control function during the approach and landing manoeuvre is required on a highly repetitive basis, and although a number of parameters are to be controlled simultaneously, such control is only necessary for a comparatively short period of time, and is therefore most suited to automatic control.

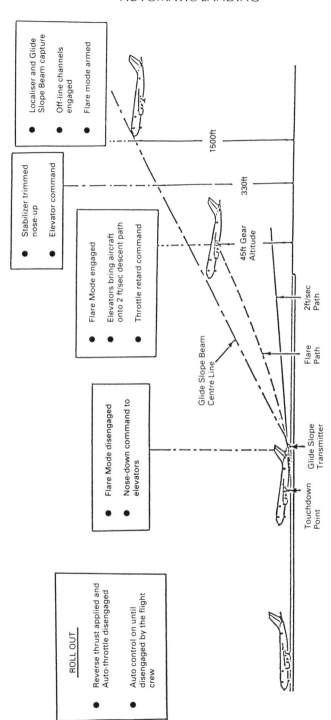

Localiser and Glide Slope Beam capture
- Off-line channels engaged
- Flare mode armed

1500ft

- **Stabilizer trimmed nose-up**
- Elevator command

330ft

45ft Gear Altitude

- **Flare Mode engaged**
- Elevators bring aircraft onto 2 ft/sec descent path
- Throttle retard command

2ft/sec Path

Flare Path

Glide Slope Beam Centre Line

- **Flare Mode disengaged**
- Nose-down command to elevators

Glide Slope Transmitter

Touchdown Point

ROLL OUT
- Reverse thrust applied and Auto-throttle disengaged
- Auto control on until disengaged by the flight crew

Figure 6–1 Automatic Approach, Flare and Land.

291

6.3 Automatic Landing Sequence

Figure 6-1 shows the flight profile of an automatic approach, flare and touchdown. This is based on a system that utilises triple digital flight control computer channels, allowing for redundancy to operate in the **fail operational** and **fail passive conditions**.

Fail operational means a system in which one failure (sometimes more) can occur, but leaves the overall system still functioning, and without causing degradation of performance beyond the limits required for automatic landing and roll-out. (Alternative terms are: fail-active and fail-survival).

Fail-passive (USA terminology: or Fail-soft in UK) means the ability of a system to withstand a failure without endangering passenger safety, and without excessive deviations from the flight path.

Depending on the number of channels that are armed and engaged, the system performs what are termed a LAND 2 status or LAND 3 status autoland. LAND 2 signifies there is dual redundancy of engaged flight control computers, sensors and servos (fail-passive operation) whereas LAND 3 signifies triple redundancy of power sources, engaged flight control computers, sensors and servos (fail-operational). Each status is displayed on an autoland status annunciator.

During the cruise and initial stages of approach to land, the control system operates as a single channel system, controlling the aircraft about its pitch and roll axes and providing the appropriate flight director commands. Since multichannel operation is required for automatic landing, at a certain stage of the approach the remaining two channels are armed by pressing an APPR (Approach) switch on the flight control panel.

The operation of the switch also arms the localiser and glide slope modes. Both of the 'off-line' channels are continually supplied with the relevant outer-loop control signals and operate on a **comparative basis** the whole time.

Altitude information, essential for vertical guidance to touchdown, is always provided by signals from a radio altimeter that become effective as soon as the aircraft's altitude is within the altimeter's operating range, typically 2500 feet.

When the aircraft has descended to 1500 feet radio altitude, the localiser and glide slope beams are captured and the armed 'off-line' control channels are then automatically engaged. The localiser and glide slope beam signals control the aircraft about the roll and pitch axes so that any deviations are automatically corrected to maintain alignment with the runway.

At the same time, the autoland status annunciator displays LAND 2 or LAND 3 depending on the number of channels 'voted into operation' for landing the aircraft, and computerised control of flare is also armed.

At a radio altitude of 300 feet, the aircraft's horizontal stabiliser is automatically repositioned to begin trimming the aircraft to a nose-up attitude. The elevators are also deflected to counter the trim and to provide subsequent pitch control in the trimmed attitude.

When an altitude is reached at which the landing gear is 45 feet above the ground (referred to as gear height) the flare mode is automatically engaged. The gear altitude calculation, which is pre-programmed into the computer, is based upon radio altitude, pitch attitude and known distance between the landing gear, the fuselage and radio altimeter antenna.

The flare mode takes over pitch attitude control from the glide slope, and generates a pitch command to bring the aircraft onto a 2 feet per second descent path, at the same time, a 'throttle retard' command signal is supplied to the auto-throttle system to reduce engine thrust to the limits compatible with the flare path.

Prior to touchdown, and at about 5 feet gear altitude, the flare mode is disengaged and there is a transition to the touchdown and roll-out mode. At about 1 foot gear altitude, the pitch attitude of the aircraft is decreased to 2° and at touchdown, a command signal is supplied to the elevators to lower the aircraft's nose and so bring the nose landing gear wheels in contact with the runway and hold them there during the roll-out.

When reverse thrust is applied, the auto-throttle system is automatically disengaged. The automatic flight control system remains on until disengaged by the flight crew.

Key Points

Electrics

1. Generators are normally AIR cooled.

2. As loads are increased in a SHUNT-WOUND GENERATOR supply system current increases and voltage decreases.

3. Loads are normally connected to the bus-bar in parallel to allow load shedding to take place.

4. When FIELD FLASHING is carried out, the polarity of the magnets of the generator reverse.

5. When a shunt-wound generator is over-volting, field current is reduced.

6. In normal flight the lower screen of an EICAS is blank.

7. The HSI of the EFIS has four modes – MAP, PLAN, ILS & VOR.

8. LAND 3 on the ADI indicates FAIL OPERATIONAL

9. Aircraft attitude in AUTOFLIGHT is a function of the INNER LOOP.

10. Failure annunciations on the EFIS are indicated by yellow flags.

11. Engine vibration is indicated on the EICAS Lower Display.

12. Caution messages are indicated on the EICAS Upper Display Left-Hand Side.

13. LAND 2 is fail passive.

14. The RAD ALT is shown on the ADI at 1 o'clock.

15. The RAD ALT changes to a circular scale at 1000ft.

Test Yourself Six   Automatic Landing

1. Fail operational is also known as:
   (a) fail active.
   (b) fail passive.
   (c) fail soft.
   (d) serviceable.

Ref 6.3.

2. During the autoland sequence the horizontal stabiliser automatically commences to trim the aircraft Nose Up at:
   (a) 1000ft.
   (b) 100ft.
   (c) 300ft.
   (d) 3000ft.

Ref 6.3.

3. Just prior to touchdown the aircraft's rate of descent should be reduced to:
   (a) 10ft per second.
   (b) 2ft per second.
   (c) 8ft per second.
   (d) 5ft per second.

Ref 6.3.

4. On touch-down in autoland a command signal is supplied to the elevators to:
   (a) maintain flare attitude.
   (b) increase Nose Up by 2°.
   (c) lower the nose.
   (d) increase Nose Up by 5°.

Ref 6.3.

5. Auto-throttle is automatically disengaged when:
   (a) the main undercarriage touches the runway.
   (b) the nose undercarriage touches the runway.
   (c) selected OFF only.
   (d) reverse thrust is selected.

Ref 6.3.

Test Yourself   Final Practice Questions

1. Normally the EICAS Upper Display Unit displays:
   (a) FF, EPR and Vibration.
   (b) FF, EGT and EPR.
   (c) EGT, EPR and N1 speed.
   (d) N1, N2 and N3 speeds.

Ref 4.10.

2. Warning messages on the EICAS Upper Display Units are indicated in:
   (a) Yellow.
   (b) Amber.
   (c) White.
   (d) Red.

Ref 4.10.

3. If the Lower Display Unit of the EICAS fails during operation then a warning display is illuminated in:
   (a) the form of a red warning light.
   (b) the upper display unit in amber.
   (c) the upper display unit in red.
   (d) the lower display unit top left corner in red.

Ref 4.15.

4. In the event of total failure of the EICAS, information is:
   (a) displayed on the Standby Engine Indicator.
   (b) displayed on conventional instruments.
   (c) by a system of warning lights.
   (d) by a standby image generator.

Ref 4.18.

5. The ADI of the EFIS RAD ALT is displayed on the instrument's face at:
   (a) 1 o'clock position.
   (b) 6 o'clock position.
   (c) 7 o'clock position.
   (d) 9 o'clock position.

Ref 4.22.

6. The HSI of the EFIS consists of:
   (a) Three Modes.
   (b) Two Modes.
   (c) Four Modes.
   (d) Six Modes.

Ref 4.23.

7. The HSI displays a dynamic map background in:
   (a) Map and Plan Modes.
   (b) Map Mode.
   (c) Map, Plan and VOR Modes.
   (d) Map, Plan and ILS Modes.

Ref 4.23.

8. Failure of DATA Signals on the HSI is shown as:
   (a) red warning lights.
   (b) red flags.
   (c) yellow flags.
   (d) amber warning lights.

Ref 4.23.

9. Weather returns are available on the HSI:
   (a) in all modes at all times.
   (b) in MAP and PLAN modes only.
   (c) on VOR and ILS in expanded Mode only.
   (d) on the MAP Mode only.

Ref 4.23.

10. The RAD ALT is displayed below 1000ft as a circular scale in increments of:
    (a) 100ft.
    (b) 50ft.
    (c) 500ft.
    (d) 250ft.

Ref 4.22.

11. In the HSI PLAN Mode the active route date is orientated to:
    (a) Magnetic North.
    (b) True North.
    (c) True or Magnetic North.
    (d) a diagramatic heading.

Ref 4.23.

12. An aural alarm is sounded on the ADI when the:
    (a) DH is reached.
    (b) DH + 50ft is reached.
    (c) height of 50ft above the ground is reached.
    (d) DH minus 50ft is reached.

Ref 4.22.

13. The Circular Scale of the RAD ALT changes from magenta to amber at:
    (a) DH + 50ft.
    (b) DH.
    (c) DH –50ft.
    (d) 50ft above the ground.

Ref 4.22.

14. The DH Marker of the ADI RAD ALT is positioned on the scale at:
    (a) 1 o'clock.
    (b) 6 o'clock.
    (c) 12 o'clock.
    (d) 7 o'clock.

Ref 4.22.

15. Decision height is selected on the:
    (a) EFIS control panel.
    (b) ADI Instrument.
    (c) HSI Instrument.
    (d) AFCS control panel.

Ref 4.22.

16. Radio Altitude is indicated above 1000ft on the ADI at:
    (a) 1 o'clock.
    (b) 6 o'clock.
    (c) 12 o'clock.
    (d) 7 o'clock.

Ref 4.22.

17. When Automatic Flight is employed with a single axis system automatic stabilisation is normally provided in the:
    (a) roll and yaw axis.
    (b) yaw axis.
    (c) pitch axis.
    (d) roll axis.

Ref 5.5.

18. Auto Trim is normally a function of:
    (a) Pitch and Roll.
    (b) Pitch and Yaw.
    (c) Roll and Yaw.
    (d) Pitch only.

Ref 5.6.

19. Primary Control Functions of Automatic Flight are controlled within the:
    (a) Outer Loop.
    (b) Inner and Outer Loop.
    (c) Inner Loop.
    (d) Auxiliary and Inner Loop.

Ref 5.4.

20. Raw Air Data to the Outer Loop is termed:
    (a) Outer Loop Data.
    (b) Air Data.
    (c) Pressure Data.
    (d) Manometric Data.

Ref 5.9.

Part 3

Instruments

1

Pressure Sources

Aircraft pressure instruments – altimeter, airspeed indicator, vertical speed indicator and (in high speed aircraft) Machmeter – all measure changes of pressure. Before looking at each instrument in detail, it is important to understand the pressures involved and how they are sensed. Errors common to all the pressure instruments are also discussed in this chapter.

1.1 Static Pressure

Static pressure is that which is exerted by the weight of the Earth's atmosphere on everything, everybody, every aircraft and every instrument. Static pressure varies from place to place and from time to time as meteorological conditions change; it also decreases as altitude increases.

Static pressure is sensed through one or more small holes or **static vents** which are connected to the aircraft's pressure system. Usually the vents are fitted in the side of the fuselage, and often there are two – one on each side – to balance out errors. Some aircraft, however, have the static vents incorporated in a pressure head (see Fig 1-1).

1.2 Dynamic Pressure

Dynamic pressure is that which is caused by the forward motion of the aircraft through the air. The faster the aircraft goes, the greater the dynamic pressure.

It is impossible to sense dynamic pressure directly. As previously stated, static pressure is ever-present, so the pressure experienced by a moving aircraft is the **sum** of static and dynamic pressures. This is called **pitot pressure** and is sensed by the **pitot tube**, an open tube facing into the

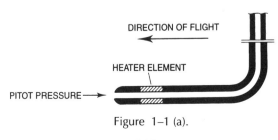

Figure 1–1 (a).

airflow and connected to the pressure system – see Fig 1-1(a). To prevent the pitot tube becoming blocked by ice, a **pitot heater** is usually fitted.

As mentioned earlier, some aircraft are fitted with a **pressure head** which combines the functions of pitot tube and static vents. See Fig 1–1(b).

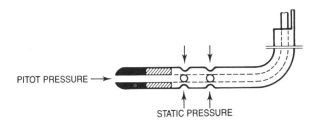

Figure 1–1 (b).

Pitot pressure (P) = Dynamic Pressure (D) + Static Pressure (S)

therefore **D = P - S**

So by comparing the pitot pressure with the static pressure we can get a measure of the dynamic pressure.

1.3 Pressure Systems

Once sensed, the pressures are fed to the instruments by a **pressure system**. A schematic of a simple light aircraft system is shown at Fig 1-2.

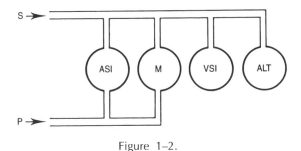

Figure 1–2.

1.4 Sensing Errors

Some errors are common to all pressure instruments.

1.5 Instrument Error

All instruments are subject to errors caused by manufacturing faults, design weaknesses and wear – such errors can be calibrated.

1.6 Position Error

The pressure sensors, static vents and pitot heads, can never be in perfect positions on the airframe and so the pressures which they sense will frequently be incorrect. Such position error at the pitot head is usually very small and is ignored. For static vents to sense the correct pressure they must be positioned in air which is entirely free from disturbances caused by movement of the air over the airframe – an all but impossible task. Furthermore, position errors will change with changes in configuration (flaps, gear etc). Position error can be calibrated, however, and the combined effects of instrument and position error are promulgated in the aircraft manual.

1.7 Manoeuvre Error

Whenever the aircraft is not in straight-and-level flight the sensed pressures will be inaccurate because of the aerodynamic disturbances caused by manoeuvre.

It is for this reason that many aircraft have two static vents – to cancel out errors in a turn. Residual error will inevitably remain, however, and it cannot be calibrated.

Manoeuvre error and position error are often referred to in combination as **pressure error**.

1.8 Blockages

Any blockages (such as bugs or ice) in the pressure sensors will cause errors. Hence the use of pitot heaters, pitot head covers, static vent plugs and the like. Some aircraft are fitted with an alternative static source, but its use tends to cause substantial errors.

1.9 Calibration Errors

Pressure instruments are calibrated on the assumption that certain atmospheric conditions prevail. These conditions define the International Standard Atmosphere (ISA) and are:

At mean sea level:

=   A pressure of 1013.2 mb
=   A density of 1225 gm/m^3
=   A temperature of + 15°C

A temperature lapse rate of 1.98°C per thousand feet up to 36,090 feet (11km), above which the temperature is constant at –56.5°C.

Any differences between ambient conditions and those for which the instruments are calibrated will induce errors. These are discussed in more detail in the subsequent chapters which describe each instrument in detail.

2

The Altimeter

As described in Chapter 1, static pressure varies as altitude changes. The altimeter makes use of this phenomenon – it measures changes of static pressure and relates these to changes of vertical distance from a chosen pressure datum.

2.1 Principle of Operation

Basic Altimeter
A schematic diagram of a simple altimeter is given in Fig 2-1.

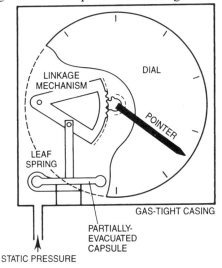

Figure 2–1.

The sensing element is a partially-evacuated, sealed capsule (an aneroid capsule). A leaf spring is used to prevent the capsule collapsing. The capsule is mounted within a case which is sealed, apart from a feed of static pressure. If static pressure decreases, the spring will be strong enough to expand the capsule. The movement of expansion is fed through a system of linkages which cause a needle to rotate over the altimeter dial. If static pressure increases its effect causes the capsule to contract, against the spring, and the needle will move in the opposite direction.

303

2.2 Sensitive Altimeter

The sensitive altimeter works on exactly the same principle as the basic instrument. However, to improve sensitivity, the single capsule is replaced by multiple capsules in a stack. (Fig 2-2.)

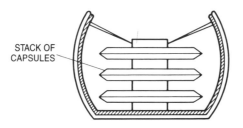

STACK OF CAPSULES

Figure 2–2.

This arrangement provides a much larger movement for a given change of pressure and so makes feasible the use of a three-needle indicator (Fig 2-3).

Sensitive altimeters incorporate error-reducing devices such as jewelled bearings in the linkages, and temperature compensators to allow for expansion and contraction of the linkages. A sub-scale setting knob is fitted to allow the pilot to set the datum pressure (QFE, QNH etc) he chooses.

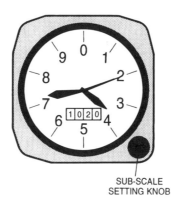

SUB-SCALE
SETTING KNOB

Figure 2–3.

2.3 Servo Altimeter

The modern servo altimeter retains the capsule stack as a sensing element but the 'suitable system of levers' is replaced by a servo mechanism based on an 'I and E bar' system. (Fig 2-4)

The centre arm of the E bar is wound with a primary coil which is excited by an alternating current. Secondary coils, wound around the outer arms of the E, will thus have voltages induced into them. If the I bar is equidistant from the arms of the E these voltages will be equal, though of opposite polarity.

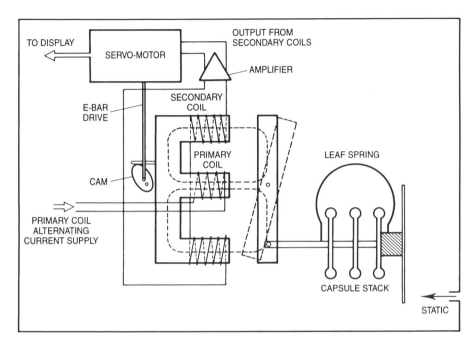

Figure 2–4.

Expansion or contraction of the capsules moves one end of the I bar, which is pivoted at its centre. The air gaps between the I bar and the outer arms of the E will no longer be equal, so neither will the induced voltages. The difference in voltage is amplified and used both to turn the altimeter indicator and to drive the E bar, via the reset cam, back to the null position relative to the I bar.

In, say, a climb this process will be continuous. However, at top of climb the capsule will stop expanding and the I bar will stop moving. The voltages will be equal, so the E bar will stop and the altimeter will show a steady reading.

Servo altimeters offer considerable advantages over their conventional cousins:

(a)   More accurate, and usable to higher altitudes.

(b)   Digital indicators can be used (though a 'hundreds of feet' pointer is normally retained more readily to indicate small changes (Fig 2-5).

(c)   Output can be fed to remote systems, eg the transponder for Mode C.

(d)   Correction for position error can be incorporated, as can altitude alerting devices.

Figure 2–5.

2.4 Accuracy

The table below gives illustrative figures for the accuracies of the different types of altimeter together with an indication of the maximum altitude to which they can be used.

Type	Error		Max Alt
	At MSL	At Altitude	
Simple	± 100ft	± 1000ft at 35,000ft	35,000ft
		± 600ft at 20,000ft	
Sensitive	± 70ft	± 1500ft at 80,000ft	80,000ft
		± 1000ft at 40,000ft	
Servo	± 30ft	± 300ft at 60,000ft	100,000ft
		± 100ft at 40,000ft	

2.5 Errors

Source Errors

The source errors discussed in Chapter 1 are all present. The following additional points should be noted:

(a) Instrument Error

(i)   Simple instruments, which employ a single capsule, are insensitive to small pressure changes.

(ii) Calibration assumes a constant decrease of pressure per unit of altitude. However, as altitude increases the atmosphere becomes rarer, the rate of fall of pressure decreases and simple altimeters become increasingly insensitive. This is not a problem in servo altimeters.

(iii) There will be lag in the instrument caused by the fact that it takes some time, however small, for pressure changes to travel through the system. Additionally, there is hysteresis in the capsule: that is, it will initially resist the effects of pressure changes. Lag is largely overcome in servo altimeters.

(b) Manoeuvre Error

Manoeuvres, particularly steep climbs and descents, aggravate the lag such that the altimeter underreads in a climb and overreads in a descent.

(c) Blockages

Should the static vent or line become blocked 'old' static will be trapped in the instrument. Consequently, any change of altitude will **not be indicated**; a climb (or descent) which is initiated after the blockage occurs will cause the altimeter to underread (or overread).

2.6 Temperature Error

Altimeters are calibrated in accordance with the ISA MSL temperature and lapse rate, which prescribes the assumed temperature at any altitude. Any difference between the ambient temperature and ISA will cause an error in the altimeter such that if the air is **colder** than ISA the instrument will **overread** – the dangerous case.

2.7 Barometric Error

The altimeter really only measures **changes** of pressure. For it to provide a meaningful indication it must be provided with a pressure datum (see Fig 2-8) from which to measure and the sub-scale setting knob facilitates this. Any difference between sub-scale setting and the actual pressure at, say, mean sea level will cause the altimeter to be in error. If the actual pressure is **lower** than the one set then the altimeter will **overread** – again, the dangerous case. In other words, if the actual pressure is **lower** than the sub-scale setting you are **lower** than the altimeter is indicating.

The sub-scale range of UK altimeters is 800 to 1050mb. However, some

US specification instruments have a more restrictive range, starting at 950mb.

2.8 Pressure Datums

The need to provide the altimeter with a pressure datum against which it can do its measurement has already been stated. There are three datums in common use:

QFE   The barometric pressure at airfield level. With QFE set, the altimeter will indicate zero when the aircraft is on the ground and, when airborne, **height** above the airfield.

QNH   The airfield pressure reduced to sea level using the ISA formula. For all practical purposes it is mean sea level pressure and when it is set on the sub-scale the altimeter will indicate **altitude** above MSL.

In the UK **Regional QNHs** are also available, providing lowest forecast MSL pressure within an altimeter setting region. The forecast is made two hours ahead and is valid for the second of those two hours. For example, the forecast made at 1200 is valid 1300 to 1400.

1013mb   The 'standard' pressure setting which, when set on the sub-scale, causes the altimeter to indicate **flight level** or pressure altitude. The reading of the altimeter when so set is called QNE (used at high altitude airfields when QFE is so low that it cannot be set on the sub-scale).

The relationship between these three settings can perhaps be more readily appreciated by reference to Fig 2-6.

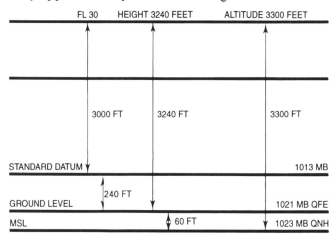

Figure 2–6   Chart of Atmospheric Pressure Datums.

2.9 Altimetry

It was stated when discussing Barometric Error, that if the actual pressure is different from that set on the subscale then the altimeter will be in error, overreading when the pressure is low and vice versa. This can also be related to drift – see Fig 2-8. In the northern hemisphere, if an aircraft has persistent starboard drift it must be flying into an area of low pressure and the pilot should expect the altimeter to read too high.

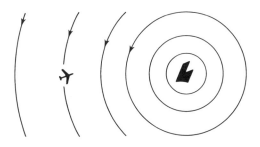

Figure 2–7.

The converse is true with port drift and, of course, everything is the other way round in the Southern Hemisphere.

To re-emphasise the point, take the case depicted in Fig 2-8.

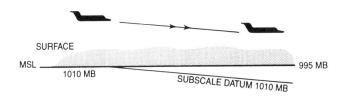

Figure 2–8.

The aircraft is flying from an area where the QNH is 1010mb to another area where the QNH is 995mb. However, the sub-scale setting is left on 1010. Flying at a constant **indicated** altitude the aircraft will maintain constant vertical separation from the 1010mb datum but, as can be seen from the diagram, its **actual** altitude will fall – that is, the altimeter will overread.

The above factors, together with the inter-relationship between the different pressure datums, provide a ready source of questions for the examiner – questions which you can expect to meet in Meteorology as well as in Instruments. The following examples are typical and, as you will see, a sketch diagram is all but essential if you are not to get muddled.

Example 1

An aircraft on a track of 230° (M) is required to fly at a flight level such that it will clear by at least 1500ft high ground rising to 1800 metres amsl. The regional QNH is 990mb.

(i) What is the minimum appropriate flight level at which the aircraft may fly?

(ii) Assuming that the flight is made at the level given in (i) what will be the aircraft's approximate clearance above the high ground? (Assume that 1mb = 28ft).

Solution

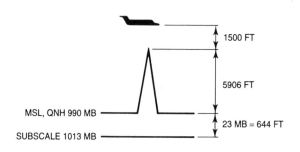

Figure 2–9.

a The aircraft is required to fly at an even flight level (the third quadrant).

b The high ground rises to 1800 metres, which is equal to 5906 feet amsl.

c The difference between the QNH (990mb) and the QFF (1013mb) is 23mb which represents a vertical difference in datums of 23 × 28 = 644ft.

d The aircraft must fly above a level of 644 + 5906 + 1500 = 8050ft on a 1013mb subscale setting.

e The next appropriate even flight level is FL 1000.

f At FL 100 the aircraft's approximate clearance above the ground is 10,000 – (644 + 5906) = 3450ft.

Therefore the required answers are:

(i) **FL 100**

(ii) **3450ft**

Example 2

One aircraft is flying in the vicinity of an airfield (elevation 360ft amsl) at 3000ft on the QFE of 995mb. A second aircraft is overflying at FL 35.

What is the approximate vertical separation between the two aircraft? (Assume that 1mb = 27 feet).

Solution

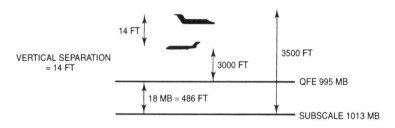

Figure 2–10.

a Note that airfield elevation is irrelevant and that knowledge of the QNH is not needed. The problem concerns the difference between QFE and the standard setting (1013mb), the latter being used by the aircraft at FL 35.

b $1013 - 995 = 18 \times 27 = 486$ft.

c By inspection from the diagram, the aircraft at 3000ft QFE is 3000 + 486 = 3486ft above the 1013mb datum.

d The separation is therefore 3500 – 3486 = 14ft.

Example 3

The altimeter of an aircraft standing at an airfield indicated 360ft when the subscale of the instrument was set to 989mb.

If the QNH at the time was 1005mb and a change of pressure of 1mb represents a height change of 28ft, what was the elevation of the airfield?

Solution

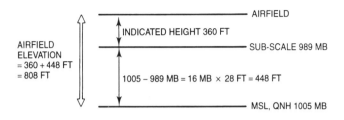

Figure 2–11.

Example 4
The altimeter of an aircraft at an airfield indicated 350ft when the QNH was 982mb.

If the elevation of the airfield was 70 feet and a change of pressure of 1mb represents a change of height of 28 feet, what was the setting on the subscale of the altimeter?

Solution

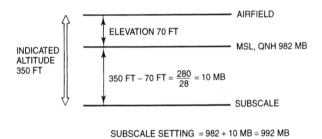

Figure 2–12.

Example 5
The altimeter of an aircraft at an airfield indicated 140ft when the subscale of the instrument was set to 990mb.

If the elevation of the airfield was 476 feet and a change of pressure of 1mb represents a height change of 28 feet what was the QNH at the airfield?

Solution

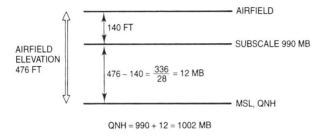

Figure 2–13.

3

The Airspeed Indicator

We saw in Chapter 1 that, as an aircraft moves through the air, it experiences an additional **dynamic** pressure. The magnitude of the dynamic pressure is proportional to the speed of the aircraft and the Airspeed Indicator (ASI) uses this relationship to measure airspeed.

3.1 Principle of Operation

A simple ASI is shown schematically at Fig 3-1.

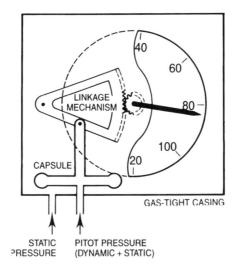

Figure 3–1.

When an aircraft is stationary, the only pressure it will experience is the atmospheric or **static** pressure. When the aircraft moves through the air the additional **dynamic** pressure discussed above is also experienced.

The pitot head (see Fig 1-1(b)) senses the total pressure – pitot pressure (P) – which is the sum of the static (S) and dynamic (D) pressures. Hence:

$$D = P - S$$

This equation is mechanised in the ASI by placing a capsule in an airtight case. Pitot pressure is fed to the capsule and static pressure is fed to the inside of the case.

There is thus static pressure both on the inside and the outside of the capsule, which cancels out, and the capsule will expand and contract in response to increases and decreases of dynamic pressure. Capsule movement is therefore proportional to airspeed; the movement is fed through a 'suitable system of linkages' to a needle that moves over a calibrated dial from which we can read Indicated Airspeed (IAS).

3.2 Calibration

Dynamic pressure – and hence capsule movement – is dependant not only on speed but also on the density of the air. In fact:

$$D = \tfrac{1}{2}\, \rho\, V^2$$

Where ρ is the ambient air density and V is the **true** airspeed (TAS).

The ASI can be calibrated for only one value of density. As you might expect, the value chosen is the density at sea level in the ISA, 1225gm/m³. Only when the air is actually at this density will IAS equate to TAS. If the density is of some different value there will be a **density error**, of which more later.

3.3 Errors

Source Errors

Instrument and position errors combined can be measured and a correction graph or table is usually to be found in the aircraft manual. An example is shown at Fig 3-2.

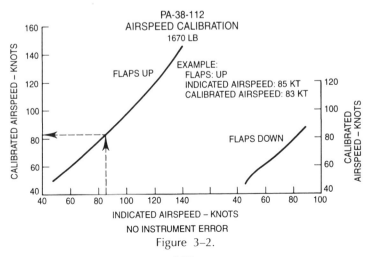

Figure 3–2.

When these corrections are applied to IAS the result is known as **Rectified Airspeed (RAS)** which sometimes, especially in the USA, is called **Calibrated Airspeed (CAS)**.

3.4 Density Error

We have seen that if the ambient air density is other than 1225gm/m³ there will be a density error. The major cause of changes in air density is changes in altitude and at the levels used by jet aircraft the IAS will be considerably less than TAS (eg at FL 350 with an IAS of 250kt, the TAS could be 440kt). The error can be calculated manually on your navigation computer or, in more sophisticated aircraft, automatically in an air data computer.

3.5 Compressibility Error

As the aircraft moves through the air, the air is brought to rest in the pitot head and is compressed. The compression causes the pitot pressure to increase, giving an incorrectly high value of dynamic pressure, and so too high an airspeed is indicated.

The error, which is insignificant at TAS below 300kt, can be corrected for on your navigation computer. When RAS is corrected for compressibility error the result is known as Equivalent Airspeed (EAS). As a figure, EAS is of little interest to aviators though very important to aircraft designers. What is important is that you remember that, when converting RAS to TAS, you must **allow for compressibility if the TAS is 300kt or more**.

3.6 Summary

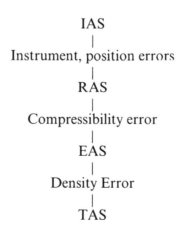

IAS
|
Instrument, position errors
|
RAS
|
Compressibility error
|
EAS
|
Density Error
|
TAS

3.7 Blockages

Blocked Pitot – A blockage in the pitot tube will mean that whatever pressure is in the capsule becomes trapped there. The ASI reading will thus remain constant, whatever the actual speed, so long as altitude is also constant. A change of altitude will result in a change of static pressure. In a descent, for example, the static in the case will increase but the static trapped in the capsule will stay the same. The ASI will **underread**. In a climb the ASI will overread.

Blocked Static – A blockage in the static line will again cause a constant reading in level flight. During a descent the pressure in the capsule will rise with the static part of pitot pressure. However, the static pressure in the case will not change and the ASI will overread – the dangerous case. The reverse holds good in a climb.

4

The Vertical Speed Indicator

Like the altimeter, the Vertical Speed Indicator (VSI) measures changes of static pressure. However, it is so constructed that it indicates, rather than altitude, rate of climb of descent. Not surprisingly, it is sometimes referred to as a Rate of Climb and Descent Indicator (RCDI).

4.1 Principle of Operation

A simple VSI is illustrated at Fig 4-1.

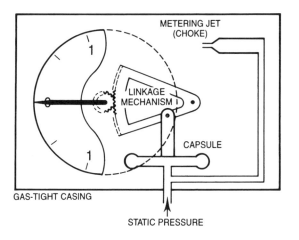

Figure 4–1.

A capsule inside a sealed case is fed with static pressure. Static pressure is also fed to the inside of the case but via a metering jet (choke) which permits changes of static pressure to pass only after a calibrated delay.

When the aircraft climbs (or descends) the consequent change of static pressure will be felt by the capsule almost instantaneously. But the change will reach the inside of the case only after a slight delay. During the delay the capsule will contract (or expand) in response to the pressure differential inside the case. The movement of the capsule is fed through linkages to cause the needle to move over a calibrated dial. The faster the

318

climb/descent the greater will be the movement of the capsule and there-fore the needle. The instrument dial usually has a logarithmic scale to give greater clarity at low rates of climb and descent – see Fig 4-2.

Figure 4–2.

4.2 The Metering Jet

The metering jet (choke) is designed to provide a rate of change of pressure directly related to a given rate of climb or descent **regardless of altitude**. That is, it must compensate for the variations of temperature and density which occur at altitude changes. It does this by making part of the air flow through a capillary tube (see Fig 4-3), while the rest of the air passes through a knife-edge orifice.

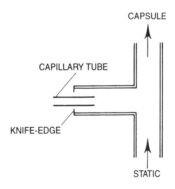

Figure 4–3.

The capillary tube allows the pressure difference to increase as the altitude increases and to decrease with decreasing temperature.

The orifice allows the pressure difference to decrease as altitude increases and to increase with decreasing temperature.

If you appreciate that the system **'balances the reduction in viscosity with reducing temperature against the reducing pressure differential with increasing altitude'**!

4.3 Errors

The VSI is susceptible to all the basic source errors. Note the following points:

(a) Instrument Error

(i) An adjustment screw permits the pointer to be reset to zero, if necessary.

(ii) Lag in the system is apparent when beginning or ending climb or descent.

(b) Manoeuvre Error
Changes of attitude can cause large errors. These are particularly apparent in the go-around situation and can persist for up to 3 seconds even at low altitudes.

(c) Blockages
A blockage of the static feed would cause the VSI to read zero.

4.4 Accuracy

The VSI should read zero ± 200 fpm when the aircraft is on the ground at temperatures between –20°C and +50°C. Outside these limits ± 300 fpm is permitted.

4.5 The Instantaneous VSI

To overcome the problem of lag in the normal VSI, the instantaneous (or instant lead) VSI (IVSI) incorporates an accelerometer unit in the static feed to the capsule (Fig 4-4).

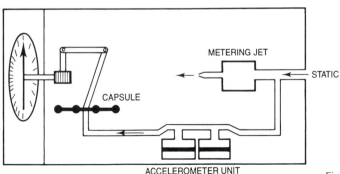

Figure 4–4.

320

The accelerometer unit comprises two dashpots. Each has an inertial mass piston and a balance spring, but one spring is stronger than the other. When a change of vertical speed occurs the pistons are displaced because of their inertia causing in, say, a descent an immediate increase of air pressure in the capsule.

After a short time the pistons settle again but by then the normal operation of the instrument has caught up.

4.6 Errors of the IVSI

The IVSI suffers from all the errors of the normal instrument except that lag is virtually eliminated. One new error is introduced:

Turning Error   The dashpots respond to the 'g' force in turns, causing erroneous readings. At bank angles of more than 40° the IVSI is unreliable.

5

The Machmeter

For a variety of reasons – mainly aerodynamic – it is important for the pilot of high speed aircraft to know how fast his aircraft is travelling in relation to the speed of sound. The speed of sound is not constant, but varies with temperature – it is the speed of sound in the airmass in which he is flying that is of interest to the pilot – that is the **local speed of sound (LSS)**.

The Machmeter presents the aircraft's speed (TAS) as a ratio of the LSS, the result being called the Mach (M) Number. So M 1.0 is the LSS and, more generally:

$$M = \frac{TAS}{LSS}$$

You may well be asked in the examination to calculate LSS, either directly or en-route to solving another problem. The relationship between temperature and LSS is given by the formula:

$$\textbf{LSS} = \textbf{39} \ \sqrt{\textbf{T}}$$

where T is the air temperature in **degrees absolute** (°A) or Kelvin. To convert °C to °A, simply add 273 (eg + 25°C = 298°A; –35°C = 238°A).

5.1 Principle of Operation

Both TAS and LSS can be related to dynamic (D) and static (S) pressures:

(a) From D = ½ ρ V² we can deduce that the TAS (V) is proportional to $\underline{D}$, ie $\underline{\text{Dynamic}}$
ρ   Density

(b) LSS is proportional to temperature which itself is proportional to density and static pressure. It can be shown that LSS is proportional to $\underline{S}$, $\underline{\text{Static}}$
ρ Density

From the foregoing we can deduce that:

$$M = \frac{TAS}{LSS} = \frac{D}{\rho} \div \frac{S}{\rho} = \frac{D}{S}$$

or, more practically,

$$M = \frac{P-S}{S}$$

The Machmeter makes use of this relationship by combining an airspeed capsule (P - S) and an altitude capsule (S) to produce Mach Number. A schematic is shown in Fig 5-1.

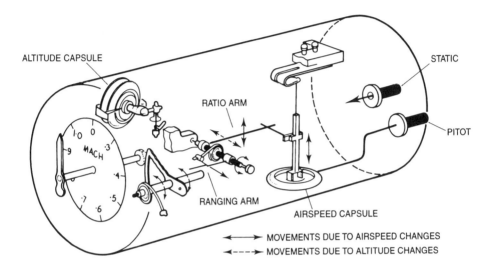

Figure 5–1 Schematic diagram of a Machmeter.

Movement (expansion or contraction) of the airspeed capsule is transmitted via the main shaft to the **ratio arm**. Movement of the altitude capsule is also transmitted to the ratio arm, but via a pin which is held in place by a retaining spring.

Note that the two capsules are mounted at 90° to each other, so the movements of the capsules cause the ratio arm to move in two planes, each at 90° to the other.

The ratio arm connects to the **ranging arm**. Because the movement of the ratio arm is in two planes, movement of the airspeed capsule causes the ratio arm to **move** the ranging arm and movement of the altitude capsule moves the ratio arm **along** the ranging arm.

The result is that the pointer movement is proportional to the ratio of the movements of the two capsules – that is, $\frac{P-S}{S}$, or Mach number.

The principle is perhaps best illustrated by reference to the simplified diagram at Fig 5-2.

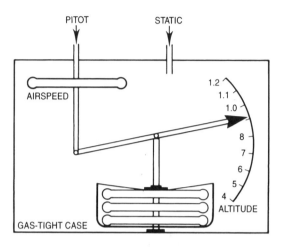

Figure 5–2.

An increase in altitude will cause the altimeter capsule to expand and show an increased Mach Number. Similarly, an increase in speed will cause the airspeed capsule to expand, which will also show an increased Mach Number. At speeds below M 0.4 the ratio and ranging arms are not in contact and no reading is indicated.

5.2 Errors

The Machmeter does not suffer from density, temperature or compressibility errors because these are all related to density which, as we saw, is cancelled out of the Machmeter equation.

Instrument, position and manoeuvre errors remain but, as they are small compared with the TAS, they are ignored in practice and the indicated Mach Number is taken as accurate (to ± M 0.01).

5.3 Blockages

Blocked Pitot – will cause the same error as in the ASI. That is, the Machmeter will overread in a climb, underread in a descent.

Blocked Static – will again cause the Machmeter to be in error in the same sense as the ASI. That is, it will overread in a descent and underread in a climb.

5.4 Mach Number, TAS, RAS Relationship

Mach Number, TAS and RAS are all inter-related by temperature and you must be able to work out how the three speeds change in relation to each other.

5.5 Level Flight

Flying at a constant RAS, in level flight, both the TAS and Mach Number will change if the temperature changes. A **decrease** in temperature will cause a decrease in TAS and increase in Mach Number, and vice versa. So as temperature decreases, to maintain a constant Mach Number, TAS (and RAS) must be reduced. This results in the apparent anomaly that if two aircraft at different levels are flying at the same Mach Number the one at the lower (warmer) level will have the higher TAS.

5.6 Climbs and Descents

In a 'constant speed' climb or descent the pilot has a choice of datums for speed control – constant RAS, constant TAS or constant Mach Number. Unfortunately (for us) if one value is held constant the others will change. How they change is a favourite exam question. You may find the following helps keep the relationship in mind.

| Climb | + | MTR | – |
| Descent | + | RTM | – |

For example – climbing at a constant RAS (R) both the TAS (T) and Mach Number (M) will increase. Descending at a constant TAS, the RAS increases but the Mach Number will decrease.

An alternative, graphical, way of presenting the same information is shown below.

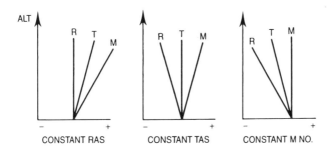

Figure 5-3.

325

At constant RAS, in a climb, both TAS and Mach Number increase, the Mach Number at the greater rate. In a descent, the opposite happens.

At constant RAS in a climb, the RAS decreases but the Mach Number increases.

At constant Mach Number in a climb, both RAS and TAS decrease, RAS at the greater rate.

Effects of Inversions/Isothermal Layers
The above arguments supposed that an increase in altitude was accompanied by a decrease in temperature. This is not always the case, and exam questions have cropped up concerning the RAS/TAS/nm relationship during a descent through an inversion. The graphs and mnemonics do not work in this case – a little logic must be applied!
You need to keep in mind that:

$$M = \frac{TAS}{LSS} \qquad - \quad (1)$$

$$LSS = 39\sqrt{T} \qquad - \quad (2)$$

$$RAS = \tfrac{1}{2}\rho\,(TAS)^2 \qquad - \quad (3)$$

Now, consider a descent at **constant RAS** through an inversion layer, bearing in mind that the air is warmer above the inversion layer than below it and that the colder air below the inversion is the more dense.

From (2) above, as temperature decreases through the inversion so LSS must reduce.

From (1), if LSS reduces **Mach Number must increase**

From (3), if density increases **RAS must increase**

The same sort of logic can be applied to climbs and to isothermal layers.

5.7 Mach Number Calculations

Calculations involving the Mach Number formulae frequently occur in the examination. The following examples will help familiarise you with what is required. Note that temperature is often quoted as **temperature deviation** – that is, the difference between ambient temperature and the **Jet Standard Atmosphere (JSA)** which assumes a sea level temperature of + 15°C and a lapse rate of 2°C per thousand feet with no tropopause. Note also that some problems can be readily solved using your navigation computer; others require you to do the sums.

Example 1
At FL 330 the ambient temperature is –53°C. What is the temperature deviation?

Solution
JSA temperature at 33,000ft is + 15 –(33 × 2) = –51°C
Ambient temperature is given as –53°C
Ambient is 2°C **colder** than JSA
∴ Temperature deviation is –2°C

Example 2
You are flying at FL 310 at RAS 265kt. The temperature deviation is +10°C. Determine:
    (a)   TAS
    (b)   Mach Number
    (c)   LSS

Solution
JSA temperature FL 310 = + 15 –(31 × 2)   =   –47°C
Temperature deviation   =   +10°C

Ambient temperature   =   –37°C

    (a)   From nav computer, RAS 265kt, –37°C, FL 310:

          TAS = 430kt (Don't forget compressibility)

    (b)   From nav computer, TAS 430kt, –37°C

          M = 0.72

    (c)   LSS = 39 $\sqrt{T}$

          = 39 $\sqrt{-37 + 273}$

          = 39 $\sqrt{236}$

          = **599 kt**

Example 3
What is the LSS at F260 when the temperature deviation is –4°C?

Solution
JSA temperature at F260 = +15 – (26 × 2) =   –37°C
Temperature Deviation   .=   –4°C

Ambient Temperature   = –41°C

Convert to °A = –4.1 + 273 = 232°A

LSS = 39 $\sqrt{T}$ = 39 $\sqrt{232}$ = **594 kt**

Example 4
What is the temperature deviation at FL 390 if a TAS 460 kt gives a Mach number of 0.82?

Solution
$$M = \frac{TAS}{LSS}, \text{ so LSS} = \frac{TAS}{M} = \frac{460}{0.82} = 561 \text{ kt}$$

$$LSS = 39 \sqrt{T}, \text{ so } T = \frac{LSS^2}{39} = \frac{561^2}{39} = 207°A$$

Temperature (°C) = °A – 273 = 207 – 273 = –66°C
JSA Temperature FL 390 = +15 – (2 × 39) = –63°C
Temperature deviation = **–3°C**

Example 5
An increase in Mach Number of 0.15 results in an increase in TAS of 84 kt. What is the LSS?

Solution
$$M = \frac{TAS}{LSS}, \text{ so LSS} = \frac{TAS}{M} = \frac{84}{0.15} = \textbf{560 kt}$$

6

Air Temperature Measurement

You know from your studies of meteorology, flight planning and aero-dynamics how significant a part air temperature plays in aircraft performance. But measuring the temperature of the air which surrounds an aircraft in flight is not as simple as it might seem. This is particularly so at higher airspeeds when air compressibility and heating, because of friction, become significant.

6.1 Types of Thermometer

Temperature can be measured by several different means, based on the following principles:

(a) Both solids and liquids expand as their temperature increases.

(b) The electrical resistance of substances changes with change of temperature.

(c) When dissimilar metals are joined, as in a thermocouple, an electromotive force (emf) is produced; the magnitude of the emf is dependant on temperature difference.

(d) Many liquids change state from liquid to vapour as temperature increases. If enclosed, the change of vapour pressure is related to change of temperature.

(e) The radiation emitted by a body is indicative of its temperature.

Different types of thermometer have evolved. In aircraft, those commonly used for measurement of outside air temperature (OAT) are:

(a) Expansion type, using solid or liquid elements. The former, employing a bi-metallic helical element, is common in light aircraft. Neither type is practical when TAS exceeds about 150kt.

(b) Electrical type, using either the resistance or the thermo-electric principles. Resistance types, usually employing a platinum element, are common in larger aircraft.

In light aircraft the sensing element protrudes through the aircraft skin

(or window) and is connected directly to a dial on the inside. Larger aeroplanes usually use electrical type thermometers with the sensing element
mounted either flush with the fuselage skin or in probes (see Fig 6-1).
Probes have advantages in that they can:

(a)   Shield the sensor from the effects of the sun's heating

(b)   Reduce errors induced from the heating of the aircraft's skin

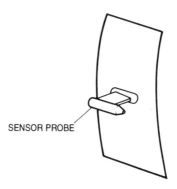

SENSOR PROBE

Figure 6–1.

6.2 Ram Air Temperature

The temperature that we need to measure is that of the ambient air – that
is, the temperature unaffected by the movement of the aircraft and
referred to as **Static Air Temperature (SAT)**.

Despite careful siting of temperature sensors, thermometers in higher
speed aircraft will not indicate the SAT, mainly because of compressibility effects.

The temperature of air brought completely to rest at stagnation points
is referred to as the **Total Air Temperature (TAT)**. The difference between
SAT and TAT is sometimes called stagnation rise and the relationship is
given by:

$$SAT = TAS - \frac{(V)^2}{(100)}$$

Where V is the TAS.

The proportion of the stagnation temperature that is sensed by the thermometers is known as the recovery factor or **K**. The value of K will
depend on the type of thermometer used; it is usually about 0.85 but with
a particularly sophisticated sensor known as a **Rosemount Probe**, can be
assumed to be 1.

In practice, the air around the temperature sensor is not brought completely to rest. The temperature actually measured is called the **Ram Air Temperature (RAT)** and the difference between SAT and RAT is known as the Ram Rise.

6.3 Corrected Outside Air Temperature

We, of course, are interested in knowing the actual ambient air temperature, the SAT. This is obtained as best we can by applying corrections to the temperature indicated on the thermometer. The result is called, for navigational purposes, the Corrected Outside Air Temperature (COAT).

6.4 Errors

Instrument Error:
There will be small instrument errors caused by manufacturing imperfections. The errors can be measured and corrected for in combination with position error.

Position Error
As already discussed, despite careful positioning of the sensor, some errors will arise. It can be measured and corrected either manually, using graphs or tables, or automatically in the aircraft's electronics.

6.5 Lag

There is minimal lag in the more sophisticated measuring devices but it can be significant in those fitted to light aircraft.

Test Yourself   Air Data Instruments 1

1. Dynamic Pressure is:
   (a)   Density and static pressure
   (b)   Pitot pressure plus static pressure
   (c)   Static pressure minus pitot pressure
   (d)   Pitot pressure minus static pressure

Ref 1.2

2. A pitot tube will sense:
   (a)   Dynamic pressure only
   (b)   Static pressure only
   (c)   Pitot and static pressure
   (d)   Static and dynamic pressure

Ref 1.2

3. The pressure experienced in the capsule(s) of an altimeter is:
   (a)   Less than static pressure
   (b)   More than static pressure
   (c)   Static pressure
   (d)   Dynamic plus static pressure

Ref 2.1

4. The subscale of an altimeter is set to 1018mb and reads 3900ft when the QNH is 992mb. Assuming 1mb equals 30ft, the true height of the aircraft AMSL is:
   (a)   3120ft.
   (b)   3440ft.
   (c)   4680ft.
   (d)   5370ft.

Ref 2.9

5. Which of the following errors is reduced significantly in the servo-altimeter to make it more accurate than the mechanical version?
   (a)   Barometric.
   (b)   Hysteresis.
   (c)   Time Lag.
   (d)   Temperature.

Ref 2.3

6. Four errors which affect the ASI are:
   (a) Instrument, Density, Compressibility, Position.
   (b) Instrument, Time Lag, Position, Compressibility.
   (c) Density, Instrument, Position, Temperature.
   (d) Time lag, Position, Instrument, Barometric.

Ref 3.3 to 3.6

7. During a descent the static vent becomes blocked by ice. The airspeed indicator will:
   (a) Underread due to static pressure increasing.
   (b) Fall rapidly to zero due to differential pressures equalising.
   (c) Overread due to static pressure increasing.
   (d) Continue to indicate correctly because the instrument only uses pitot pressure.

Ref 3.7

8. A correction for compressibility error must be applied:
   (a) At a TAS of 300kt only.
   (b) If the TAS is 300kt or more.
   (c) If the RAS is 300kt or more.
   (d) If the TAS is 250kt.

Ref 3.5

9. An IVSI, compared with a normal VSI, suffers virtually no lag. The lag is minimised by using:
   (a) A servo feed-back system.
   (b) A metering jet.
   (c) A temperature compensating device.
   (d) A double dashpot acceleration pump.

Ref 4.5

10. You are flying a constant rate of descent at 650fpm when the static vents become blocked. A few seconds after the blockage occurs the most likely VSI indication will be:
    (a) Zero.
    (b) 550fpm descent.
    (c) 650fpm descent.
    (d) 750fpm descent.

Ref 4.3

11. The term Mach No expresses:
    (a) The ratio of TAS in knots to the local speed of sound in knots.
    (b) The ratio of rectified airspeed in knots to the local speed of sound.
    (c) The ratio of the local speed of sound in mph to the TAS in knots.
    (d) The ratio of the equivalent air speed in knots to the local speed of sound in knots.

Ref 5.0

12. Errors affecting the Machmeter include:
    (a) Instrument and Position.
    (b) Density and Instrument.
    (c) Position and Temperature.
    (d) Density and Temperature.

Ref 5.2

13. The TAS of an aircraft which is flying at Mach 0.86 and a temperature of –55°C is:
    (a) 477kt.
    (b) 607kt.
    (c) 494kt.
    (d) 575kt.

Ref 5.7

14. An aircraft is climbing at a constant Mach No below the tropopause in ISA conditions. During the climb the RAS will:
    (a) Increase due to decreasing static pressure.
    (b) Increase due to decreasing temperature.
    (c) Decrease due to decreasing static pressure.
    (d) Decrease due to decreasing temperature.

Ref 5.6/5.7

15. An aircraft is fitted with an unsophisticated thermometer to measure outside air temperature (OAT). The indicated OAT will be:
    (a) Too low because reduced air density at altitude.
    (b) Too high because of skin friction and compressibility effect.
    (c) Too high only because of the heating from the sun.
    (d) Too low because of skin friction and compressibility effect.

Ref 5.6/5.7

7

The Gyroscope

A gyroscope (gyro for short) is a rotating mass which has freedom to move in one or more planes perpendicular to the plane of rotation. This freedom is provided by mounting the spinning mass in a system of gimbals, as illustrated at Fig 7-1, which are pivoted at right angles to each other.

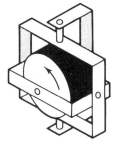

Figure 7–1.

Any gyroscope possesses two fundamental properties – **rigidity in space** and **precession**. More of these later. For the moment it is sufficient to know that these properties make gyros extremely useful as the basis for instruments which measure and display aircraft attitude and direction.

7.1 Types of Gyro

7.2 Free Gyro   A free gyro has **complete freedom** in three planes at right angles to each other. Also known as a **space gyro**, it has no practical application that concerns us.

7.3 Tied Gyro   A tied gyro also has freedom in three planes but is constrained in one plane to some external reference. An example is the Directional Gyro Indicator which has its spin axis constrained in the aircraft's yawing plane.

7.4 Earth Gyro   An Earth gyro again has freedom in three planes but is constrained by **gravity**. An example is the Attitude

335

Indicator which has its spin axis constrained to the Earth vertical.

7.5 Rate Gyro A rate gyro has freedom in only one plane (in addition to its plane of rotation) and is constructed so as to measure **rate** of movement about an axis which is at right angles both to the spin axis and the axis of freedom. An example is the turn co-ordinator.

7.6 Gyroscopic Theory

We mentioned earlier that a gyro has two important characteristics – rigidity and precession. We must now examine these in a little more depth.

Rigidity
A gyro's rigidity in space, or gyroscopic inertia, means that when the rotor of a free gyro is spinning its plane of rotation will remain fixed in space. If mounted in an aircraft the gyro will maintain its alignment unaffected by the motion of its parent craft.

You do not need to understand why this occurs. You **do** need to know the factors which affect the degree or amount of rigidity. These are:

Speed of rotation
Mass of the rotor
Radius of the rotor

The greater any of these factors, the greater is the rigidity.

The gyro designer, then, will make his rotor spin as fast as possible. He would also like it to have a huge, heavy rotor but, for aircraft instruments, this is not practical. Instead he makes the effective radius of rotation of the mass as big as possible by concentrating the mass to the outside of the rotor, as shown in Fig 7-2.

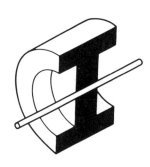

Figure 7–2.

Precession

If an external force is applied to a gyro it will **apparently** act at a point which is removed from the **actual** point of application by 90° in the direction of rotor rotation. Luckily you do not have to know why this occurs, only that it does. Follow through Fig 7-3 and the subsequent explanation.

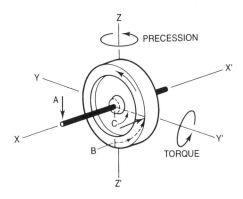

Figure 7–3.

In this illustration the spin axis (XX') is shown to be horizontal (it could be anywhere) and the gyro rotor is spinning anti-clockwise as you look at it. Now consider a force A applied to the spin axis as shown. This force has the same effect as pushing against the bottom of the rotor at B, and producing a torque about the YY' axis. You would expect this torque to cause the spin axis to tilt. But the laws of gyrodynamics cause the effect of the applied force to be moved through 90° in the direction of rotor spin, so the force is apparently acting at C, and the rotor **precessed** about the ZZ' axis.

Precession and rigidity are inter-related in that the more rigid the gyro the greater the applied force needed to produce a given amount of precession.

Secondary Precession

The above description assumes that unrestricted movement of the gyro axis can take place in the direction of precession.

If, however, the precession is impeded or opposed in any way, the force producing the opposition will in turn produce its own **secondary precession**. Secondary precession obeys exactly the same rules as primary precession and, since it is caused by an existing primary precession, its magnitude is proportional to the primary precession.

The principle of operation of the rate gyro makes use of secondary precession.

7.7 Gyro Wander

We have seen that, because of its rigidity, a gyro will retain a fixed alignment **in space** unless acted on by some external force. Any movement of the gyro away from its initial orientation is known as **wander**.

If the spin axis is moved in the horizontal plane the wander is known as **drift** (Fig 7-4).

Figure 7–4.

If the spin axis is moved in the vertical plane, the wander is known as topple – Fig 7-5.

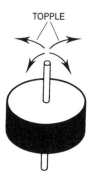

Figure 7–5.

Note that a gyro with its spin axis vertical can only topple – it cannot drift because movement in the horizontal plane would be movement about the spin axis. However, a gyro with its spin axis in anything but the vertical can both topple and drift.

Wander can be further divided into **real wander** and **apparent wander**.

Real Wander
Real wander is the **actual** movement of the spin axis away from the initial orientation in space. It can be drift, topple or a combination of the two. Unwanted, random real wander is caused by imperfections in the gyro such as friction in the bearings or imbalance of the rotor or gimbals.

Real wander can also be deliberately induced for correction purposes. We shall discuss this later.

Apparent Wander
Apparent wander occurs when the spin axis of a gyro **appears** to move **in relation to an observer on the Earth** (or in an aircraft). In fact, it is not that the gyro which is moving but that the observer's view of it is changing. Apparent wander can also be drift, topple or a combination.

Apparent wander is induced by the rotation of the Earth and by movement of the observer over the Earth. Consider Fig 7-6.

Earth Rate

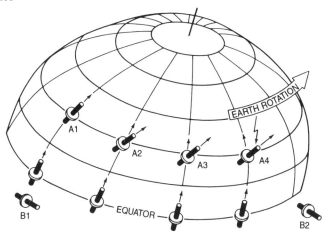

Figure 7-6.

Suppose gyro A at position 1 has its spin axis aligned with True North at that point. With the passage of time, although the gyro will maintain its alignment in space the direction of True North (relative to the gyro) will change as the Earth rotates and the observer's position **in space** moves through 2 and 3 to 4. This is **apparent drift**, which will be zero at the Equator (where the meridians are parallel) and maximum at the poles. The specific term for this apparent wander is **Earth Rate**.

Now consider gyro B which is at the Equator and has its spin axis aligned East–West. As the Earth rotates, and the gyro maintains its alignment in space, the gyro will appear to topple through 90° for each quarter revolution of the Earth – **apparent topple**. The same gyro at the pole would not appear to topple at all.

To summarise. In general terms, **apparent drift** due to Earth Rate is zero at the Equator and maximum at the poles. **Apparent** topple is maximum at the Equator and zero at the poles.

Transport Wander

Just as movement of the Earth 'under' the space orientated gyro will cause wander, so too will transporting the gyro over the Earth – **transport wander**. Movement with an easterly component creates apparent drift in the same sense as Earth Rate; a westerly component causes the drift to be in the opposite sense.

Wander – A Summary

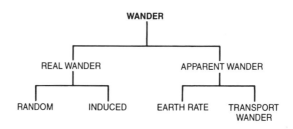

Figure 7–7.

7.8 Power Sources

In light aircraft, most gyros are air driven. That is, air is sucked out of the gyro case by a **vacuum pump**; replacement air rushes into the case to fill the vacuum and in so doing drives the gyro rotor, which has 'buckets' shaped into its rim to catch the air.

In larger aircraft, all gyros are electrically driven by induction motors which are designed into the rotor. The main advantages of electrically-driven gyros are:

- A higher speed can be used, giving a greater rigidity.

- Constant speed whereas the air-driven rotor slows at altitude as the air density falls.

- Less prone to ingestion of dust and moisture because the gyro case is sealed. Life and reliability are enhanced.

- Greater freedom of movement: the motor is part of the rotor, so there is no need for wiring or piping which restricts movement.

- Faster erection and re-erection.

7.9 Ring Laser Gyros

Ring laser gyros (RLG) are solid-state instruments which cannot, strictly speaking, be considered to be gyroscopes. However, they do the same job as a rate gyro – measure rates of rotation – and so have assumed the name. They were developed for use in inertial navigation systems where they have considerable advantages over conventional instruments.

The RLG consists of three optical tubes arranged in a triangle (Fig 6-8) to form a continuous path. Two laser beams travel around this path in opposite directions. If there is any rotation of the triangle, one beam will take longer than the other to complete its journey. The time difference, which can be measured by an optical sensor, is proportional to rate of rotation.

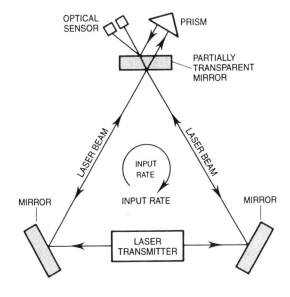

Figure 7–8.

A problem can arise if there is no rotational movement at all – the laser beams suffer from 'beam interlock'. This is overcome by fitting a **dither motor**.

8

The Direction Indicator

The Direction Indicator (DI) – sometimes known as the Directional Gyro Indicator (DGI) – makes use of the rigidity of a gyro to provide a heading reference. Unlike the magnetic compass, the gyro does not suffer from turning and acceleration errors and so can provide a stable display of heading to the pilot.

8.1 Principle of Operation

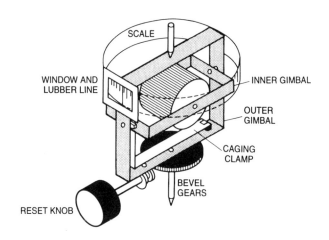

Figure 8–1.

The diagram at Fig 8-1 shows an early type of DI which is easier to illustrate than more modern instruments. However, the principle of operation is the same.

The DI is designed to measure change of heading – that is, motion in the aircraft's yawing plane. A free gyro (three planes of movement including the plane of rotation) is mounted in two gimbals with its spin axis in the yawing plane. The spin axis is constrained in this plane and is, therefore, a **tied gyro**.

The gyro rotor is mounted in the inner gimbal, which itself is in the yawing plane. The inner gimbal is pivoted in the outer gimbal, which itself is pivoted in the case of the instrument to allow 360° movement in azimuth. The outer gimbal also carries the compass card or scale. Note that the freedom of the inner gimbal is limited such that, if pitch or roll exceeds **55°**, the inner gimbal will contact a mechanical stop and the gyro will precess.

The gyro is rigid in space, so any movement of the aircraft in its yawing plane – ie any **change of heading** – can be measured relative to the direction of the gyro. But when it is first run-up, the gyro will erect on any random direction, whereas we need to know direction relative to a useful datum, usually Magnetic North. The DI is therefore provided with a **reset knob**. When this is pushed in, the gyro is 'caged' and can be rotated until the gyro reading agrees with an external reference such as the magnetic compass. The resetting action also acts as a fast re-erection device which can be useful if the gyro limits are exceeded in flight.

The DI can be air driven or electrically driven. We are concerned only with the air-driven version which spins at about **12,000 rpm**.

8.2 Gyro Control

The DI, we said, is designed to measure movement in the aircraft's yawing plane, or in other words, movement about the **aircraft's vertical axis**. However, when the aircraft banks in a turn, the gyro – because of its rigidity – tries to stay in the **true or Earth** vertical. Some form of control is needed to **tie** the gyro to the aircraft vertical.

The method of control makes use of the property of precession. In normal flight (Fig 8-2) the gyro is driven by two air jets which impinge equally on 'buckets' cut into the rim of the rotor. The jets are mounted on the outer gimbal which, remember, is attached to the instrument case.

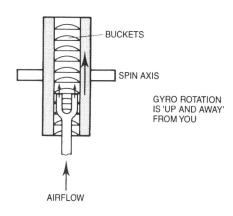

Figure 8–2.

When the aircraft banks (Fig 8-3) the force of the driving airflow is divided into two components. One, X, continues to drive the rotor

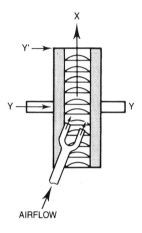

Figure 8–3.

but the second Y acts on the rim of the rotor in the direction of the spin axis. Because of the law of precession, this force is moved through 90° in the direction of rotation. It appears to act as Y^1, a force which will push the gyro rotor back into the aircraft vertical, which is where we want it.

8.3 Errors

Gimballing Error
Gimballing errors occur **during manoeuvre** because of the **geometry of the gimbal system**. That's all you need to know.

Real Wander
Real wander is caused by mechanical imperfections in the gyro. Real topple will be corrected by the air jets as described earlier. Real drift will cause errors in the indicated heading and is corrected by periodically resetting the gyro reading to synchronise it with the magnetic compass.

Apparent Wander
As we saw in the previous chapter, a gyro with its spin axis horizontal will suffer from apparent wander because of Earth Rate and Transport Wander. Apparent topple will be corrected by the air jets. Apparent drift will cause heading errors and needs to be looked at in more detail.

Earth Rate
To revise and expand on our discussion in Chapter 7, consider Fig 8-4.

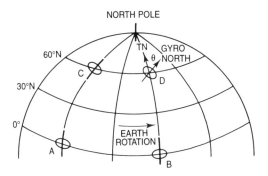

Figure 8–4.

The gyro at A, at the Equator, is aligned with the meridian. Because the meridians are parallel at the Equator, it will maintain this alignment when the Earth's rotation moves it to B. On the other hand, a gyro at the pole would **appear** to drift at a rate equal to the Earth's rotation rate – that is, 360° in 24 hours or **15° per hour** – in fact, the rate is 15° times the sine of the latitude (15° sin lat) per hour.

The numbers are not particularly important. What **is important** to note is the difference between Gyro North and True North for the gyro at D. Because of the effect of Earth Rate between C and D, a heading measured from Gyro North at D will be **less than** the same heading measured from True North. In other words, in the northern hemisphere:

Earth Rate causes the gyro to Underread

The opposite will be true in the southern hemisphere.

Earth Rate Correction
The effect of apparent drift caused by Earth Rate can be corrected for by inducing real drift in the opposite direction. This is done by using a **latitude nut** which will correct for Earth Rate at **one particular latitude**, usually that of the aircraft's home base.

A nut is fitted to one side of the inner gimbal on a spindle. (Fig 8-5).

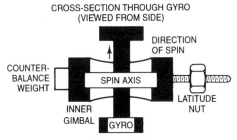

Figure 8–5.

345

On the opposite side is a counter-weight that exactly balances the nut when the nut is mid-way along the spindle. This would be the setting for the Equator, where no correction is required.

Now suppose that the nut is adjusted so that it is nearer the outer end of its spindle (Fig 8-6).

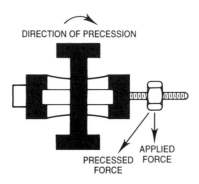

Figure 8–6.

A torque is set up because of the weight of the nut that, because of the law of precession, will cause the gyro to precess (drift) in a clockwise direction. This is a correction for Earth Rate in the southern hemisphere, and the amount by which the nut is moved from its mid-way (Equator) setting depends on the latitude for which the correction is required. Adjusting the nut in the opposite direction produces corrections for the northern hemisphere.

Note carefully that the apparent drift due to Earth Rate is reduced to zero **only at the latitude for which the nut is set.** For instance, in the northern hemisphere, to the North of the set latitude the gyro will still underread and to the South of the set latitude the gyro will overread.

Figure 8-7 illustrates the case for a gyro with its latitude nut set for 30°N.

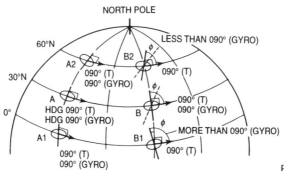

Figure 8–7.

In effect – as far as the gyro is concerned – the Equator has been 'moved' to 30°N.

Transport Wander

As we saw in Chapter 7, transporting the gyro over the surface of the Earth also induces apparent drift known as Transport Wander. Like Earth Rate, it happens because of the convergency of the meridians and its magnitude is proportional to the East/West component of ground-speed, and latitude.

With an easterly component, transport wander is in the same sense as Earth Rate in the northern hemisphere. That is, in the northern hemisphere it causes the gyro to underread. Westerly movement has the opposite effect.

Sense of Apparent Drift

You may find the following table helpful in remembering the sense of the apparent drift and the latitude nut correction.

	N	S
EARTH RATE	–	+
LAT NUT	+	–
TW-E	–	+
TW-W	+	–

Notice that if you can keep in your head the fact that Earth Rate in the northern hemisphere caused an underread (-) then all the other signs can be filled in by flip-flopping plus and minus.

8.4 Drift Assessment

Examination questions crop up frequently where you will be asked to assess the total effect of Earth Rate, Transport Wander and the latitude nut. You will not have to do any calculations – just decide whether the overall effect will cause the gyro to underread or overread at an increasing or decreasing rate. Inevitably, the question will put you at a latitude other than the one for which the nut is set!

Example

A perfectly balanced (ie no random drift) DI has its latitude nut set for 50°N.

Would the indicator reading increase, decrease or remain the same when:

(a) Flying on a track of 090°(T) in latitude 70°N

(b) Flying on a track of 270°(T) in latitude 20°N

(c) Flying on a track of 090°(T) in latitude 40°S

Solution to (a)
Based on the diagram below, a flight to the North of the set latitude causes a decrease in reading, as does a track of 090°(T) in the northern hemisphere, therefore the DI underreads and the readings will decrease.

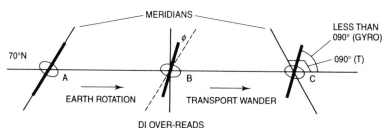

DI OVER-READS
(EARTH ROTATION AND TRANSPORT WANDER ERRORS ARE COMPLEMENTARY)

Solution to (b)
When South of the set latitude the latitude nut will cause an overreading. Flight on a track of 270°(T) in the Northern Hemisphere also causes the gyro to overread. The overall effect is therefore to cause the DI readings to increase.

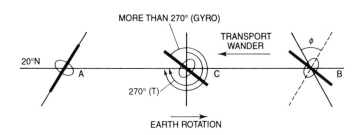

DI OVER-READS
(EARTH ROTATION AND TRANSPORT WANDER ERRORS ARE COMPLEMENTARY)

Solution to (c)
Flight to the South of the set latitude causes overreading, flight on a track of 090°(T) in the southern hemisphere will also cause an overreading. The DI readings will increase.

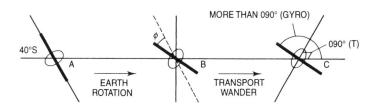

9

The Attitude Indicator

The Direction Indicator (DI) discussed in the previous chapter provides the pilot with indication of changing heading – that is, movement in the yawing plane. To complete a three dimensional picture he also needs indication of movement in the pitching and rolling planes and these are provided by the **Attitude Indicator (AI)** – known in earlier times as the **Artificial Horizon**.

9.1 Principle of Operation

The pilot needs to know his attitude in pitch and roll with reference to the 'real' horizon, the Earth horizontal. Accordingly, the AI uses an **Earth gyro**, one that is constrained to the Earth reference by gravity.

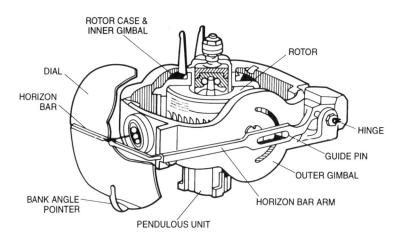

Figure 9–1.

The gyro is mounted with its plane of rotation in the horizontal (spin axis is vertical) in two gimbals; the AI thus has freedom of movement in all three planes. The gyro remains rigid in space and provides the datum against which pitch and roll attitude can be measured and displayed.

The gyro can be driven by air or electricity. We are concerned primarily with the air-driven version which has a rotor speed of about 15,000 rpm.

The gyro rotor is enclosed in a sealed case which also acts as the inner gimbal. The driving air is let into the case then, having spun the rotor, escapes from the case through four **exhaust ports** in a **pendulous unit** mounted below the gyro (of which more later).

The inner gimbal is mounted, with its axis athwartships, within the outer gimbal. The outer gimbal is mounted in the instrument case with pivots in the aircraft's fore-and-aft axis. A horizon-bar is hinged to the outer gimbal at the rear of the instrument. A guide pin, which is fixed to the inner gimbal, passes through slots in the outer gimbal to engage the horizon-bar. Fixed to the horizon-bar is a dial which, as the aircraft manoeuvres, moves behind the glass instrument face on which is marked an aircraft symbol (representing the real thing).

Pitch Indication

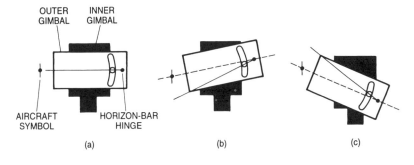

Figure 9–2.

In level flight (Fig 9-2(a)) the aircraft's horizontal axis is perpendicular to the spin axis. The guide pin is in the centre of the slot in the outer gimbal; the horizon-bar is horizontal and coincident with the aircraft symbol on the face of the dial.

If the aircraft pitches up (Fig 9-2(b)), the outer gimbal and the instrument case move with the aircraft. The gyro rotor and inner gimbal remain rigid. The relative motion between inner and outer gimbals causes the guide pin to be displaced (downwards) in its slot. The displaced guide pin takes with it the horizon-bar which, because it is hinged at the rear (right in the diagram), moves down. On the instrument the horizon-bar is below the aircraft symbol indicating a pitch-up.

If the aircraft pitches down, the opposite occurs (Fig 9-2(c)).

9.2 Roll Indication

When the aircraft banks the rotor and inner gimbal, the outer gimbal and horizon bar remain in the horizontal because of gyroscopic rigidity.

The instrument case and the miniature aircraft move with the aircraft. The miniature aircraft therefore indicates the angle of bank relative to the gyro horizon.

9.3 Presentation

Examples of how altitude is presented to the pilot are shown in Fig 9-3.

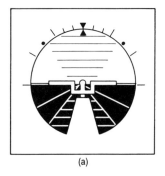
(a)

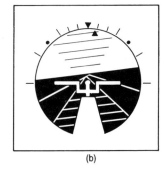
(b)

Figure 9-3 (a) Straight and Level (b) Descending right turn (c) Climbing left turn.

9.4 Gyro Control

An air-driven AI is powered by air which is drawn into the sealed gyro case and exhausted through a pendulous erection unit at the base of the inner gimbal. There are four exhaust ports in the unit, two in the fore-and-aft axis (one forward, one aft) and two athwartships (one left, one right). Pivoted at the top of each port is a vane which, in straight and level unaccelerating flight covers half of its port. Air escapes equally from all four ports (Fig 9-4).

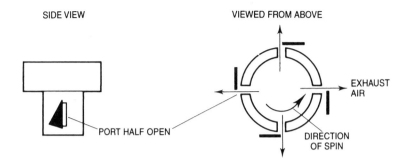

Figure 9–4.

Should the rotor spin axis move out of the Earth vertical (Fig 9-5) the vanes, under the influence of gravity, will stay in the vertical. This results in one pair of exhaust ports being put out of balance – one port will be more than half open, its partner more than half closed, and the airflow through the open port will be excessive. A reaction force will be set up against the closed port. This force will be moved 'gyrodynamically' through 90° in the direction of rotor spin and hence will push the gyro back to the vertical.

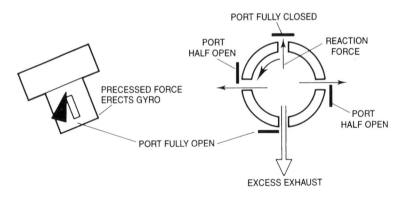

Figure 9–5.

9.5 Errors

The AI suffers from turning and acceleration errors. The sense of some of the errors is dependent on the direction of spin of the rotor; in the subsequent discussion we will assume that the gyro is rotating **anti-clockwise as viewed from above**. This is the usual direction for air-driven instruments.

353

9.6 Acceleration Errors

Acceleration error is in two parts, resulting in false indications of pitch **and** roll.

The presence of the pendulous erection unit under the gyro makes the assembly 'bottom heavy'. So the effect of an acceleration is to produce a force on the bottom of the assembly, acting towards the pilot. This force is moved gyroscopically through 90° in the direction of rotation and causes the whole assembly to rotate anti-clockwise (as viewed by the pilot). The resulting indication is that of a turn to the right.

The acceleration is also felt by the vanes on the erection unit. Both will move back towards the pilot so the right port becomes fully open and the left port fully closed. The resulting force, moved through 90°, causes the AI to indicate a climb.

Decelerations have exactly the opposite effect. Just remember that **acceleration** causes an air-driven AI to indicate a **false climbing right turn**.

9.7 Turning Errors

Like a linear acceleration, the centrifugal force in a turn will affect both the pendulous mass of the erection unit and the vanes.

The fore and aft vanes will be displaced away from the centre of the turn. One port will be open and its partner closed and the resulting reaction force, moved through 90°, will rotate the outer gimbal. A false indication of bank angle will occur, the sense depending on the direction of the turn.

The effect of the centrifugal force acting on the erection unit is to cause a false indication of climb or descent, again depending on the direction of the turn.

Turning errors are transitory (maximum after 180° of turn, reducing to zero after 360°). In modern instruments the errors are minimised by offsetting the rotor axis, but the correction is valid only for a **specific rate of turn at a specific speed**. Note that the offsetting of the rotor will not affect straight-and-level indications because the scales on the instrument are offset by a similar amount.

9.8 Operating Limits

Air-driven AIs have freedom in pitch of about ±60°, with complete freedom in roll and yaw.

The instrument will be ready for use about five minutes after starting the engine (and hence the engine-driven vacuum pump). During this period the horizon-bar may oscillate violently at first but should settle within a minute or two.

9.9 The Electrically-Driven AI

The principle of the electrically-driven AI is similar to that of the air-driven type. It uses an Earth Gyro, spinning in the horizontal plane, with a centre of gravity below the geometric centre. It spins in a **clockwise** direction viewed from above.

The erection system consists of tilt-switches and torque motors (see Fig 9-6). Two switches, containing mercury, are mounted in the base of the inner gimbal; one fore-and-aft, one athwartships. If the rotor starts to 'topple' the mercury will cover two contacts and a current will flow to the torque motor, causing it to rotate the gimbal. The rear motor controls pitch by turning the outer gimbal – the starboard motor controls roll by turning the inner gimbal.

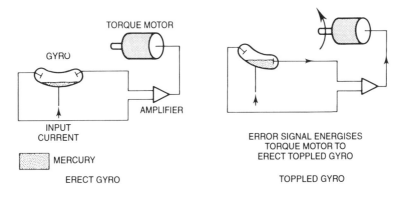

Figure 9–6.

A 'fast erection button' is usually fitted. This passes an extra current to the torque motors, re-aligning the rotor very rapidly on start-up and if it topples in flight. Overheating can be caused by this extra current and it must not be used for more than 15 seconds. If it is used in any attitude other than straight and level flight the rotor will be re-erected to a false vertical.

9.10 Advantages
The electric instrument has the following advantages as opposed to an air-driven type:

- Fast spin-speed giving greater rigidity and less precession.

- Constant spin-speed at all heights, regardless of air density.

- The case is sealed and not affected by moisture, dust or corrosion.

- Runs at constant temperature which improve accuracy.

- Fast erection and re-erection.

- Acceleration errors are much smaller because there is no large erection chamber or vanes to be affected by inertia. Furthermore, cut-out devices in the levelling circuit cause it to be de-activated when subject to large accelerations and large angles of bank. However, in less violent conditions, some errors will persist.

9.11 Operating Limits

Modern electrically-driven AIs have ±85° freedom in pitch with full freedom in roll and yaw.

After switch-on, all warning/failure flags should disappear and the gyro will run-up to speed. If the 'off' flag does not disappear, you **must** switch off **immediately** to avoid damaging the instrument.

The AI will settle after about 90 seconds. The fast-erect button can be used 15 seconds after switch on – if used earlier it will cause wild oscillations and damage.

10

The Turn and Slip (Balance) Indicator

The turn and slip (or turn and bank) indicator is actually two instruments in one:

- The **Turn Indicator** is a gyro instrument which measures rate of turn.

- The **Slip Indicator** uses a balance ball or pendulum to measure any slip or skid.

10.1 The Turn Indicator

The turn indicator measures **rate** of change of heading – that is, it measures movement in the yawing plane. It consists of a gyro positioned with its spin axis horizontally athwartships in the aircraft (Fig 10-1).

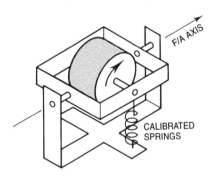

Figure 10–1.

The gyro is mounted in a single gimbal which is pivoted fore-and-aft in the instrument case. The gimbal is also attached to the case by two springs, one on each side. The direction of rotor spin is 'up and away' from the pilot. Note that the gyro has freedom of movement in only two planes, one of which is the plane of rotation – it is, therefore, a **rate gyro**.

Turn indicators usually employ electrically-driven gyros. DC power is used so that they can operate from the aircraft batteries in an emergency. Spin speed is about 9000 rpm.

A scale (not shown) is fixed to the gimbal, and moves against a lubber line on the instrument case.

The scale is graduated in rates of turn on the basis that:

Rate 1 =   3 degrees per second, 180° in 1 minute, 360° in 2 minutes

Rate 2 =   6 degrees per second, 360° in 1 minute

Rate 3 =   9 degrees per second, 540° in 1 minute, 360° in 40 seconds

10.2 Principle of Operation

Figure 10-1 shows the turn indicator in straight and level flight. Now consider Fig 10-2, which illustrates operation in a turn.

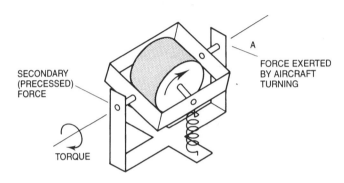

Figure 10–2.

Suppose the aircraft turns left. The gyro's orientation in the fore-and-aft axis is fixed, so the gyro is forced to turn with the aircraft by the force A. By the law of precession this force is moved through 90° in the direction of spin, hence producing a torque which rotates the rotor clockwise (from the pilot's point of view). This is the **primary precession**.

If no springs were involved, the rotor would continue to tilt until its spin axis was vertical – when it would be no use at all for sensing turns! However, we have springs.

As the rotor begins to tilt, one spring is stretched. The stretched spring exerts a balancing force downwards on the gyro axle. This vertical force will also be moved through 90° in the direction of spin, ending up as a secondary force in the direction of the original turning force.

When a steady rate of turn has been established, all forces are constant and in balance and the gyro is tilted at a constant angle proportional to the rate of turn.

10.3 Errors

The springs in the Turn Indicator are calibrated such that the instrument will give correct readings only at a specific TAS. The calibration assumes a constant gyro rigidity. Errors will consequently be introduced when flying at different speeds and if the rigidity changes. Furthermore, the spring tension is adjusted for a given rate of turn, normally Rate One, and although the spring has a theoretically linear response, in practice there will be an error at other turn rates.

10.4 Airspeed Error
Turns executed whilst flying at a TAS other than that for which the instrument is calibrated will produce a small error, perhaps 5% for a speed range of ± 100kt. The error can be ignored in practice.

10.5 Rotor Speed Error
The rigidity of the gyro rotor is proportional to its speed of rotation. A change in the spin speed will therefore cause a mismatch between the actual rigidity and the tension of the springs. Reductions in rotor speed are more likely in air-driven instruments which will be affected by leaks in the vacuum system and the reduction in air density at high altitudes.

If the rotor speed is low, the primary and secondary precession forces will be less; the spring will not be stretched as much and the indication of turn rate will be less. Hence:

Underspeed = Underread

10.6 Pitching Error
The pitching up which is necessary to maintain altitude in a turn will result in additional precession which causes the instrument to **overread**.

In steep turns the error is significant, but at the low rates of turn used when instrument flying it can be ignored.

10.7 Relationship Between Bank Angle and Rate of Turn

As TAS increases, the bank angle needed to achieve a given rate of turn will increase.

The rule of thumb for a **rate one** turn is:

$$\frac{\text{TAS (in knots)}}{10} + 7 = \text{bank angle required}$$

For example, at 90kt:

$$\text{Bank Angle} = \frac{90}{10} + 7 = 16°$$

10.8 Indication

Figure 10-3 shows a typical Turn Indicator.

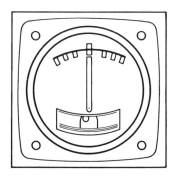

Figure 10–3.

The situation illustrated is when no turn is taking place, hence the needle is central. In a turn the needle will be displaced left or right, indicating the direction of turn, by an amount proportional to the rate of turn. The graduated marks represent rates one, two and three, moving outwards from the centre.

10.9 The Balance Indicator

In a turn, an aircraft is banked and is yawing. The turn will be **balanced** only when the inputs of bank and yaw are correctly matched. The balance indicator provides information to the pilot to enable him to achieve the match.

The instrument can consist of a weighted pendulum attached to a pointer.

Nowadays, however, it is more usual to use a ball-shaped weight in a curved glass tube. Movement of the ball within the tube is damped by a liquid. In straight and level flight the ball will be in the centre of the tube (Fig 10-4).

Figure 10–4.

When the aircraft turns (Fig 10-5) the centripetal force acting towards the centre of the turn creates a centrifugal force acting outwards. Weight continues to act vertically. If the turn is balanced the resultant of weight and centrifugal force will act through the aircraft vertical and the ball will remain centred.

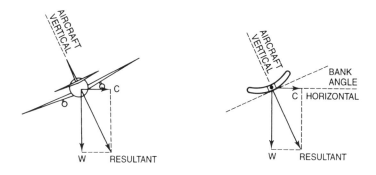

Figure 10–5.

When the turn is not balanced the forces will no longer be matched and the ball will appear to move left or right (Fig 10-6).

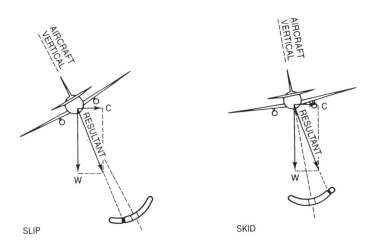

Figure 10–6.

The diagram on the left illustrates the situation when the aircraft is over-banked (or too little rudder is applied). The aircraft is **slipping into** the turn and the ball is displaced **into** the turn.

On the right we have the opposite case. The aircraft is under-banked (too much rudder applied). The aircraft is **skidding out** of the turn and the ball is displaced **out** of the turn.

Figure 10-7 illustrates a number of situations. The key fact to remember is:

Slip IN, Skid OUT

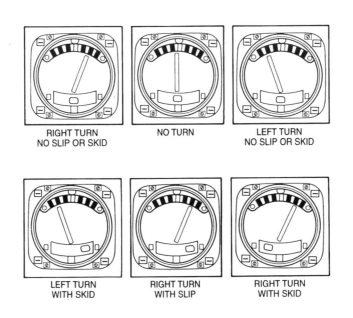

RIGHT TURN
NO SLIP OR SKID   NO TURN   LEFT TURN
NO SLIP OR SKID

LEFT TURN
WITH SKID   RIGHT TURN
WITH SLIP   RIGHT TURN
WITH SKID

Figure 10–7.

10.10 The Turn Co-ordinator

The Turn Indicator senses only **yaw**. It will give no indication of bank because, with the gyro gimbal in the aircraft horizontal, it is insensitive to roll.

To overcome this deficiency, the **Turn Co-ordinator** was developed. The gimbal is tilted through some 30° such that the foremost end is highest. It can now detect yaw and roll.

A typical presentation is shown at Fig 10-8. When the aircraft turns the aircraft symbol tilts left or right as appropriate. There are graduated marks for only a **Rate One turn**. This is because, with the gimbal tilted, the geometry is such that it 'hits the stops' at about Rate 1½.

The Turn Co-ordinator is therefore suitable for use only in light aircraft.

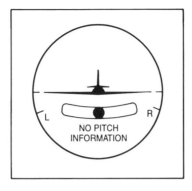

Figure 10–8.

Test Yourself   Gyro Instruments 2

1. A space gyro can also be referred to as:
   (a)   A Tied gyro.
   (b)   An Earth gyro.
   (c)   A Rate gyro.
   (d)   A Free gyro.

Ref 7.2

2. Which of the following cause Real Wander?
   (a)   The rotation of the earth.
   (b)   Movement of the aircraft over the Earth.
   (c)   Precession when torque is applied.
   (d)   Mass imbalance and bearing friction.

Ref 7.7

3. The term 'drift' refers to the wander of the axis of a gyro in:
   (a)   The vertical plane only.
   (b)   Any plane.
   (c)   The horizontal plane only.
   (d)   The vertical and horizontal plane.

Ref 7.7

4. A Direction Indication gyro suffers no random drift and Earth Rate is accurately compensated for by the latitude nut. The effect of Transport Wander will be:
   (a) Always to increase the gyro reading.
   (b) Always to decrease the gyro reading.
   (c) An increase or decrease in gyro reading, depending on track and groundspeed.
   (d) Apparent topple.

Ref 8.3

5. A 'perfect' directional gyro has its latitude nut set to compensate for Earth Rate at 30°N. If stationary at the Equator the gyro readings would:
   (a) Stay constant.
   (b) Increase.
   (c) Decrease.
   (d) Vary randomly.

Ref 8.3

6. If the gyro described in Question 5 were taken to 50°N and flown on a track of 090°(T) the DI readings would:
   (a) Stay constant.
   (b) Increase.
   (c) Decrease.
   (d) Vary randomly.

Ref 8.3

7. The Attitude Indicator employs a:
   (a) Free gyro.
   (b) Earth gyro.
   (c) Tied gyro.
   (d) Rate gyro.

Ref 9.1

8. During the take-off ground roll, the air-driven Attitude Indicator will indicate a:
   (a) Climbing turn to the left.
   (b) Climbing turn to the right.
   (c) Descending turn to the right.
   (d) Descending turn to the left.

Ref 9.5

9. The electrically-driven Attitude Indicator has several advantages over the air-driven version. These advantages include:
   (a) Faster spin speed hence greater rigidity.
   (b) Acceleration errors reduced because of reduced rigidity.
   (c) Turning error reduced because the rotor spins in the opposite direction.
   (d) Less subject to lag because an accelerometer unit is fitted.

   Ref 9.10

10. The Turn Indicator utilises a:
    (a) Free gyro.
    (b) Earth gyro.
    (c) Tied gyro.
    (d) Rate gyro.

    Ref 10.1

11. If a descending aircraft is making a Rate 1 turn with 25° left bank and is unbalanced due to slip, the ball of the balance indicator will be:
    (a) Displaced to the left.
    (b) Displaced to the right.
    (c) Displaced to the right or left.
    (d) At the centre.

    Ref 10.1

12. The Turn Co-ordinator is sensitive to:
    (a) Yaw only.
    (b) Roll only.
    (c) Pitch and roll.
    (d) Yaw and roll.

    Ref 10.10

11

Magnetism

The magnetic compasses that are used in aircraft depend for their operation on the way in which magnets behave. So before looking at the compasses themselves, we need to understand something of the theory of magentism, bearing in mind that the Earth itself can be considered to be a magnet.

11.1 Theory of Magnetism

A magnet is a piece of material, metallic in nature, which has certain properties:

(a) It attracts other materials that are **ferrous** (that is, containing iron).

(b) The powers of attraction are concentrated near the ends of the magnet, at its **poles**.

(c) If freely suspended over the Earth, one end tends to point North: this is the North-seeking or **red** pole. The other, South-seeking, end is the **blue** pole.

(d) The area of magnetic influence around a magnet is known as its **magnetic field**. The field is three dimensional and extends outwards from the magnet with progressively decreasing strength.

(e) If two magnets are close enough (ie within each other's fields), the similar poles will **repel** each other whilst the dissimilar poles will **attract** each other.

Some magnetic materials occur naturally, but magnetism can be **induced** in other metallic materials. A metal that can be easily magnetised (but will just as easily lose its magnetism) is known as **soft iron**. It is difficult on the other hand, to induce magnetism into **hard iron** but, once it is done, it can be considered permanent.

11.2 Terrestrial Magnetism

The Earth's magnetic field can be considered that of a gigantic bar magnetic within the Earth such that its blue pole is near (but not at) the True North Pole (Fig 11-1).

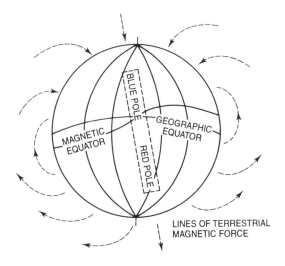

Figure 11–1.

11.3 Dip

Notice that the magnetic field, as represented by the **lines of magnetic force**, is parallel to the Earth's surface only near the Equator. At the magnetic poles the field will be vertical. At any particular point on the Earth, the total magnetic force (T) can be divided into two components (Fig 11-2).

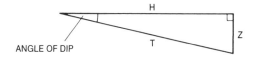

T   TOTAL FORCE
H   HORIZONTAL COMPONENT OF THE TOTAL FORCE
Z   VERTICAL COMPONENT OF THE TOTAL FORCE

Figure 11–2.

One component (H) is parallel to the Earth's surface, ie horizontal. The other component (Z) is vertical. The angle between H and T is known as the **Angle of Dip**.

The value of dip will be 90° at the poles. At 50°N it is approximately

62°. Near the Equator it will be zero and the line joining places of zero dip (an **aclinic** line) is the **Magnetic Equator**.

Note (for future reference) that: **Tan dip** $= \dfrac{Z}{H}$

11.4 Variation

As noted earlier, the Magnetic North Pole is near to but not coincident with the True North Pole. Therefore, at a given point on the Earth's surface, the direction to Magnetic North is unlikely to be the same as the direction to True North. The difference between the two directions is known as **magnetic variation**, usually referred to just as variation. When Magnetic North lies to the **East** of True North, variation is **East**; when Magnetic North lies to the West of True North, variation is **West**. (Fig 11-3).

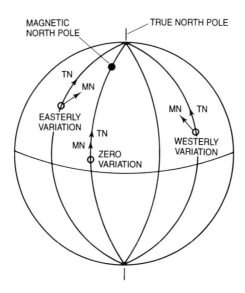

Figure 11–3.

The value of variation is shown on charts by lines joining places of equal variation; these lines are known as **isogonals**.

The Magnetic North pole is not in a fixed position. It revolves around the True Pole once every 970 years (approximately!). This movement causes the variation to change with time and the change is noted on charts by indicating the consequent movement of the isogonals.

True direction (eg heading) can be calculated from magnetic direction, and vice versa, by the application of variation. To remember which way is what, use the mnemonic:

Variation West, Magnetic Best
Variation East, Magnetic Least

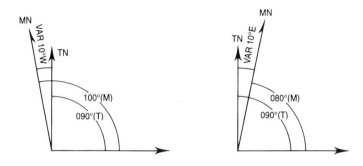

Figure 11–4.

11.5 Deviation

A magnet (compass needle) suspended inside an aircraft will not necessarily indicate the direction of Magnetic North with absolute accuracy. Magnetic fields emanating from the aircraft structure and from electrical equipment cause **deviation** of the compass needle. We shall discuss aircraft magnetism in more detail later. For the moment we are concerned only with its effect.

The direction actually taken up by the compass needle is known as **Compass North**. The angular difference between Compass North and Magnetic North is **deviation** and it can be applied in a similar manner to variation:

Deviation West, Compass Best
Deviation East, Compass Least

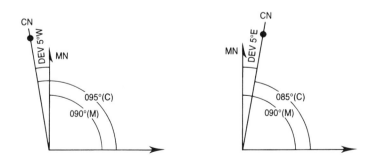

Figure 11–5.

To calculate True direction from Compass Direction you can use the mnemonic:

Cadbury's Dairy Milk Very Tasty

to help you remember that:

Compass + Deviation = Magnetic + Variation = True

For example, a pilot is steering 034° on his compass. Deviation is 3°W and variation is 13°E. What is the True heading of the aircraft?

$$034°(C) - 3°W = 031°(M) + 13°E = 044°(T)$$

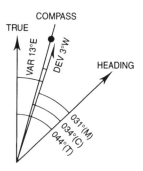

Figure 11–6.

11.6 Aircraft Magnetism

Deviation was discussed briefly earlier in this chapter, when we noted that it is caused both by the aircraft being made of metal components and by the use of electrical equipment which generate their own magnetic fields. These magnetic fields are, together, referred to as **aircraft magnetism** and it is now necessary to examine this in a little more depth.

Aircraft magnetism can be considered as being made up of hard iron and soft iron. Hard iron magnetism can be thought of as permanent, made up of the effects of the aircraft structure, wiring looms, electronic equipment and the like, which generate their own magnetic fields. Soft iron, on the other hand, can be considered (broadly) as temporary in that it consists of the magnetic fields which are **induced** into the aircraft by the effects of the Earth's own magnetism. And because the Earth's magnetic field changes (eg differences in Z and H with change of latitude), so will the intensity of the soft iron magnetism.

For analytic purposes, both sorts of iron are considered to have horizontal and vertical components. Our study can be limited to the two components which cause compass deviation, and these are **horizontal hard iron** and **vertical soft iron**.

Some elements of aircraft magnetism can be minimised by care during design and manufacture. Part of what remains can be removed by a process called 'de-gaussing' after the aircraft has been built. Some magnetism will invariably remain but its effects can be measured and calibrated. The process is known as **compass swinging** and is discussed later. One of the occasions when a compass should be swung is following a change in the aircraft's home base which involves a significant change in magnetic latitude (That is, you would **not** swing the compass during the turn-round on a London – Capetown – London trip, but you would if you intended to move the aircraft's base from UK to South Africa).

It is important (because exam questions are asked) to look at the effect of change of latitude on compass deviation.

11.7 Change of Latitude – Horizontal Hard Iron (HHI)

By definition, the strength of hard iron magnetism is permanent. However, the strength of the directive force on a compass needle – the horizontal component of the Earth's field (H) – varies with magnetic latitude. It is at its maximum at the magnetic Equator and is zero at the magnetic poles. The **deviating effect** of the HHI will be inversely proportional to H, that is:

$$\text{Deviation from HHI is proportional to } \frac{1}{H}$$

The value of H at any place is known. Given the deviation from (HHI) at one place, the deviation at another can be calculated from:

$$\frac{\text{New Deviation}}{\text{Old Deviation}} = \frac{\text{Old H}}{\text{New H}}$$

11.8 Change of Latitude – Vertical Soft Iron (vsi)

As before, the deviation will be inversely proportional to the strength in the direction force, H. However, in the case of soft iron, the deviating force strength will depend on the strength of that part of the Earth's field that is inducing it. We are concerned with vsi which is induced by the vertical component, Z, which is zero at the magnetic Equator and maximum at the magnetic poles. Deviation due to Z will thus be directly proportional to Z. We can therefore say that:

$$\text{Deviation from vsi is proportional to } \frac{Z}{H}$$

But (see Fig 11-6), $\dfrac{Z}{H}$ = tangent of dip

Dip is also known at any place so, given a change of magnetic latitude, the new deviation from vsi can be calculated from:

$$\dfrac{\textbf{New Deviation}}{\textbf{Old Deviation}} \quad = \quad \dfrac{\textbf{Tan new dip}}{\textbf{Tan old dip}}$$

11.9 Compass Swinging

Compass Swinging is the term given to the procedure whereby deviation is measured, corrected for as much as possible, and any residual deviation calibrated. The end result is a compass correction card which is placed in the aircraft to show the pilot how much deviation remains on a particular heading (nb **deviation is different on different headings**).

BCARs lay down maximum permissible deviations. These depend on the type of compass and are:

    Direct Reading Compass   -   **Maximum 3° on any heading**
    Remote Indicating Compass   -   **Maximum 1° on any heading**

There are specific occasions (also laid down in BCARs) when a compass must be swung. These are:

(a)   On acceptance of a new aircraft from the manufacturer
(b)   When a new compass is fitted
(c)   Every 3 months
(d)   After a major inspection
(e)   After any change of magnetic material in the aircraft
(f)   If transferred to another base when a large change of magnetic latitude is involved
(g)   After a lightning strike or flying in static
(h)   After standing on one heading for more than four weeks
(i)   When carrying magnetic freight
(j)   Whenever specified in the maintenance schedule
(k)   For the issue of a C of A
(l)   Following a heavy landing
(m)   At any time when the compass or the previously recorded deviation is suspect.

11.10 Compass Safe Distance

No metallic object should be put closer to a compass than the 'compass safe distance'. JARs state that:

"The change of deviation due to the proximity of any item of equipment containing magnetic material should not exceed 1°, and the combined change for all such equipment should not exceed 2°".

12

Direct Reading Compasses

A magnetic compass in its simplest form is a magnet freely suspended in the Earth's magnetic field. Such a magnet, if free from other influences, would align itself with the total component of the Earth's field; that is, in the horizontal plane it would point to Magnetic North but in the vertical plane it would be out of the horizontal by an amount equal to the dip angle.

The information pilots want from the compass is direction in the horizontal plane – the direction of Magnetic North. So to maximise the influence of the horizontal component of the Earth's field, the compass needle must be kept as **horizontal** as possible.

The compass must also be as **sensitive** as possible to the direction of the Earth's field. And if it is displaced from its proper direction, the compass needle must swiftly settle back into proper alignment without undue oscillations; that is, it must be **aperiodic** or **dead-beat**.

12.1 Construction

Horizontality
The compass needle is held as horizontal as possible by using a **pendulous suspension** (Fig 12-1).

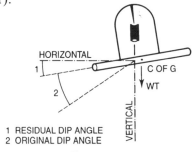

HORIZONTAL

C OF G

WT

VERTICAL

1 RESIDUAL DIP ANGLE
2 ORIGINAL DIP ANGLE

Figure 12–1.

The compass is so constructed that the centre of gravity of the magnet is below the pivot point. The weight of the magnet creates a mechanical force to counter the magnetic force of the vertical component of the Earth's field. In mid-latitudes this brings the magnet to within 3° of the horizontal.

12.2 Sensitivity

To keep the compass needle firmly aligned with the horizontal component of the Earth's field the magnet must be as strong as possible. In
practice four magnets are usually employed – Fig 12-2.

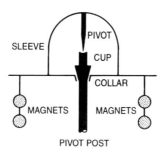

Figure 12–2.

To minimise the effects of friction on the pivot, the magnets are made
as light as possible and a jewelled bearing is used. In addition, the system
is placed in a fluid-filled bowl. The fluid not only lubricates the pivot but
also reduces the effective weight by 'floating' the magnets.

The magnets are held in position by a collar and sleeve arrangement.

The fluid must be transparent and be resistant to expansion/contrac-
tion caused by temperature change. Silicon fluid is favoured.

The fluid must completely fill the bowl. If it does not, the fluid will swirl
during turns, causing errors. Accordingly, an expansion bellows or
'sylphon tube' is fitted to keep the bowl full despite expansion/contrac-
tion of the fluid.

12.3 Aperiodicity

To reduce any oscillation of the magnets, **damping wires** are attached
which act in the fluid as brakes.

Additionally, the magnets – already made as light as possible – are
made as short as possible to reduce their moment of inertia.

12.4 Types of Compass

P-Type Compass

The grid ring compass, of which the P-type is an example, is now little
used except in historic aircraft. It has several disadvantages; perhaps the
main one is that it has to be mounted horizontally – Fig 12-3.

When the pilot wants to turn onto a new heading he must unlock the
grid ring, turn it until the desired heading is against the lubber line and

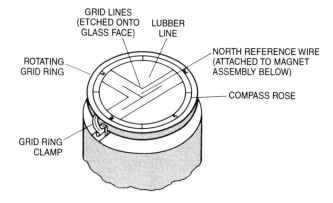

Figure 12–3.

re-lock the ring. He then turns the aircraft until the North reference wire is against the North index on the grid ring.

12.5 The E-Type Compass

The E-type compass is widely used as the main heading reference in light aircraft and as a standby system in larger types. It is a 'vertical card' or 'vertical reading' compass (Fig 12-4) with a quoted accuracy of ± 10°, although you can expect better than this in steady flight.

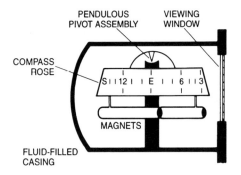

Figure 12–4.

The magnet system is pendulously suspended in a fluid-filled transparent bowl. A compass card is fixed to the magnets and the pilot can read the aircraft's heading against a fixed lubber line inscribed on the face of the instrument (Fig 12-5).

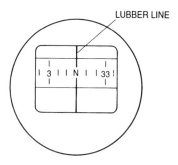

Figure 12–5.

Note that if the magnet system is for any reason deflected **clockwise** (as viewed from above), the reading presented to the pilot will be **less** than the correct one. **Anti-clockwise** deflection will cause the reading to be too great.

12.6 Errors

We have seen that Direct Reading Compasses employ pendulous suspension to counteract dip and keep the magnet nearly horizontal. Unfortunately, the pendulous suspension makes the compasses prone to errors when the aircraft is subject to accelerations – be they linear (changes of speed) or centripetal (turns). Any swirl of the fluid in the bowl will cause additional errors. There will also be a small error because of the effect of the Z component on a tilted magnet but we shall not consider this in further detail.

12.7 Acceleration Error

Acceleration errors (and the turning errors we shall examine shortly) result from the fact that the pendulous suspension leaves some residual dip in the system. Note that at the Magnetic Equator, where there is no dip, there will be no errors.

Consider first an aircraft in the mid-latitudes of the Northern hemisphere (Fig 12-6).

The side view of the magnet system at (a) shows that, because of residual dip, the centre of gravity of the magnets is displaced to the South (right in the diagram) of the pivot. At (b) is a plan view of the same arrangement with the aircraft in unaccelerating flight on an Easterly heading. If the aircraft now accelerates we shall have the situation illustrated at (c). The **acceleration** will be exerted on the pivot, which is attached to the aircraft. The **reaction** to the acceleration, acting in the opposite direction, will be exerted through the C of G of the magnets.

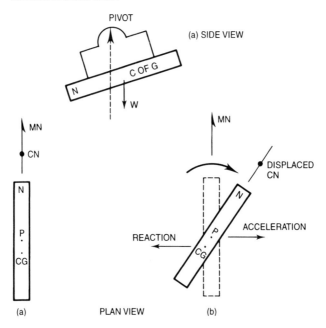

Figure 12–6.

Because the C of G is not directly below the pivot, a force couple will be set up that will turn the magnet **clockwise**. The compass will underread, indicating an **apparent turn towards North**.

Had the aircraft been heading West, the magnets would have rotated anti-clockwise. The compass would overread but again would indicate an **apparent turn towards North**.

On northerly or southerly headings the accelerations will be along the pivot/C of G line and so there will be no error.

Decelerations, of course, are 'accelerations in reverse' and the same logic can be applied.

Now consider what happens in the southern hemisphere (Fig 12-7).

The side view at (a) shows that the residual dip is in the opposite sense from that in the northern hemisphere. The C of G is therefore on the northern side of the pivot (b). An acceleration on East will now cause an anti-clockwise rotation of the magnets – the compass will **overread**, indicating an **apparent turn to the South**.

Similarly, on a westerly heading, an acceleration would cause the compass to **underread**, again causing an **apparent turn to the South**.

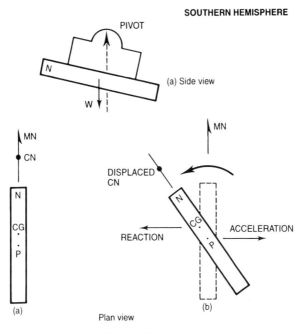

Figure 12–7.

12.8 Summary of Acceleration Errors
In **both** hemispheres: **Acceleration = apparent turn towards nearer pole**
Deceleration = apparent turn towards the Equator

The magnitude of acceleration errors depends on:

(a) The magnetic latitude.
(b) The magnitude of the acceleration.
(c) Heading – maximum on East and West.
(d) The moment of inertia of the magnet system.

12.9 Turning Errors
Turning errors are caused by just the same mechanism as linear acceleration errors except that now the accelerating force is the centripetal force
acting towards the centre of the turn. This force will act along the pivot/C
of G line when the turns are through East and West; maximum errors will
arrive during turns through North and South. Consider Fig 12-8 which
illustrates the effect in the northern hemisphere.

In a right turn through North, the centripetal force acting into the turn
will cause the magnet to rotate clockwise. The compass will **underread**
the turn and, because the needle is turning in the same direction as the

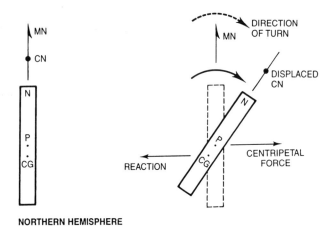

Figure 12–8.

aircraft, the pilot must roll-out of the turn **before** his new desired heading is indicated. The compass is said to be **sluggish**.

In a turn through North in the southern hemisphere, (Fig 12-9) the opposite occurs.

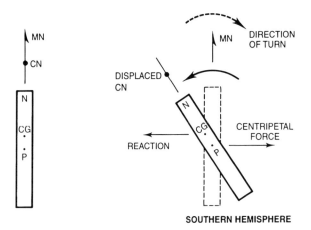

Figure 12–9.

The centripetal force again causes the compass needle to rotate clockwise but now the needle rotates in the opposite direction to that in which the aircraft is turning. The result is an over indication of the turn and the pilot must turn through his (indicated) desired heading before rolling out. The compass is said to be **lively**.

In the **southern** hemisphere, as usual, everything is the other way round.
It is convenient to discuss the effects of liquid **swirl** in conjunction with
turning errors. In turns, friction between the liquid and the bowl sets a
swirl **in the same direction as the turn**. Thus when the compass needle is
turning in the same direction as the aircraft the swirl will add to the
turning error; when the compass needle is turning in the opposite direction to the aircraft, swirl will reduce the error.

12.10 Summary of Turning Errors

Hemi-sphere	Turn	Hdg	Magnet Swings	Error	Reaction	Effect of Swirl
North	Right	N	Clockwise	Underread	Sluggish	Increases
North	Left	N	Anti-clockwise	Overread	Sluggish	Increases
North	Right	S	Anti-clockwise	Overread	Lively	Reduces
North	Left	S	Clockwise	Underread	Lively	Reduces
South	Right	N	Anti-clockwise	Overread	Lively	Reduces
South	Left	N	Clockwise	Underread	Lively	Reduces
South	Right	S	Clockwise	Underread	Sluggish	Increases
South	Left	S	Anti-clockwise	Overread	Sluggish	Increases

The magnitude of turning error depends on:

(a) The magnetic latitude.
(b) The rate of turn.
(c) Heading – maximum on North or South.
(d) The moment of inertia of the magnet system.

12.11 Serviceability Checks

The following checks should be made to ensure the serviceability of
DRCs:

(a) Check that the liquid is free from bubbles, discolouration and
sediments.
(b) Examine all parts for luminosity.
(c) If fitted, ensure that the grid ring rotates freely through 360° and
that the locking device functions properly.
(d) Test the suspension of the bowl by moving it gently in all directions, checking that there is no metal contact.
(e) Test for pivot friction. Deflect the magnet system through 10° or

15° each way, release and note the readings when it has swung back, which should be within 2° of each other.

(f) Test for damping. Deflect the system through 90°; hold for 30 seconds to allow the liquid to settle, then release; time its return through 85°. Maximum and minimum permissible times are laid down by the manufacturer.

Test Yourself   Magnetism & DRCs 3

1. Hard iron is the name given to a metal which:
    (a)   Is difficult to magnetise and loses its magnetism easily.
    (b)   Is difficult to magnetise and retains its magnetism.
    (c)   Is easy to magnetise and loses its magnetism easily.
    (d)   Is easy to magnetise and retains its magnetism.

Ref 11.1

2. As 'magnetic latitude' increases the horizontal component (H) of the Earth's magnetic field..........and the vertical component (Z)..........The missing words are:
    (a)   Decreases, increases.
    (b)   Decreases, decreases.
    (c)   Increases, increases.
    (d)   Increases, decreases.

Ref 11.3

3. At a given place, compass deviation will:
    (a)   Be constant always.
    (b)   Vary with aircraft heading.
    (c)   Depend on the value of variation.
    (d)   Be constant in unaccelerated flight.

Ref 11.5

4. In a direct reading compass, horizontality is achieved by:
    (a)   Suspending the magnet system in a liquid-filled bowl.
    (b)   Using jewelled bearings.
    (c)   Using a sylphon tube.
    (d)   Using pendulous suspension.

Ref 12.1

5. When accelerating on an easterly heading in the northern hemisphere, the magnet system of a direct reading compass will:
    (a)   Turn clockwise, indicating an apparent turn towards North.
    (b)   Turn clockwise, indicating an apparent turn towards South.
    (c)   Turn anti-clockwise, indicating an apparent turn towards South.
    (d)   Turn anti-clockwise, indicating an apparent turn towards North.

Ref 12.7

6. Whilst flying on a northerly heading in the southern hemisphere, an aircraft decelerates. Its direct reading compass will indicate:
   (a) An apparent turn towards East.
   (b) An apparent turn towards West.
   (c) No error because the force acts along the magnet.
   (d) No error because the C of G and the pivot are coincident.

   Ref 12.7

7. Whilst flying in the southern hemisphere, an aircraft turns right from a heading of 135°(M) to 235°(M). During the turn the magnet system of the direct reading compass will rotate _____ (when viewed from above), the compass will _____ and the effect of liquid swirl _____ the error. The missing words are:
   (a) Clockwise, Underread, Reduces.
   (b) Clockwise, Overread, Increases.
   (c) Anti-clockwise, Overread, Reduces.
   (d) Clockwise, Underread, Increases.

   Ref 12.10

8. The purpose of fitting a sylphon tube to a direct reading compass is to:
   (a) Compensate for leaks in the system.
   (b) Compensate for expansion/contraction of the liquid.
   (c) Minimise liquid swirl.
   (d) Maintain the liquid at constant temperature.

   Ref 12.2

9. You are flying over the UK. When using the direct reading compass to turn left from 030°(M) to 330°(M) you should roll out of the turn:
   (a) When 330° is indicated.
   (b) Before 330° is indicated.
   (c) After 330° is indicated.
   (d) After one minute if turning at Rate One.

   Ref 12.10

10. You wish to fly a heading of 076°(T). Variation is 13°W, deviation is 3°E. The compass heading to fly is _____:
    (a) 086°.
    (b) 092°.
    (c) 060°.
    (d) 066°.

    Ref 12.9/12.10+

13

Remote Indicating Compasses

You will know, from the previous chapter, that Direct Reading Compasses have some severe disadvantages:

They suffer from turning and acceleration errors.

They must be positioned, so that they can be easily read in the flight deck. In such a position they are particularly prone to deviating effects.

They can only display compass heading. If magnetic or true headings are needed they must be calculated.

They cannot pass their heading information to other instrument systems.

In light aircraft, a directional gyro is used as the primary heading reference. This overcomes the problem of acceleration and turning errors. However, because the gyro is subject to wander – both real and apparent – it must be compared frequently with the compass and be manually reset.

It would be advantageous to have a system which could continuously compare magnetic and gyro headings and automatically update the gyro. This, in effect, is what the gyro magnetic Remote Indicating Compass does – combining the short-term stability of the gyro with the long-term accuracy of a magnetic sensor. In the bargain, it also provides a means of overcoming all the disadvantages of Direct Reading Compasses.

For the examination you will need a good understanding of the principles of operation, but a superficial knowledge of the mechanics will suffice.

13.1 Components

A basic gyro-magnetic Remote Indicating Compass (RIC) consists of the components shown in Fig 13-1.

The basic principle is that the detector unit senses magnetic direction which it passes to the selsyn. Gyro direction is also fed to the selsyn. Any difference between magnetic and gyro is fed, via the amplifier, as an error signal to the gyro. The gyro is made to turn to agree with the magnetic

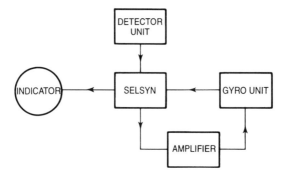

Figure 13-1.

information. In the process, it 'zeros' the selsyn and turns the heading indicator.

13.2 Detector Unit

The detector unit senses the direction of **Magnetic North** *not*, note carefully, magnetic heading as such. It is usually placed well away from deviating influences – typically in the wing tip or the fin. It consists of three 'flux valves'.

13.3 Flux Valve

If an easily magnetised metal bar is placed horizontally in the Earth's magnetic field, the bar will acquire magnetic flux proportional to the amount of the horizontal component (H) of the field passing through it.

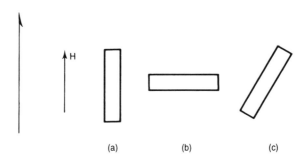

Figure 13-2.

In Fig 13-2 the bar (a) is aligned with H and so will acquire maximum flux. The bar (b) is perpendicular to H and will acquire no flux. The bar at (c) is at, say, 30° to H and will acquire flex proportional to H cos 30°. So, if the bar were to be fixed to the fore-and-aft axis of an aircraft the induced flux would be proportional to magnetic heading!

This is the basis of the detector unit. Unfortunately, in practice things are not so simple because a flux can only be detected if it is changing – no good with the aircraft on a steady heading. So it is necessary to make the flux change even if the heading does not.

Now, if an electric current is passed through a coil (or winding) which is wound around a soft iron core, the core will become magnetised (Fig 13-3).

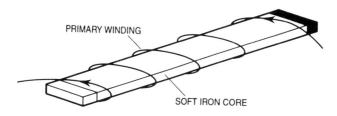

PRIMARY WINDING

SOFT IRON CORE

Figure 13–3.

If two cores are used, wound with a continuous winding, two magnets of equal and opposite polarity are produced (Fig 13-4).

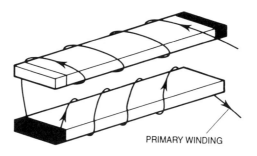

PRIMARY WINDING

Figure 13–4.

And if the current used in the winding were AC, the polarity of the magnets would be reversed every time the direction of current flow changed – ie changing flux has been produced. Furthermore, the value of the current can be adjusted so that the cores become magnetically saturated; that is, any further increase in current will not result in a corresponding increase in the strength of the magnetic fields produced. So, as shown in Fig 13-5, if external magnetic influences are ignored, the cores would become saturated at the 90° and 270° phase points of the winding current.

Now comes the clever bit! We know that an electric current can be used to produce a magnetic field (or flux). The converse is also true – if a

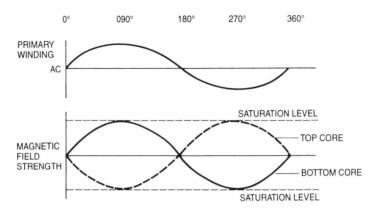

Figure 13–5.

magnetic field of changing strength of polarity cuts a wire, an AC current will be induced into the wire. Suppose, then, that another (secondary) coil is wound around the outside of our construction so far – see Fig 13-6.

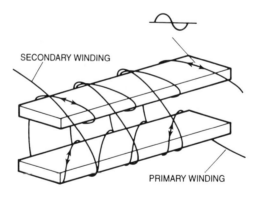

Figure 13–6.

If there were no external influences, nothing would happen because the cores are producing equal and opposite fields which cancel each other. But what happens if the contraption – which can now be called a **flux valve** – is placed in the Earth's magnetic field? The equality of the magnetic fields in the cores is disturbed and a current is induced into the secondary coil (Fig 13-7).

Assuming that the cores are horizontal, the magnitude of the induced current will be proportional to the amount of H being 'sensed'. Just as with our original metal bar (Fig 13-2), the output is **proportional to the**

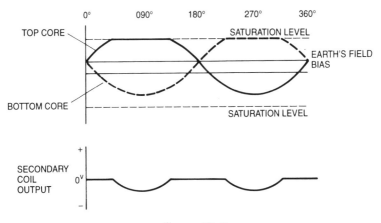

Figure 13–7.

orientation with respect to magnetic North. Unfortunately, it would be ambiguous, with identical currents being produced on reciprocal headings. To overcome this, three flux valves are used in the Detector Unit.

13.4 Detector Unit

The three flux valves are positioned at 120° to each other and 'collector horns' are added to concentrate the amount of flux collected by each leg (Fig 13-8) where the primary windings are not shown for sake of clarity.

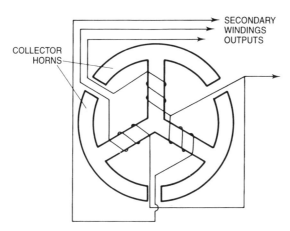

Figure 13–8.

When resolved together, the outputs of the 3 flux valves can be shown to represent the direction of the Earth's field, or magnetic North (Fig 13-9).

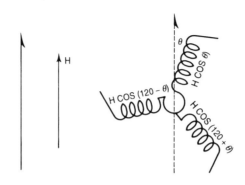

Figure 13–9.

The unit's alignment to the fore-aft axis of the aircraft is fixed, so changes of heading can be **detected**. Remember though that the Detector Unit merely **senses the direction of Magnetic North**.

For it to work properly, the Detector Unit must be horizontal, so that it senses only the horizontal component of the Earth's field. Accordingly, it is suspended pendulously by a device known as a **Hooke's Joint** which allows freedom of movement up to ±25°. If this limit is exceeded, the output of the Unit is isolated to prevent the effect of sensing the vertical (Z) component of the Earth's field affecting the system.

Even if the 25° limit is not exceeded, turns and accelerations will force the Detector Unit out of the horizontal. To minimise the effect of such a manoeuvre, the rate at which the gyro is permitted to respond to signals from the Detector Unit is limited to **2° per minute**. Short duration manoeuvres will therefore not cause significant errors in the system.

13.5 Signal Selsyn

The Signal Selsyn – often called the **Synchronising Unit** – can be thought of as a Detector Unit in reverse. It replicates the Earth's magnetic field, as sensed by the Detector Unit. It consists of three **stators**, mutually at 120°, and a **null seeking rotor** at their centre (Fig 13-10).

The currents induced into the secondary coils of the Detector Unit are passed to the stator coils of the selsyn. A magnetic field is therefore produced which in turn will induce a current in the rotor coil **unless the rotor is at 90° to the field**. This current is fed to the gyro unit; the gyro is turned (precessed); the precession is used via a linkage to turn the rotor. When the rotor is at 90° to the selsyn field, no current will flow and the gyro is **synchronised**.

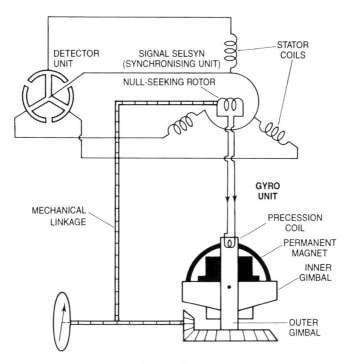

Figure 13–10.

13.6 Amplifier

The amplifier – often referred to as the **precession amplifier** – is used to amplify (and rectify) the error signals from the selsyn on their way to the Gyro Unit.

13.7 Gyro Unit

The gyro unit consists of an electrically-driven tied (spin axis in yawing plane) gyro which is fitted with a precession mechanism (Fig 13-10). Amplified signals from the selsyn rotor are fed to the **precession coil** through which runs a permanent magnet which is attached to the gyro's inner gimbal. A signal in the precession coil will induce a field around the coil which will cause the permanent magnet to move, so attempting to topple the gyro. This will effect a precession of the gyro in the horizontal plane. This precession is fed to the rotor of the selsyn (driving it back to null) and to the heading indicator.

13.8 Heading Indicator

The heading indicator, as we have seen, is always fed with gyro heading which, in normal operation, is the same as magnetic heading.

On some systems, variation can be fed into the system, enabling a display of true heading. The feed from the Detector Unit can usually be manually disconnected, allowing the system to operate in the pure gyro (DG) mode if required (for instance, in high latitudes).

The indicator can be placed anywhere in the aircraft, and can be of any design.

Given a suitable transmission system, any number of repeaters can be used and heading can be fed to other systems such as an autopilot. The main indicator will be designated the **Master Indicator**.

A typical indicator is shown at Fig 13-11.

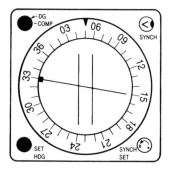

Figure 13–11.

13.9 Data Selsyn Transmission

In Fig 13-10, and so far discussed, a mechanical linkage is used to drive the heading indicator and the rotor of the signal selsyn. This is often not practicable and a **Data Selsyn** system is used instead (Fig 13-12).

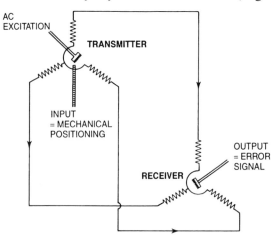

Figure 13–12.

The data selsyn system is rather like two signal selsyns linked by wires. The rotor of the transmitting selsyn, which is positioned by mechanical input, is fed with AC current which will induce a magnetic field around the rotor. This field will be sensed by the stator coils, in which currents will be induced proportional to their orientation to the rotor field. These induced currents are fed to the stators of the receiver selsyn where they in turn produce magnetic fields. The resultant field is sensed by the rotor of the receiver selsyn into which a current will be induced unless it is in the null position. This current, or error signal, is the output. The use of data selsyn in a gyro-magnetic compass is illustrated at Fig 13-13.

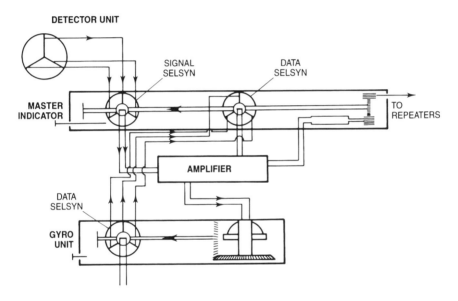

Figure 13–13.

13.10 Bits and Pieces

The Annunciator

The state of synchronisation of the system – the state of alignment or misalignment between gyro and magnetic inputs – is shown by the **annunciator**.

If the system is synchronised, an alternating dot-cross will be displayed in an annunciator window on the heading indicator. De-synchronisation is indicated by a steady dot or steady cross. If required, the system can be manually synchronised by turning the synchronising control (also on the heading indicator) in the appropriate direction.

13.11 Manual synchronisation

Automatic synchronisation is limited, as we have seen, by the 2°/min maximum gyro precession rate. However, when first switched on, the system will probably be grossly desynchronised. Hence the need for a manual synchronisation control, the operation of which de-clutches the gyro and permits manual rotation of the heading shaft and null rotor.

13.12 Gyro Erection

The gyro is designed to measure change of heading – it is therefore important to keep the spin axis in the aircraft's yawing plane. Commutator switches detect any topple of the gyro (relative to the aircraft) and pass a signal to a torque motor which applies a precessing force to the gyro to bring it back to level (Fig 13-14).

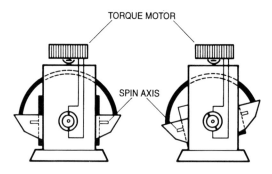

Figure 13–14.

13.13 Accuracy

RICs are inherently accurate to about ±½°.

BCARs require that residual deviation, after calibration, be no more than 1° on any heading.

13.14 Advantages & Disadvantages of the RIC

Compared with Direct Reading Compasses, the RIC has the following advantages:

The magnetic sensing element, the Detector Unit, can be placed well away from the worst deviating effects.

The gyro is continuously and automatically monitored.

Headings relative to any datum, eg True North, can be displayed.

Turning and acceleration errors are reduced to a minimum (slow gyro follow-up rate of 2°/min; detector unit cut-out >25° manoeuvre).

The magnetic influence can be manually disconnected if required (high latitudes, electrical storms).

Indicators can be placed anywhere in the aircraft.

More than one indicator can be used and heading information can be fed to other equipment.

However, the RIC is:

Heavier

More expensive to buy and maintain

Electrical dependent

More complicated

13.15 Principle of Operation – Reminder

The system is up-and-running and synchronised. With everything working perfectly, and with no gyro drift, the rotor of the signal selsyn will stay in the null position whatever the aircraft's heading. If the gyro drifts, however, the selsyn rotor will be driven out of null; an error signal will be generated by the rotor which is fed through the amplifier and used to precess the gyro and turn the rotor back to correct alignment.

If the aircraft turns, the orientation of the detector unit relative to the Earth's magnetic field will change, and the field created by the stators of the signal selsyn will change in sympathy. But, the gyro will maintain the system in North alignment and, as the aircraft 'turns round the gyro', the selsyn rotor will be turned at the same rate and so will stay in the null position.

Test Yourself   Remote Indicating Compasses 4

All questions refer to Remote Indicating Compasses.

1. The detector unit is normally:
   (a)   Fixed in the vertical plane only.
   (b)   Fixed in azimuth.
   (c)   Free in both the vertical and horizontal planes.
   (d)   Located in the flight deck area.

2. The gyro rotor is prevented from wandering in the vertical plane by means of:
   (a)   Pendulous suspension.
   (b)   Bevel gears and gimbals.
   (c)   A levelling switch and torque motor.
   (d)   The precession circuit.

3. The gyro rotor is prevented from wandering in the horizontal plane by means of:
   (a)   A levelling switch and torque motor.
   (b)   A commutator type alignment switch.
   (c)   The precession circuit.
   (d)   The latitude nut.

4. The rate of precession of the gyro is limited to:
   (a)   1° per second.
   (b)   2° per minute.
   (c)   2° per second.
   (d)   5° per minute.

5. The function of the synchronising system is to:
   (a)   Maintain the gyro in alignment with the magnetic reference.
   (b)   Hold the gyros in the aircraft's yawing plane.
   (c)   Ensure the gyro spin speed remains constant.
   (d)   Maintain the detector unit in the horizontal.

6. A DG flag in the annunciator window indicates that the system is:
    (a) Unserviceable.
    (b) Not using information from the detector unit.
    (c) Not aligned with the magnetic meridian.
    (d) Being manually synchronised.

7. In moderate to severe turbulence, the annunciator indications will:
    (a) Remain steady.
    (b) Alternate regularly.
    (c) Alternate irregularly.
    (d) Show a DG flag.

8. BCARs require that residual deviation shall not exceed:
    (a) ½°.
    (b) 1°.
    (c) 2°.
    (d) 3°.

9. Compared to a Direct Reading Compass, an RIC will:
    (a) Suffer the same acceleration and turning errors.
    (b) Be sensitive only to acceleration errors.
    (c) Be sensitive only to turning errors.
    (d) Suffer minimally from acceleration and turning errors.

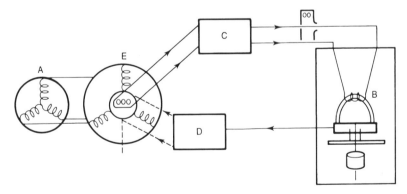

10. In the above diagram, the letters A and B refer to:
    (a) Detector Unit/Gyro Unit.
    (b) Detector Unit/Signal Selsyn.
    (c) Signal Selsyn/Amplifier.
    (d) Gyro Unit/Heading Indicator.

Instruments   Practice Paper

1. Air data instruments are calibrated to the International Standard
   Atmosphere which assumes a temperature lapse rate in the tropo-
   sphere of ....°/1000 feet and a mean sea level density of ....gm/m³:
   (a)   2,1525.
   (b)   1.98,1225.
   (c)   1.98,1525.
   (d)   1.89,1225.

2. The values of aerodrome QNH, QFE and Standard Setting:
   (a)   Can never be the same.
   (b)   Could only be the same in ISA conditions.
   (c)   Could only be the same for an aerodrome at 0ft elevation.
   (d)   Could only be the same in isothermal conditions.

3. Errors can be caused in the static system by aircraft manoeuvre.
   These errors:
   (a)   Can be corrected by calibration.
   (b)   Can possibly be sustained in straight and level flight.
   (c)   Can affect the ASI and the Machmeter.
   (d)   Only affect the Altimeter and the VSI.

4. You are flying a constant flight level, from a high pressure area
   towards a low. You would expect a pressure altimeter set to your
   departure QNH to:
   (a)   Indicate a higher than true altitude.
   (b)   Read true altitude.
   (c)   Underread the true altitude.
   (d)   Indicate height above the departure airfield.

5. An aircraft is on the ground with its altimeter subscale set to 1013mb;
   the altimeter reads 250ft. The airfield QNH is 1006mb. Airfield
   elevation, assuming 1mb = 30 feet, is:
   (a)   460ft.
   (b)   210ft.
   (c)   160ft.
   (d)   40ft.

6. If an aircraft static source becomes blocked during a climb, the pressure instruments will read as follows:

	Altimeter	ASI	VSI
(a)	Underread	Underread	Zero
(b)	Underread	Overread	Underread
(c)	Underread	Overread	Zero
(d)	Overread	Correctly	Overread

7. The ASI is subject to compressibility error. The error cannot be ignored if the .... is ....
   (a) RAS, 300kt or more.
   (b) TAS, 300kt or more.
   (c) TAS, 200kt or more.
   (d) RAS, 200kt or more.

8. The interior of the capsule in an ASI is:
   (a) Connected to the static line.
   (b) Partially evacuated.
   (c) Connected to the pitot head.
   (d) Connected to the static line via a metering jet.

9. Equivalent Airspeed (EAS) is:
   (a) RAS corrected for density error.
   (b) RAS corrected for compressibility error.
   (c) IAS corrected for compressibility error.
   (d) IAS corrected for instrument, pressure and density errors.

10. The diagram below illustrates a Machmeter. The components labelled B, D and E are:

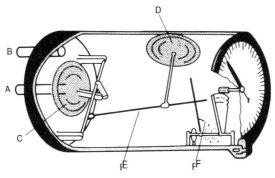

	B	D	E
(a)	Pitot feed	Airspeed capsule	Ratio arm
(b)	Static feed	Altimeter capsule	Ranging arm
(c)	Pitot feed	Airspeed capsule	Ranging arm
(d)	Static feed	Altimeter capsule	Ratio arm

11. The speed of sound:
    (a) Varies with the atmospheric pressure.
    (b) May increase with altitude.
    (c) Varies as the square root of temperature in °C.
    (d) Varies as the square of temperature in °C.

12. It is found that an increase of 0.15 Mach Number increases the TAS by 93kt. The local speed of sound is:
    (a) 1613kt.
    (b) 614kt.
    (c) 620kt.
    (d) 810kt.

13. When climbing at a constant RAS, below the tropopause in ISA conditions the TAS will .... and the Mach Number will ....
    (a) Increase, increase.
    (b) Increase, decrease.
    (c) Decrease, increase.
    (d) Decrease, decrease.

14. Lag error in the VSI:
    (a) Causes the instrument to lag behind the correct rate of change of height.
    (b) Causes the instrument to underread the correct rate of change of height.
    (c) Is reduced by using the static vents connected in parallel.
    (d) Is calibrated out for the lower rates of climb and descent, using a logarithmic scale.

15. The main advantage of the IVSI over its 'normal' counterpart is that the IVSI will:
    (a) Give an immediate indication of change in pitch altitude.
    (b) Given an immediate indication of vertical speed when a climb or descent is initiated.
    (c) Automatically initiate climbs and descents by providing inputs to the flight control system.
    (d) Almost totally remove barometric error.

16. To compensate for changes in the viscosity of the air the VSI incorporates:
    (a) An accelerometer unit in the static feed.
    (b) A restrictive choke.
    (c) A logarithmic scale.
    (d) A capillary tube and knife-edge orifice in the metering jet.

17. A gyroscope which is constrained by an external reference but which has freedom of movement in three planes is a:
    (a) Space gyro.
    (b) Earth gyro.
    (c) Tied gyro.
    (d) Rate gyro.

18. Apparent wander of a gyro can be caused by:
    (a) Friction in the rotor or gimbal bearings.
    (b) The effect of the latitude nut.
    (c) The Earth's rotation.
    (d) Movement of the gyro over the Earth on North/South tracks.

19. The gyro of a Direction Indicator, corrected for Earth Rate at 30°N, has no random drift. When flying a track of 270°(T) at 30°N the gyro readings will:
    (a) Increase.
    (b) Decrease.
    (c) Vary randomly.
    (d) Remain constant.

20. The gyro described in Question 19 is taken to 60°S. When flying on a track of 090°(T) the gyro readings will:
    (a) Increase.
    (b) Decrease.
    (c) Vary randomly.
    (d) Remain constant.

21. The spin axis of the gyro in an Attitude Indicator is:
    (a) Tied in one vertical plane.
    (b) Tied in two vertical planes.
    (c) Maintained horizontal by gravity.
    (d) Tied to the horizontal plane.

22. During a turn, an air-driven AI which is compensated for turning error will give:
    (a) Correct indications for a selected speed and rate of turn.
    (b) Correct indications for all speeds.
    (c) Approximate indications in the pitch plane only.
    (d) Approximate indications in the roll plane only.

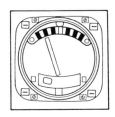

23. The Turn and Balance Indicator illustrated above is indicating:
    (a) Left turn with too much bank.
    (b) Right turn with too little bank.
    (c) Right turn with too much bank.
    (d) Left turn with too little bank.

24. A fault occurs in the vacuum pump, causing it to run too slowly. A consequent effect is that the Turn Co-ordinator will:
    (a) Over-indicate turns.
    (b) Under-indicate turns.
    (c) Indicate turns in the wrong direction.
    (d) Indicate turns accurately.

25. The vertical angle between the horizontal component (H) of the Earth's magnetic field and the direction of the total field is known as:
    (a) Variation.
    (b) Deviation.
    (c) Dip.
    (d) Vertical error.

26. An aircraft's compass should be swung:
    (a) When carrying a magnetic payload in the aircraft.
    (b) If a base change involves a large change of magnetic latitude.
    (c) If the aircraft has been left standing on one heading for 4 weeks or more.
    (d) All of the above.

27. An aircraft at 30°S turns anti-clockwise from 225°(M) to 155°(M). The magnet system of its direct reading compass would turn .... causing the instrument to .... the amount of turn. The missing words are:
    (a) Clockwise   Overread
    (b) Anti-clockwise   Overread
    (c) Anti-clockwise   Underread
    (d) Clockwise   Underread

28. In direct reading compasses, the magnets are made as short but as magnetically strong as possible and the magnet system is suspended in a fluid. The purpose of these features is to:
    (a) Increase sensitivity.
    (b) Reduce aperiodicity.
    (c) Improve horizontality.
    (d) Reduce deviation.

29. An aircraft flying over the UK, steering 270°(M), accelerates. The magnet system of its direct reading compass will rotate .... (as viewed from above), which will cause the compass to ....:
    (a) Clockwise, overread.
    (b) Anti-clockwise, overread.
    (c) Anti-clockwise, underread.
    (d) Clockwise, underread.

30. In a Remote Indicating Compass the rate of precession of the gyro
(in degrees/min) is normally limited to:
    (a) ½°.
    (b) 1°.
    (c) 2°.
    (d) 5°.

31. In a Remote Indicating Compass the prime function of the precession system is to use signals directly from .... to ....
    (a) Detector Unit   Maintain a correct heading indication
    (b) Signal selsyn rotor   Precess the gyro in azimuth
    (c) Signal selsyn stators Maintain a low rate of horizontal cover
                                over the gyro
    (d) Follow up amplifier   Maintain the master indicator aligned
                                with the gyro unit

Instruments Practice Examination Answers

1. (b)
2. (c)
3. (c)
4. (a)
5. (d)
6. (a)
7. (b)
8. (c)
9. (b)
10. (d)
11. (b)
12. (c)
13. (a)
14. (a)
15. (b)
16. (d)
17. (c)
18. (c)
19. (a)
20. (a)
21. (b)
22. (a)
23. (a)
24. (b)
25. (c)
26. (d)
27. (c)
28. (a)
29. (b)
30. (c)
31. (b)